# MONSTERS TO DESTROY

# MONSTERS TO DESTROY

## UNDERSTANDING THE WAR ON TERROR

### NAVIN A. BAPAT

# OXFORD
UNIVERSITY PRESS

Oxford University Press is a department of the University of Oxford. It furthers the University's objective of excellence in research, scholarship, and education by publishing worldwide. Oxford is a registered trade mark of Oxford University Press in the UK and certain other countries.

Published in the United States of America by Oxford University Press
198 Madison Avenue, New York, NY 10016, United States of America.

© Oxford University Press 2019

All rights reserved. No part of this publication may be reproduced, stored in a retrieval system, or transmitted, in any form or by any means, without the prior permission in writing of Oxford University Press, or as expressly permitted by law, by license, or under terms agreed with the appropriate reproduction rights organization. Inquiries concerning reproduction outside the scope of the above should be sent to the Rights Department, Oxford University Press, at the address above.

You must not circulate this work in any other form
and you must impose this same condition on any acquirer.

Library of Congress Cataloging-in-Publication Data
Names: Bapat, Navin A., author.
Title: Monsters to destroy : understanding the War on Terror / Navin A. Bapat.
Description: New York, NY : Oxford University Press, [2019] |
Includes bibliographical references and index.
Identifiers: LCCN 2019015335| ISBN 9780190061456 (hardback) |
ISBN 9780190061463 (pbk.) | ISBN 9780190061470 (updf) |
ISBN 9780190061487(epub) | ISBN 9780190061494 (online)
Subjects: LCSH: Terrorism—Economic aspects—United States. |
Terrorism—Political aspects—United States. | War on Terrorism,
2001-2009—Economic aspects. | United States—Foreign relations—21st century.
Classification: LCC HV6432 .B364 2019 | DDC 363.3250973—dc23
LC record available at https://lccn.loc.gov/2019015335

1 3 5 7 9 8 6 4 2

Paperback printed by Marquis, Canada
Hardback printed by Bridgeport National Bindery, Inc., United States of America

*To Shahsultan Bapat, M.D.*

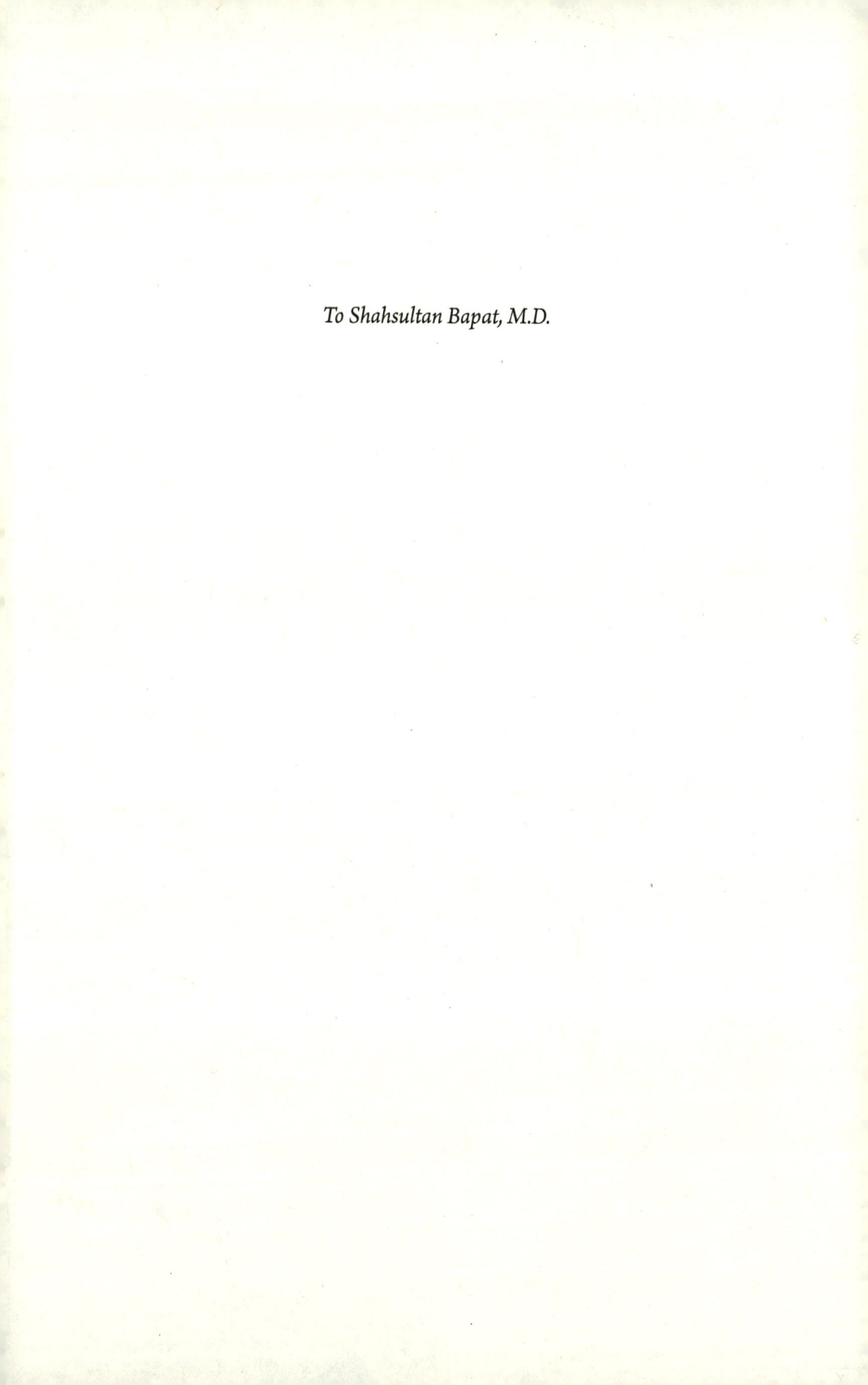

# CONTENTS

Acknowledgments ix

**1**
INTRODUCTION 1

**2**
THE ECONOMIC ORIGINS OF THE "WAR ON TERROR" 8

**3**
TERRORISM AND THE PROBLEM OF MORAL HAZARD 39

**4**
THREATENING ALLIES 70

**5**
HEGEMONIC DECLINE AND THE ESCALATION OF VIOLENCE 110

**6**
CONCLUSION: THE WAR FOR EXORBITANT PRIVILEGE 141

Appendix: Game Theoretical Solutions and Statistical Models 155
Notes 181
Bibliography 199
Index 211

# ACKNOWLEDGMENTS

This book represents the combination of two puzzles that I've examined for most of my career. The first is why terrorism creates such large effects on policy, investment, and on decisions to go to war. The second is why the U.S. is as powerful and as influential as it is, even though Americans only constitute 5% of the world's population. This work proposes answers to both of these questions, though I am not entirely comfortable with their implications. I've come to think of this book as one that is about privilege, and what people will do to maintain their social and economic superiority relative to others. As someone with privilege in a global sense, I certainly understand that one cannot credibly commit to surrendering it. Yet, while researching what is done to protect it, I've found it increasingly difficult to conclude that this position is justifiable, and that these behaviors are defensible.

I have many people to thank for allowing me to create this manuscript that has contributed to my ongoing moral anguish and torment. My colleagues at the University of North Carolina at Chapel Hill have been invaluable to me in terms of pushing the project forward, especially Mark Crescenzi, Stephen Gent, Patricia Sullivan, Layna Mosley, Cameron Ballard-Rosa, Sean Zeigler, Frank Baumgartner, and Tom Carsey, who unfortunately left us far too soon. Thank you also to my students Lucia Bird, Menevis Cilizoglu, Chelsea Estancona, Bailee Donahue, Dan Gustafson, and Rob Williams for listening to me blabber on about energy markets far too many times over the last few years. I also have to thank numerous scholars in the field who patiently listened to my ideas, pointed out their deficiencies, and forced me to make improvements. These include Cliff Morgan, Sara Croco, Faten Ghosn, Kathy Powers, Will Winecoff, Songying Fang, Glenn Palmer, Doug Lemke, Jim Piazza, Errol Henderson, Pat Regan, Michael Bernhard, Bill Reed, Andy Enterline, Walter Enders, Ed Kaplan, Jeannie Murdock, and especially Todd Sandler, who has made an enormous difference in my career and intellectual development.

The second group to thank are the many editors that have helped me immensely in clarifying my ideas and arguments. I am very grateful to my editors David McBride and Emily Mackenzie for all of their help in developing the project. I am also thankful to both Heather Thompson for the last edits, and to John Lovette for his assistance with the maps. I would also like to send a special thank you to Mitchell Mass. As a student in my classes on terrorism and national security, Mitchell would always stay late and probe arguments harder than anyone else. He read and edited every part of this project, and it would not be anywhere close to coherent without his help.

I would also like to thank the Institute of Defense and Business in Chapel Hill. This organization offered me to opportunity to lecture on this material to career officers of various ranks over the last several years. The feedback I got from these groups of officers, along with the sometimes open hostility, always forced me to better justify my arguments and the evidence that supported them. I was also able to gain invaluable insights from the participants, many of which are reflected in the final draft. I am deeply thankful to Ambassador David Litt, Zebrina Warner, and Van Noah for allowing me to work with these students over the years.

Finally, I would like to thank my immediate and extended family, especially my father Avinash Bapat, my mother Shahsultan Bapat. Thank you for all you've done for me throughout my life, but in particular, thank you for exposing me to the world and helping me to see it through a global lens. A great many thanks are also owed to Anil Bapat, Rozmin Bapat, Delia Campos, Salvador Campos, Isabel Huerta, and Juan Campos. And of course, the biggest possible thank you to Catarina Inés, Naima Isabel, and Neela Valentina, the three most perfect daughters I could ask for. Last, but certainly not least, I would like to thank Dr. Carmen Huerta-Bapat, my spouse and partner in crime. This book would not have been completed without her support and unwavering faith in me, which is far too great to justify. No one has taught me more about the power of privilege than her, and no one has forced me to face and think about the morality behind the analysis. Her support has been invaluable, and the book would not have been finished without her. Thank you all.

# INTRODUCTION

> We cannot erase every trace of evil from the world, and small groups of killers have the capacity to do great harm. That was the case before 9/11, and that remains true today. That's why we must remain vigilant as threats emerge.
>
> —U.S. President Barack Obama
> September 10, 2014

In 2001, the United States began the global war on terror in response to al Qaeda's attacks in New York and Washington. The war has been responsible for the deaths of thousands of American military personnel, as well as tens of thousands of civilian fatalities throughout the Middle East, Asia, and Africa. As of 2019, the estimated cost of war had reached about $5.9 trillion, or about $18,000 per American.[1] Yet, despite this immense effort, the number of worldwide terrorist attacks increased exponentially in the years after the 9/11 attacks. The U.S. came to be locked into conflicts with the Islamic state (ISIS), the ongoing Taliban insurgency in Afghanistan, Boko Haram in Nigeria, and a multitude of al Qaeda offshoots and other terrorist groups throughout northern Africa. Given that terrorist attacks have become more frequent, there are more active terrorist groups in the world, Iraq and Afghanistan are still embroiled in internal conflicts, and former allied regimes have destabilized, the verdict seems clear: the war on terror appears to be an unmitigated foreign policy disaster.

Figure 1.1 demonstrates that prior to 9/11, there were fewer than 2,000 terrorist incidents globally per year. The number of terrorist attacks precipitously increased after the George W. Bush administration initiated Operation Iraqi Freedom in 2003, and it continued throughout the decade and into the era of the Obama administration, reaching a peak in 2011 with over 5,000 annual incidents. Although this data demonstrates that the U.S. failed to diminish the threat of terrorism, there is little disagreement that the war on terror was worth fighting. The risk that terrorists could repeat another 9/11-style attack, or attack with a weapon of mass destruction, meant that any cost was worth the price to protect civilian lives.

However, consider the data presented in Figure 1.2, which compares the annual number of fatalities resulting from terrorism during the period 1968–2011 against the number of fatalities resulting from

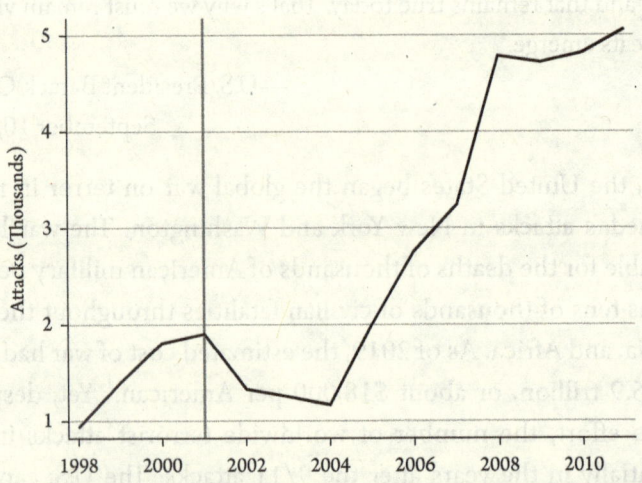

Figure 1.1. Terrorist Attacks Worldwide 1998–2011.
Note. Data obtained from the Global Terrorism Database (GTD), includes both domestic and transnational terrorist attacks; see Global Terrorism Database: Codebook: Inclusion Criteria and Variables (https://www.start.umd.edu/gtd/downloads/Codebook.pdf). The GTD defines terrorist attacks as the threatened or actual use of illegal force and violence by a non-state actor to attain a political, economic, religious, or social goal through fear, coercion, or intimidation. GTD further assumes that the violence is intentional, and it excludes state terrorism, such as repression or genocide. Solid line indicates the start of the George W. Bush administration in 2001.

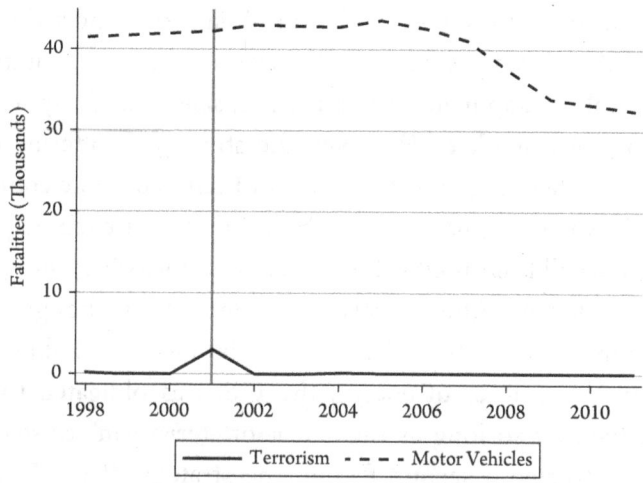

Figure 1.2. U.S. Fatalities from Transnational Terrorist Attacks Worldwide Compared to Motor Vehicle Accidents in the United States, 1998–2011.
Note. Solid line represents American fatalities from terrorist attacks based on the Global Terrorism Database; see National Consortium for the Study of Terrorism and Responses to Terrorism (START). 2018. Retrieved from https://www.start.umd.edu/gtd. Global Terrorism Database [data file]. Dashed line represents traffic fatalities data from the National Highway Transportation Safety Administration. Solid line represents 2001, when the 9/11 attacks contributed to a significant increase in fatalities from terrorism.

motor vehicle accidents. Consistently, motor vehicles on average kill tens of thousands more people annually than terrorism.[2] This disparity raises the question: why is there a "war on terror" instead of a "war on traffic"? Why is the U.S. willing to expend so many of its resources and sacrifice the life and limb of its military personnel to fight this war when terrorism poses such an insignificant threat? Further, given that the U.S. chose to fight this war, why are American policies worsening the problem of terrorism, given the disproportionate level of resources the U.S. is allocating?

### THE ARGUMENT

This study argues that the war on terror can be explained as an effort to expand American control over the global energy markets, thereby cementing the place of the U.S. dollar as the world's foremost reserve currency. By destroying al Qaeda, the Taliban, and Saddam Hussein's government in Iraq, the U.S. gained control not only over the bulk of Middle Eastern oil reserves but also the key transit routes needed to exploit new energy reserves in Central Asia. To support this adventure, the U.S. offered permanent military protection to a multitude of states critical to supporting the extraction, sale, and transportation of energy to global markets. However, the strategy of offering military protection to these states in exchange for their economic cooperation contained two critical flaws. First, the war on terror encouraged these states to label all their political opponents as "terrorists," even if these adversaries showed little interest in violence. Even though many of these groups were motivated by local grievances, and showed little interest in the politics of energy, the U.S. was obligated to defend the host regimes so long as the threat of "terrorism" existed. These incentives revealed a second flaw in the strategy: if the U.S. would pay to defend regimes from all terrorist threats, but would reduce its military support if the threat of terrorism receded, these states had little incentive to disarm their terrorists. Instead, these regimes demanded continued U.S. protection from their terrorist threats, even as they grew increasingly corrupt, repressive, and unresponsive to their populations.

In the years following the invasion of Iraq, several of these terrorist groups transitioned into insurgencies and developed the power to significantly challenge the sovereignty of the states under U.S. protection. By the mid-2000s, increasing military strain and a political backlash against the war on terror forced the U.S. to weaken its commitment to defend the regimes under its umbrella. Although this forced some cooperation on the part of the regimes, the decline of U.S. military support precipitously weakened the key energy states under the American security umbrella. This decline in power further encouraged rivals to initiate conflicts against the energy market states, both to destabilize their adversaries and perhaps seize their valuable territory. Facing these aggressive rivals, and with an impending loss of U.S. support, the energy states began their own preventive conflicts, before American power and influence in the region eroded completely. The reduction in American support therefore caused the insurgencies to escalate into larger interstate conflicts. This ongoing situation is paving the way for the decline of American hegemony. While the U.S. began the war on terror after

9/11 to cement its financial dominance, the U.S. now finds itself locked in a permanent war for its economic security.

## METHOD

I develop this argument using an empirical implications of theoretical models (EITM) approach. Rather than offering a descriptive account, the EITM approach seeks to identify the causal logic driving the key participants in the war on terror. Analyzing the logic allows us to make sense of situations where simply looking at the data provides us with little guidance.[3] For example, in examining American behavior in Afghanistan, those in favor of continuing to maintain the occupation may argue that it is necessary to prevent the Taliban and al Qaeda from resurfacing. By contrast, those with political inclinations against the occupation may argue that the U.S. presence is fueling the violence. Unfortunately, the empirical record provides little resolution to the dispute: weak states do increase the growth of terrorist groups, but so do military occupations. As a result, it is very difficult for any policymaker to determine a preferable course of action. Using the scientific method allows us to assess the likely outcomes for various policy choices, assess the risk of the policies, and explain their likely effects. To be sure, in examining a problem as complex as transnational terrorism, policymakers will benefit from a rational, impartial, and scientific analysis of foreign policy choices.

This scientific method involves several steps. First, we must observe our problem of interest. In this case, we have observed that terrorism appears to be rising and U.S. policy appears ineffective. Given this observation, we next analyze the problem by identifying key definitions and specifying up front what assumptions we are making. For example, when we say terrorism is rising, what exactly do we mean by "terrorism"? According to the U.S. State Department, and most scientific studies of the topic, terrorism is a tactic. Specifically, terrorism is defined as political violence used by non-state actors against non-combatant targets for the purposes of influencing an audience larger than the immediate victims.[4] This creates several restrictions that are worth mentioning. First, terrorism is an attack directed against noncombatant targets, meaning that attacks on military personnel are not considered terrorism. This implies that the attack on the World Trade Center on 9/11 can be considered an act of terrorism, but the attack on the Pentagon cannot be, given that the Pentagon is the hub of military activity in the U.S. and is a legitimate military target. Second, the definition posits that only non-state actors can be considered terrorists. Even if governments attack non-combatants, as they frequently do, governments cannot be considered terrorists. Third, terrorist attacks are not aimed only at the immediate victims. Again, in the case of 9/11, the attacks were not only aimed at the people in the World Trade Center and the Pentagon but were also intended to shock and influence the U.S. public at large. Fourth, the definition assumes that terrorism is a political activity. Therefore, attacks intended solely for economic gains cannot be considered terrorism.

Most importantly, however, we see from this definition that terrorism is a tactic. When policymakers discuss eradicating terrorism, they are probably not talking about eliminating a tactic but rather eliminating any non-state actor that engages in violence against the U.S.—whether guerrillas, insurgents, militias, or pirates. In point of fact, nearly every one of these militant groups uses the tactic of terrorism in some form as part of their military strategy. Though many groups prefer to refer to themselves as guerrillas or insurgents, many of them engage in violent activities that harm non-combatants, and these activities are often intended to influence the government's population. For example, attacks by Hamas often kill individual Israelis, but they are also intended to signal to the Israeli population that Hamas will not tolerate actions taken by the Israeli government. This fits the definition of terrorism. We also see that many other non-state actors, even those we may view as righteous, often use this tactic. For example, Nelson Mandela's African National Congress (ANC) engaged in sabotage attacks against the facilities of the South African apartheid government. In perhaps a more relevant example, the organization known as the Sons of Liberty during the American Revolution engaged in numerous acts of political violence against the colonial British government. To understand terrorism scientifically, we must acknowledge that under the cited definition of terrorism, these groups, no matter how righteous we believe their cause to be, should be classified as terrorist groups. We therefore see that if we do approach terrorism in a scientific way, the old saying that "one man's terrorist is another man's freedom fighter" appears to hold true. To maintain consistency with the policymakers, I will use "terrorists" to signify any non-state actor that is engaging in political violence against the U.S. and its allies, though it is also possible to use another more generic term, such as militants or non-state actors.

## PLAN OF THE BOOK

The argument proceeds in several steps. Chapter 2 discusses the economic foundations for why terrorism posed a fundamental threat to American security. Chapter 3 examines the fundamental flaw in the American strategy, and how this created an incentive for states with energy supplies and key transit routes to become increasingly corrupt while cultivating the growth of terrorist movements. Chapter 4 discusses how this corruption allowed terrorist movements to transition into insurgencies and how the U.S. sought to compel the states into fighting their insurgent challengers by scaling back its military commitments. In Chapter 5, I discuss how the threat of U.S. retrenchment caused these insurgencies to escalate into larger, interstate conflicts. Chapter 6 concludes by arguing that events unrelated to terrorism allowed the U.S. to maintain its financial hegemony in the short term. However, the ongoing war on terror is accelerating the transition away from American hegemony over the international system.

# 2

# THE ECONOMIC ORIGINS OF THE "WAR ON TERROR"

> These terrorists kill not merely to end lives but to disrupt and end a way of life. With every atrocity, they hope that America grows fearful, retreating from the world and forsaking our friends. They stand against us, because we stand in their way. We are not deceived by their pretenses to piety. We have seen their kind before. They are the heirs of all the murderous ideologies of the twentieth century. By sacrificing human life to serve their radical visions, by abandoning every value except the will to power, they follow in the path of fascism and Nazism and totalitarianism. And they will follow that path all the way, to where it ends, in history's unmarked grave of discarded lies.
> 
> —President George W. Bush
> September 20, 2001, speech to joint session of Congress

George W. Bush's speech before the joint session of Congress likened the new war on terror to both World War II and the Cold War. Given the trauma of 9/11, it is easy to understand how so many Americans believed that al Qaeda posed such a significant threat. However, as previously established, Americans are more likely to die from motor vehicle accidents, drowning, or choking than from terrorist attacks.[1] Additionally, as frightening as groups such as al Qaeda and ISIS appear, terrorists tend to be terribly ineffective at accomplishing their strategic objectives and often fail due to their own dysfunction.[2] This demonstrates that while each death due to terrorism is tragic, terrorist groups do not pose anything close to existential threats.

Since the risk of terrorism is so low, the simplest explanation for American behavior is that the U.S. overreacted to the trauma of 9/11. However, nearly two decades after the attacks, terrorism remains at the forefront of American policy, and American policymakers still use much of the rhetoric and the "lessons" of 9/11 continue to guide their decision-making. This suggests that we may not be observing an overreaction that will ameliorate itself with time, and it raises the question: if terrorism does not pose a significant risk to the lives of Americans, how exactly does terrorism threaten U.S. security?

This chapter argues that the root causes of the war on terror are economic. The 9/11 attacks provided an opportunity for the U.S. to expand its control over global energy markets, which in turn would cement the U.S. dollar as the world's foremost reserve currency. Since the early 1970s, the states of OPEC (Organization of the Petroleum Exporting Countries) have agreed to denominate sales of oil and energy products in U.S. dollars in exchange for American military protection. These states subsequently recycled their dollars back into American bonds and commercial banks, which allowed the U.S. to borrow at low interest rates while running substantial budget deficits. The war on terror was an effort to preserve these benefits by destroying al Qaeda, the Taliban, and Saddam Hussein's government in Iraq. These actions gave the U.S. control over both the bulk of Middle Eastern oil reserves and the key transit routes needed to exploit new energy sources in Central Asia. These victories seemingly guaranteed that energy sales would be settled permanently in U.S. dollars, so long as the U.S. provided security for the host states that were critical to the extraction, sale, and transportation of energy to global markets. Politically, the U.S. justified its forward presence by invoking the specter of another 9/11 attack. This threat gave the U.S. cover to provide permanent military protection to the host states that served as energy suppliers and provided critical infrastructure and transit routes. To make this argument, let us first examine how the U.S. became the pivotal player in the international system following World War II, and how American financial hegemony became linked to the global energy markets.

## THE BEGINNING OF AMERICAN HEGEMONY: BRETTON WOODS 1944–1971

The end of World War II is often seen as the beginning of the period of American hegemony.[3] Hegemony is defined as a situation where one state dominates the international system in terms of its economic and military power. This preponderance of power enables the hegemonic state to structure and govern the world's political and economic relationships by codifying the rules of conduct in international institutions. This hegemon designs the rules of international institutions in a way that reflects its own values and preferences, and is likely to produce its preferred outcomes.[4] These rules govern economic relationships and provide a mechanism for adjudicating security disputes between states. Other states are compelled to accept the legitimacy of the hegemon's rules due to its disproportionate power. If the rules of the institutions are followed over time, these rules will eventually become socialized and perceived as "normal," "just," and the "correct" way to run international affairs.[5]

The U.S. found itself in this position of hegemony at the end of World War II. In 1945, the U.S. generated roughly 40% of the world's total economic output and maintained 60% of the world's gold reserves.[6] The U.S. further had military forces in both Europe and Asia and maintained near total control of the Atlantic and Pacific oceans. The U.S. also maintained sole possession of the atom bomb. American factories were still operating at peak production for the war effort and the economic infrastructure of the U.S. remained intact. By contrast, the war completely devastated the major European and Asian powers, along with the Soviet Union.[7] World War II represented a total war, with attacks occurring within civilian centers in addition to the battlefield. The damage from the war therefore destroyed these states' human and economic capital as well as the infrastructure needed to rebuild from the war. Since the U.S. was the only country with a functioning economy and manufacturing base, American capital was essential to begin the rebuilding process in the combatant countries. With this remarkable power, the U.S. was in position to shape the rules and norms of the international system in a way that reflected its own interests and values.

The central objective of U.S. policymakers was to prevent the outbreak of another global conflict. These policymakers concluded that the Great Depression and the instability in the value of currencies and exchange rates had led to the onset of World War II. Prior to this conflict, the world tacitly accepted the system known as the British gold standard to shape the rules of global finance.[8] This system emerged with the passage of the Bank Charter Act in 1844, which had declared that the British pound was convertible into gold bullion. The claim appeared credible due to the substantial amount of gold held by British colonial possessions. Since global merchants knew that the British held sufficient gold reserves to convert their pounds into gold, and since gold was a commodity in high demand, countries accepted pounds in exchange for goods and services. This system made the British pound the anchor for world commerce. To obtain pounds, countries devalued their own currencies to lower the price of their commodities relative to goods produced within Britain. This allowed imports to become more competitive in the British market, which in turn allowed other countries to exchange real goods for pounds, which would then be converted into other real necessary imports. Although this created a substantial trade deficit, Britain obtained the seigniorage privilege in that it could create pounds and exchange them for real goods and services. This monetary advantage cannot be overstated: *Britain could essentially generate money for almost no cost and exchange it with the rest of the world for real goods.* This system held together so long as Britain could redeem pounds (or IOUs) into gold, which required the British to maintain an empire to protect their supplies of gold to maintain this convertibility.

While the gold standard remained somewhat functional for the latter half of the nineteenth century, the onset of World War I plunged the system into crisis. To finance the war, Britain and the other combatant states removed themselves from the gold standard and began creating large amounts of currency. This increase in the supply of pounds soon appeared to exceed British holdings of gold. This perception that the British pound lost convertibility caused other states in the system to cease accepting British pounds, which in turn caused the currency to lose value. Hyperinflation swept through the continent, and Europeans found themselves poorer as their currencies lost value. These declining economic conditions hurt the ability of the Europeans to purchase imports, which soon caused the crisis to spread to the U.S. economy. Although the U.S. economy boomed in the 1920s, demand for American goods within the U.S. market ultimately hit a plateau, which required U.S. firms to export their surplus production. The collapse of the European economies gave U.S. factories nowhere to export. American firms were forced to begin layoffs, which in turn decreased the disposable income of American families, leading to a collapse in demand. The inability to sell goods led to multiple bankruptcies, culminating in the 1929 crashing of both the London and New York stock exchanges. States such as Fascist Italy and Nazi Germany responded to the depression by adopting command economic policies and stimulating their economies through military buildups. With these large militaries, these states and Imperial Japan initiated wars of conquest, which led to World War II.

As the war drew to a close, the U.S. and the British sought to create a system that would prevent something like the Great Depression from occurring again. The key task was to stabilize exchange rates by ensuring the convertibility of world currencies into something tangible. The solution was the system of exchange known as the Bretton Woods system in 1944.[9] This system established a stable exchange rate system with currencies pegged to the U.S. dollar. The U.S. dollar maintained fixed convertibility into gold at $35 per ounce. Since all currencies became tied to the dollar, and the dollar was guaranteed to convert into gold, each of the world's currencies could retain value. Bretton Woods would therefore prevent inflation and stabilize the value of global currencies. However, Bretton Woods also established the U.S. as the world's critical economic player and central banker. The U.S. dollar became the world's most important currency with unmatched value.

To encourage global trade, the U.S. pushed for the Generalized Agreement on Tariffs and Trade (GATT) to encourage international trade by lowering tariffs between countries and establishing norms of tariff reciprocity. The U.S. also developed the International Monetary Fund (IMF) to assist countries that maintained temporary balance-of-payment problems. This would enable states in the economic system to continue their economic policies at home while keeping a stable exchange rate by borrowing from the IMF. The U.S. further pushed for the decolonization of empires, which were viewed as protectionist regional trading blocs that hampered the free flow of goods and services. Although the move to end colonial empires is often interpreted as an expression of American idealism, we must remember that colonies were the exclusive economic blocs of the European powers, and they prevented U.S. trade and investment from entering these markets.[10] The dissolution of the empires opened numerous markets for American goods and services. This was particularly advantageous at the time, given that the U.S. manufacturing base was fully operational while its competitors were digging themselves out of the war. To assist the newly independent countries in their economic development, the U.S. established the World Bank to provide capital to these states, which in turn would enable governments to rebuild their societies and invest.

The problem, however, was that most of the world's states lacked the capital to participate in the system of global trade. To solve this problem, the U.S. created the Marshall Plan, which agreed to loan money to the European and Asian states recovering from the war to finance their reconstruction. In a speech at Harvard University in June 1947, Secretary of State George Marshall argued:

> Aside from the demoralizing effect on the world at large and the possibilities of disturbances arising as a result of the desperation of the people concerned, the consequences to the economy of the United States should be apparent to all. It is logical that the United States

should do whatever it is able to do to assist in the return of normal economic health to the world, without which there can be no political stability and no assured peace. Our policy is not directed against any country, but against hunger, poverty, desperation and chaos. Any government that is willing to assist in recovery will find full co-operation on the part of the U.S.A.[11]

It is worth noting that while the plan was justified as necessary to restart European economic growth, stabilize the governments, and prevent mass starvation, these reasons appear secondary to the health of the U.S. economy. President Harry Truman and Secretary Marshall appeared far more concerned with the breakdown of the new world economic system centered on the dollar. For trade to commence, and for the U.S. to begin employing the massive number of G.I.s returning from the war, the U.S. needed export markets for its surplus production. The Marshall Plan loaned European states dollars to purchase the surplus production of American goods, which in turn would be used to rebuild the European economy. The Europeans would further be responsible for paying the loans back to the U.S. with interest. If the European states retained any surplus dollars, these dollars would then also be loaned back to the U.S. by purchasing American securities. These securities could then finance the provision of American military support to defend the European and Asian states from conventional threats from the Soviet Union and from Communist insurrections within their territories. The Marshall Plan provided a boon for American business, while simultaneously pushing the cost for maintaining the American forward defense position onto the U.S. allies.

This system was sustainable so long as American dollars could be redeemed into gold. The U.S. held roughly 60% of the world's gold reserves by 1947, which made it easy to continue issuing dollars.[12] Since dollars were guaranteed to be converted into gold at $35 per ounce, and since the U.S. controlled most of the world's gold, the U.S. could create money, exchange it for goods and services, and induce countries to send their capital back to the U.S. so the pattern could be repeated. Other states faced little alternative but to accept this system. Without American support, these states could potentially face insurrections within their territory, as many of the European states did following World War I.[13] This was particularly concerning given the increased power and influence of the Soviet Union. It appeared, based on his behavior in Eastern Europe, that Joseph Stalin sought to expand Soviet influence through Europe by supporting Communist parties in each of the states. The Asian states faced similar pressures following Mao Zedong's victory over Chiang Kai-Shek in China in 1950. These states therefore needed the American security guarantee to both finance their economic recoveries and fend off Communist insurrections.

The period 1950–1971 is often referred to as the "golden age" of the Bretton Woods system. The U.S. expanded its portfolio of allies throughout Europe and the developing world based on its willingness to defend these new states from Communist destabilization. The economies of countries allied with the U.S. grew much faster relative to the states in the Communist bloc, world trade increased substantially, and the American economy expanded at an impressive pace. Domestically, the U.S. experienced what became known as the Great Compression, when income inequality fell by 7.4%.[14] The U.S. workforce gained large access to higher education due to the financial support from the G.I. Bill. As a result, both productivity and wage growth in the U.S. markedly increased. During the 1960s, the Lyndon Johnson administration expanded on Franklin D. Roosevelt's Social Security programs with the creation of Medicare and Medicaid to provide health insurance for the elderly and disabled. These Great Society programs were very popular and quickly became integral parts of the American social order.

At the same time, the U.S. faced increasing budgetary pressures from financing these new programs and from the escalating Vietnam War. The U.S. was unable to quickly subdue the insurgency led by the Communist Vietminh in Southeast Asia and needed substantial resources to continue to fight on behalf of the fledgling South Vietnamese government. Simultaneously, the U.S. needed to finance the popular Great Society programs. Since cutting the new programs would be politically difficult, and rapidly ending the war in Vietnam would be an international humiliation, the U.S. continued creating more dollars. A problem emerged when President Charles de Gaulle of France began to question if the U.S. could convert the dollars it issued into gold at $35 per ounce. De Gaulle demanded that the U.S. redeem French holdings of $884 million in dollars for gold in 1965, followed by a further demand of $601 million in gold the following year. This led to a rush by several other states to redeem their own dollars into gold. While the U.S. could meet the demand initially, it lost the ability to do so by the early 1970s. President Richard M. Nixon announced on August 11, 1971, that the U.S. would no longer redeem dollars for gold and would instead allow the dollar to float against international currencies.[15] This decision, known as the "Nixon shock," effectively broke and ended the Bretton Woods system.

### DECLINING HEGEMONY: THE END OF BRETTON WOODS AND THE OIL SHOCKS

Following the Nixon shock, the U.S. dollar began to depreciate against gold. Americans therefore found themselves becoming much poorer as the dollar devalued against other currencies. To stem the loss in the dollar's value, the U.S. raised interest rates, which in turn increased borrowing costs. To make matters worse, the U.S. was also entering the process of deindustrialization due to the flood of cheap imports that had begun in the previous decade, a situation that was increasing layoffs and beginning to push the U.S. into a recession. The U.S. was in a position that was previously unthinkable: unemployment and inflation were simultaneously rising. This meant that as numerous Americans were losing their jobs to deindustrialization, they also found that their ability to purchase goods and services was eroding due to inflation.

The increased economic vulnerability of the U.S. was put on display during the October War between Egypt, Syria, and Israel. On October 6, 1973, the Israeli holy day of Yom Kippur, the Egyptian military crossed the Suez Canal and attacked the Israeli Defense Force (IDF) positions in the Sinai Peninsula. Simultaneously, the Syrians attacked the IDF on the Golan Heights. The two Arab states were armed with Soviet weaponry and, to the surprise of both the Israelis and the U.S., performed well in the initial phases of the war. However, the war soon stalemated as the Israelis mobilized their reserves and repelled the Syrian advance. After intelligence reports suggested that the Soviets were considering a military intervention to preserve their Egyptian and Syrian clients, the U.S. began an airlift of supplies to the Israelis known as Operation Nickel Grass. In response, the OPEC states led by Saudi Arabia announced on October 19 that they would impose a punitive embargo on oil sales to all states that were supporting Israel, including the U.S.

Although the U.S. continued to supply Israel, and the war ended in a defeat for the Arab states, the OPEC producers announced in early November that they would reduce oil production by 25%, which resulted in a nearly threefold increase in the price of oil. The OPEC embargo was particularly harmful to the U.S. for three reasons. First, the U.S. was already suffering from currency depreciation due to the abandonment of the gold standard. Second, although the U.S. had long been an oil producer itself, it had exhausted much of its domestic supply by the early 1970s.[16] Since the U.S. could not meet its oil needs from domestic sources, the increases in the price of oil produced a large outflow of dollars from the U.S. to the OPEC states. These states could not spend these dollars quickly enough, which meant that the dollars were not coming back to the U.S. In 1974, Treasury Secretary William Simon described this situation bleakly in a conversation with President Nixon:"With all the states with money and nowhere to spend it, the banks and financial markets are in trouble. Oil prices have created great instability in the international financial markets."[17]

During the golden age, the U.S. could simply borrow money to push through this difficult period based on its gold reserves. However, this was not possible with the removal of the gold standard. Interest rates on loans began to rise, and the U.S. found its budget deficit rapidly widening.

The third reason why the OPEC embargo was so painful was that the U.S. began experiencing a serious drought, which coupled with rising energy prices led to a stunning 20% increase in food prices in 1973 and a subsequent 12% increase in 1974.[18] These increases in the price of food and oil in the middle of a recession, along with increasing obligations to pay for the social safety net and war in Indochina, put the U.S. government under incredible strain. In a stark illustration of the times, New York City came to the brink of bankruptcy by 1975. Many other major cities found their tax bases dwindling as the effects of inflation became widespread. However, the pain of the oil embargo was felt most by American families, who were seeing their jobs lost and their savings depleted, while simultaneously suffering from the rising cost of basic living necessities.

The weakening U.S. economy created significant problems for American foreign policy. The ability of the U.S. to project power through the international system is a function of its economic base, which translates into resources to finance American defense positions throughout the world.[19] These resources allowed the U.S. to finance the army, navy, air force, marines, and the nation's vast intelligence-gathering establishment. However, if the value of the dollars that comprised the U.S. economy were to depreciate, this would decrease the overall strength of the U.S. economy. In other words, while the U.S. maintained a powerful military to project power during the early 1970s, the continuation of the embargo would render the U.S. unable to support this military in the coming years.

This situation is known as a "dynamic commitment problem" in studies of international relations, and it is a key cause of international conflict.[20] If a hegemon such as the U.S. precipitously weakens, rival states may opportunistically take advantage of this weakness to expand their power at the weakening hegemon's expense. With the U.S. facing economic decline in the early 1970s, the Soviet Union was in position to expand its own power in Southeast Asia and the Middle East. The Soviets maintained their own energy reserves and were less dependent on the Middle East.[21] Soviet surrogates such as Egypt and Iraq could now begin to destabilize the valuable territories of American clients, such as Iran and Saudi Arabia. Any gains made at the expense of American clients would only serve to further weaken the U.S., which in turn would allow greater Soviet advances elsewhere, perhaps even in Europe. The Nixon administration realized clearly that inflation was significantly weakening the U.S. security position.

## SAVING AMERICAN HEGEMONY

The administration's solution to the problem of rapidly rising oil prices was to push Iran and Saudi Arabia to increase their oil production to slow the rising price of oil. The U.S. maintained long ties with both regimes. American ties with Iran were an extension of the relationship between the British and Shah Mohammad Reza Pahlavi. During World War II, the Shah was removed from power due to his alleged Nazi sympathies. However, in the early 1950s, the new Iranian prime minister, Mohammad Mossadeq, initiated a plan to nationalize Iranian oil assets and limit the ability of Western oil companies to operate within the country. The Dwight D. Eisenhower administration responded by initiating Operation Ajax, which fomented a military coup in Iran using American and British intelligence services. The coup returned the Shah to power and promptly restored the ability of American and Anglo oil companies to operate. The Shah was seen by the Americans to be a staunch and progressive ally against the forces of upheaval, particularly potential nationalist and Communist impulses in the Middle East. The U.S. hoped to use its long ties with the Shah to encourage him to increase production and decrease the price of oil. However, he refused to cooperate, and instead sought to use the high price of oil and flow of dollars to invest in public goods, infrastructure, and other projects.

Saudi Arabia, on the other hand, was much more willing to assist the U.S. The U.S. enjoyed a long and friendly relationship with the House of Saud, who assumed complete control of the territory comprising their state in 1926. The U.S. soon recognized Saudi Arabia in 1933 and established the Arabian American Oil Company (Aramco) to explore for oil in the eastern part of the territory. These oil discoveries became critically important during World War II. In 1945, President Roosevelt signed a security agreement with King Abdel Aziz aboard the U.S.S. *Quincy* in the Suez Canal, cementing a relationship of friendship between the two states. However, despite the long American-Saudi friendship, the practices of the Wahhabi monarchy stood in stark contrast to Iran. The Wahhabis practiced a near Puritanical interpretation of Sunni Islam, whereas the Shah appeared far more socially progressive and secular. Although this made the Shah a more favorable ally to the

U.S., both regimes were critical in that they both possessed vast oil reserves, and both were staunchly anti-Communist.

The Saudis' enthusiasm for deepening their economic and security ties with the U.S. stemmed from their vulnerable security situation. The Soviets recognized that Saudi Arabia maintained the largest oil reserves in the world and that falling American production made the West critically dependent on the kingdom's oil. The Soviets could therefore deal a critical blow to the U.S. by seizing Saudi territory. To this end, the Soviets agreed to a fifteen-year Treaty of Friendship and Cooperation with Saddam Hussein's Iraq and began bolstering his military with their advanced weaponry. The Saudis faced another threat from instability in Yemen, where Egypt had previously intervened with the support of the Soviet Union. In addition to the threat of Communism, Saudi Arabia appeared very concerned about the possibility of Iranian aggression, given Pahlavi's open disdain for Wahhabism. Pahlavi modernized his military forces and encroached on the islands of Big Tunb, Little Tunb, and Abu Moussa, all of which were held by the United Arab Emirates (UAE), a Saudi ally. Despite these threats, Saudi Arabia could not field a military to compete with Egypt, Iraq, or Iran due to its very small population. The monarchy saw the U.S. as a solution to its security problems.

The eagerness of the Saudis to gain the backing of the U.S. military led to a remarkable agreement of cooperation. Saudi Arabia would continue to price oil exclusively in dollars and would use its power in OPEC to convince the other oil producers to do the same. In exchange, the U.S. would guarantee to defend the Saudi kingdom in perpetuity from all internal and external threats. Saudi Arabia was further given a promise that the U.S. would support the continuation of the monarchy and protect it from any internal challengers. While the deal therefore seemed quite favorable for the kingdom, it also served to halt the dollar's depreciation. If the world needed U.S. currency to purchase oil, the value of the dollar would stabilize.

For the system to work, the Saudis would have to be able to convert U.S. dollars into a commodity that would generate a return for the Saudis. Treasury Secretary Simon therefore proposed that the Saudis and other OPEC states reinvest the surplus dollars they acquired into U.S. securities and commercial banks. In his discussions with President Nixon, Simon stated, "I would like to get some commitment from them to purchase long- and short-term securities. That would be very helpful for our money markets."[22] The U.S. had a long history of meeting its obligations with respect to its securities, and it consistently delivered stable and positive rates of return. Additionally, the Federal Reserve began raising interest rates to very high levels to fight inflation in the U.S. This meant that the interest returns to the Saudis would become even greater, and their wealth would increase even more, so long as they maintained the system where oil could only be purchased with dollars. To the surprise of the administration, the Saudis were overwhelmingly enthusiastic about the proposal. Secretary Simon reported that it was received "Outstandingly. Even where I shouldn't have been." Simon further reported that other states were willing to cooperate; he told the president, "Two things will happen. We will get Arab investment in the U.S. Treasury certainly . . . They know we have the best credit and they can invest with us directly and not drive the market price up."[23]

To facilitate the recycling of the vast quantities of petrodollars from Saudi Arabia, Simon allowed for special offerings of securities beyond the normal amount the U.S. government offered publicly. Additionally, given U.S. support for Israel and the precarious security position of the monarchy, King Faisal asked the U.S. to keep the purchases of U.S. treasuries "discreet."[24] The Saudis did not want to appear to be assisting Israel's top benefactor in the region for fear of stirring internal and regional unrest against them. From the American perspective, there were also reasons to keep the arrangement quiet. First, if it became clear that the U.S. depended on Saudi Arabia to this extent, it would encourage the Soviets to use their proxies in the Middle East to attack and destabilize the kingdom. Second, the revelation that the dollar needed Arab support to prevent depreciation might cause speculators to attack by selling their dollars in exchange for gold while the dollar held some value. This in turn would exacerbate the problem of depreciation and defeat the purpose of the entire arrangement with the Saudis. In addition to these strategic reasons, the overwhelming reason to keep the arrangement quiet was the need for the Nixon and subsequent Ford administrations to avoid admitting to the American public that the U.S. economy was now more vulnerable than it had been in the past. Interestingly, some in the Nixon and then the Ford administrations advocating having open discussions with the U.S. public about these seismic changes in the global economy. For example, Ford's chairman of the Council of Economic Advisors and future chairman of the Federal Reserve, Alan Greenspan, stated that the administration should inform the public that the days where the U.S. could inoculate itself from the world were over and that oil was a key economic problem.[25] However, President Gerald R. Ford was up for reelection in 1976 and had presided over the U.S. defeat in Vietnam, the damage of the oil shocks, and the shadow of Nixon's impeachment. With all of this baggage, admitting to the American public that the government was now dependent on foreign states, particularly Arab states, would likely pose significant damage to his efforts to keep power.[26] Congressional leaders were already expressing some concern that U.S. foreign policy interests would now be held captive by the Arab states. This was especially concerning since nearly all of these states were openly hostile to Israel. Admitting that the U.S. needed the Arabs, and would in fact depend on them, would all but doom Ford's reelection effort. Since Ford preferred to hold onto power, and since the Saudis preferred to remain discreet about the arrangement, the deal to protect the kingdom in perpetuity in exchange for the oil peg remained secret.

The Shah of Iran was left out of the deal due to his unwillingness to cooperate, though President Nixon and Secretary of State Henry Kissinger, and later President Ford, all preferred working with him as opposed to the Saudis.[27] Treasury Secretary Simon pushed hard for making the Saudis the critical partner in the relationship rather than Iran. Simon argued, "Saudi Arabia has probably 150 years of production left, whereas Iran has only 15 years."[28] While the Nixon administration promised the Saudis perpetual security, the Ford administration signaled to Pahlavi that the U.S. was preparing contingency plans to invade and depose the monarchy in the event of instability in the kingdom.[29] The instability referred to a hostile takeover of the monarchy following the assassination of King Faisal in March 1975. However, despite these overtures, Pahlavi announced at his departure that he would continue to seek increases in the price of oil. Simon's argument in favor of Saudi Arabia strengthened in 1976 when the Saudis held off increases in the price of oil at the December OPEC meetings. The meetings pitted the Saudis against the Iranians in an argument over price increases. When the Saudis won over the Shah, it became clear that they would be America's key partner in the Middle East. The fall in the price of oil in the following year began accelerating the collapse of Pahlavi's regime, which culminated in 1979 during the Iranian Revolution.

Although inflation continued to plague the U.S. through the end of the decade, particularly after the Iranian Revolution of 1979, the agreement with the Saudis soon began to bear fruit. Shortly after Saudi Arabia agreed to maintain its oil sales in dollars, and the kingdom began acquiring large amounts of U.S. dollars, other states in OPEC quickly followed suit. Other commodities soon followed the lead of oil and remained exclusively priced in American dollars as well. International demand for U.S. dollars again increased. However, this time, the arrangement was far more lucrative. While the amount of gold is finite, oil production was consistently increasing. This allowed the U.S. to create more dollars to bolster its wealth. Additionally, since the dollars traded for oil were subsequently reinvested in American treasuries, the U.S. could again run budget deficits to finance large defense budgets and domestic spending with low tax rates.

From the Saudi perspective, the kingdom gained a security guarantee from a very powerful ally that could stabilize the monarchy in perpetuity. Moreover, the monarchy saw the system as a way to vastly improve its riches. The Saudis could collect steady rates of interest on their American treasuries, allowing them to further profit from their oil sales. The U.S. further accelerated Saudi monetary gains by relaxing the rules on capital controls and on the divisions between commercial and investment banking. This deregulation allowed American financial institutions to take greater risks and realize greater profits. Additionally, the price of oil soon began to fall as the Saudis and their allies in OPEC agreed to increase production. This increase in supply, the end of the embargo, and U.S. Federal Reserve Chairman Paul Volcker's decision to raise interest rates, successfully tamed inflation in the U.S.

The increase in oil production further created a financial attack on the Soviet economy, which was highly dependent on oil and other natural resources. The collapse in world energy prices, coupled with enormous defense expenditures and the disastrous war in Afghanistan, led to the dissolution of the Soviet Union and the end of its Eastern European empire in the late 1980s and early 1990s. The revolutions in Eastern Europe opened these states to multinational investment and created new trading partners for American firms. As with the Marshall Plan, these governments accepted loans to make the transition from command to market economies, which were then used to purchase goods from the U.S. that could be paid back with interest. The U.S. once again found itself with a booming economy. The U.S. continued to create dollars and exchange them for oil; the money from the oil revenues would be reinvested in the U.S. market, and American firms would consistently deliver excellent returns due to demand from the transitioning countries and increasing multinational investment in countries that were adopting market reforms. Domination of the world's energy market not only saved U.S. hegemony, it exponentially increased American economic power.

## THE BENEFITS OF HEGEMONY AND
## THE PETRODOLLAR SYSTEM

Let us consider the benefits this international order provides to most Americans. Americans represent about 5% of the world's population. Yet, at the end of the Cold War in 1990, the U.S. economy generated about 26.6% of the world's gross domestic product.[30] By 1998, 86.8% of all global foreign transactions in were conducted in dollars.[31] This position allowed all Americans to benefit from the large international demand for dollars that American economic and military hegemony provides. This demand enabled Americans to enjoy low interest rates, which in turn increased consumer spending. Lower-income Americans could not only afford luxury items at cheaper prices from imports due to the strength of the dollar and but could also simultaneously purchase automobiles and homes on credit. Additionally, all Americans enjoyed the benefits of low taxation while funding Social Security, Medicare, defense, public schools, and a police force on credit. While the benefits were fewer for the less affluent and the poor, these groups still gained a relatively higher quality of life in comparison to their counterparts overseas.

Given these benefits, a central goal of U.S. foreign policy was to maintain this financial dominance, which rested on three pillars. First, the dollar needed to remain in high demand. This demand could be supported by keeping sales of oil and all other energy products pegged to U.S. dollars. While there was some concern that Saudi Arabia would no longer need the protection of the U.S. military after the Cold War, the Iraqi invasion of Kuwait in 1990 and the increased assertiveness of Iran both reinforced the need for American protection. Saudi Arabia maintained the incentive to use its power in OPEC to keep oil sales pegged to dollars. Second, the system required dollars from abroad to be recycled into American financial institutions and securities. American multinationals therefore required profits in the domestic market as well as the stability of investments abroad. The U.S. therefore preferred supporting regimes that are willing to continue paying back loans to American financial institutions and staying in the international economic system as opposed to supporting leaders who threaten to withdraw from the system and default on their payments. As with the pricing of dollars, this situation appeared to be relatively stable.[32] These investments enabled the U.S. to make credit readily available to consumers and firms, which in turn allowed demand in the U.S. to stay high and profits to continue.[33]

The third and most often overlooked pillar of American economic success was the ability of the U.S. to project military force abroad.[34] The privileged position of the U.S. stemmed from its superiority in ground, naval, air, and space weapons and its ability to use these weapons in response to any threat. Having this power enabled the U.S. to contain any disruptions to the international economic system, such as Saddam Hussein's adventurism in Kuwait or North Korea's desire to absorb the

South. American naval power further ensured stability of the seas and the ability of commerce to flow uninterrupted. In many ways, preserving this dominance was also in the interest of many of America's financial competitors, such as the European Union and Japan, which both contended with potential threats from Russia and China, respectively. Both benefited from the U.S.'s ability to maintain hegemony over the Middle East, Asia, and Africa and secure the flow of energy supplies from these regions to the world. To maintain the ability to serve as the guarantor of the economic system, the U.S. constructed numerous forward bases throughout the world that allowed for rapid power projection in response to threats and to minimize disruptions throughout the world.[35] In other words, the international economic system depended on "stability," or the lack of any challengers to the current order.

## RISING THREATS TO AMERICAN HEGEMONY IN THE NEW CENTURY

By the end of the Cold War, the U.S. was the unchallenged military hegemon of the global system, with unrivaled power. The dollar accounted for 89.9% of the world's economic transactions,[36] the U.S. economy was booming on the strength of the Internet revolution, and the U.S. enjoyed a budget surplus. American military power was unrivaled; the U.S. could fight major military engagements while typically losing few soldiers in battle. In his final State of the Union address, President Bill Clinton declared, "The state of our union is the strongest it has ever been."[37] However, the U.S. faced three interrelated challenges over the horizon: Saddam Hussein's Iraq, the emergence of al Qaeda, and the creation of the euro.[38]

The first challenge came from Iraqi president Saddam Hussein's invasion of neighboring Kuwait in August 1990. Saddam alleged that Kuwait was exceeding oil production quotas and driving the price down, making it difficult to repay Iraqi debts from its war with Iran. Saddam believed that the Iranian war was waged on behalf of all Arabs, but he was now being squeezed economically by those states that benefited the most from it. Saddam voiced these complaints in a now-famous meeting with U.S. Ambassador April Glaspie, where he asked if the U.S. was prepared to defend Kuwait in the event of a military conflict. Glaspie replied that the U.S. did not get involved in Arab-Arab conflicts but that any dispute should be resolved peacefully. Many historians believed that this meeting encouraged Saddam to proceed with his invasion of Kuwait. The problem, however, stemmed from a combination of the Bush administration's distrust of Saddam and the American commitment to defend the security of the cooperative OPEC states. The administration looked suspiciously on Saddam's prior ties to the Soviet Union, his anti-Israeli rhetoric, and his willingness to use chemical weaponry to suppress internal revolts. Given this history, Bush appeared deeply skeptical of allowing Saddam to move from controlling 9% of the world's oil reserves to 15.1%, which would rival Saudi Arabia's 15.9%.[39] Saddam's unpredictability might have led to a destabilization of financial markets if he were to threaten a move away from the petrodollar agreements. Additionally, however, the U.S. commitment to its allies in OPEC specified that it would protect the security of each of these states. Kuwait was a key part of the petrodollar system. The Iraqi invasion therefore needed to be turned back not only because of the oil now under Saddam's control but also to affirm the credibility of the American defense guarantee. The U.S. was therefore compelled to act. The full power of the U.S. military came on display with a stunningly rapid defeat of Iraq in five weeks from January to February 1991. The U.S. overwhelmed the fourth-largest army in the world armed with Soviet weapons, all while suffering only 376 battle deaths.[40]

The second challenge to American dominance came from Osama bin Laden, a former Afghan mujahideen fighter who began organizing his former veterans into a group known as al Qaeda, or "the base." Bin Laden challenged the decision by Saudi Arabia to allow the American military to maintain a base within its territory. Bin Laden proposed initially to lead a guerrilla war to liberate the territory from Saddam. The monarchy respectfully dismissed his plan and instead chose to authorize the deployment of American forces into the kingdom. The decision created substantial unrest as numerous religious scholars protested the presence of U.S. forces in Saudi Arabia, which was home to Mecca and

Medina, the holiest sites in Islam. In response, the kingdom initiated a program of mass arrests and suppression, and soon made the decision to expel bin Laden himself for agitating propaganda against the regime. The interesting facet of this decision was that bin Laden was part of the Saudi elite and supportive of King Fahd. The regime was also a considerable benefactor to numerous religious radical groups, including bin Laden's. Yet, bin Laden publicly denounced the regime and its decision.

Bin Laden first moved to Sudan but was quickly expelled. With his organization on its knees, bin Laden was given sanctuary by the Taliban, a Pakistani-supported group that controlled a large portion of Afghanistan's territory. The Taliban saw bin Laden as someone who might provide some financial assistance in their wars against other parts of the mujahideen. From his bases in Afghanistan, bin Laden continued to wage a propaganda war against Saudi Arabia to further destabilize the monarchy. In 1998, al Qaeda staged two high-profile attacks against U.S. embassies in Kenya and Tanzania. These attacks elevated bin Laden to one of America's most wanted fugitives. American policymakers warned that bin Laden's organization was a significant threat to the U.S. and to the stability of the Saudi regime. In response, the U.S. ordered airstrikes against al Qaeda targets in both Sudan and Afghanistan. The failure of these strikes to kill bin Laden only elevated his status further. This image continued in 2000 with the suicide attack on the U.S.S. *Cole* in the Gulf of Aden. Bin Laden assumed the role of the leader of the resistance against American policies and its apostate puppet regimes in the Middle East, and became spiritual guardian of the true believers.[41]

Although bin Laden could be considered just another fanatical terrorist, his public statements and rhetoric were quite concerning to analysts in the United States. Bin Laden's stated goal was to expel the U.S. from the Middle East and destabilize the apostate regimes supporting U.S. interests. A closer examination also reveals that Bin Laden's original letter voicing his dispute with the Saudi monarchy listed almost entirely economic grievances.[42] One of them cites that the increase in Saudi oil production only benefited U.S. interests. He further argued that the system benefited American and Western citizens at the expense of the Saudi population as well as the larger Arab population in the Middle East. Additionally, bin Laden charged the monarchy with stashing its resources abroad and depleting the kingdom's real resources. These attacks indicate that bin Laden seemed to have some understanding of the economic impact of the kingdom's security arrangement with the U.S.

Even more concerning, however, was that there appeared to be some sympathy for these viewpoints within the monarchy. The royal family encouraged and cultivated numerous radical religious groups in an effort to regulate Islamist forces within the kingdom. This behavior continued into the 1990s as several members of the royal family openly gave to charities associated with these groups, including numerous affiliates of al Qaeda.[43] Since Saudi Arabia adopted this "softer" policy toward Islamic radicals, and these radicals were now demanding a severance of the cooperative relationship between the U.S. and the kingdom, American officials were concerned about Saudi cooperation with these Islamists. With the Cold War over, Saddam Hussein defeated, and the Arab-Israeli peace process underway, the Saudis could potentially view cooperation with the U.S. as more of a security liability than an asset. This could potentially jeopardize the very foundations of the security agreement supporting American hegemony.

The third threat to U.S. dominance came from the birth of the euro in 1999. The euro was a common currency that would be shared by the member states of the European Union. The combined economy of the European states was roughly equal to that of the U.S. The creation of this alternative currency posed a potential challenge to the supremacy of the dollar on the world market. Previously, there was no more attractive financial market than the U.S., giving each one of the producers in OPEC a reason to accept dollars for energy. However, with the euro forming a common market rivaling that of the U.S., OPEC could potentially price in both dollars and euros.

Despite this threat, the U.S. maintained three key advantages over the euro. First, the clear majority of the world's transactions were conducted in dollars, making the dollar the status quo. Second, states such as Saudi Arabia held investments in dollars, and seemingly had no reason to allow these holdings to lose value by weakening the dollar relative to the euro. The third, and most important, reason was that the U.S. possessed the military power to provide security to anyone whereas the Europeans did not. So long as the Saudis needed American security, the Saudis would have even less of a reason to move away from pricing oil exclusively in dollars. The Saudis faced challenges from al Qaeda, Saddam Hussein's Iraq, and Iran, all of which justified a forward U.S. presence. These threats provided ample reason for the Saudis to continue the system of dollars for oil.

A different situation existed for Saddam Hussein's Iraq. Since the first Gulf War in the early 1990s, Iraq faced crippling U.N. sanctions that prohibited trade with the major oil consumers of the world. The only exception to the sanctions came from a program known as "Oil for Food," which permitted Iraq to trade oil on a limited basis. The U.N. claimed that if weapons inspectors could certify that Saddam Hussein eliminated his arsenals of chemical and biological weapons, the U.N. would consider removing the sanctions. However, despite Saddam's declaration that he was cooperating with the effort, U.N. weapons inspectors consistently argued that Iraq was obstructing their efforts. Additionally, tensions between the U.S. and Iraq remained high. The U.S. saw several of Iraq's military maneuvers as provocative and threatening to American positions in Saudi Arabia. These tensions came to a head in late 1998. The U.S. charged that Saddam was not complying with U.N. weapons inspections, and it initiated a punitive bombing campaign known as Operation Desert Fox. Saddam responded by announcing that he would no longer cooperate with the U.N. and expelling all inspectors from his territory. This expulsion effectively guaranteed that sanctions against Iraq would remain in place and Saddam's ability to trade oil would be constrained.

Saddam responded in the fall of 2000 by announcing that he would transition from accepting dollars for oil to exclusively trading his oil in euros.[44] American companies that were importing Iraqi oil would therefore need to convert their dollars into euros to purchase Iraqi oil. This decision challenged the fundamental bedrock of American hegemony. Iraq was estimated to have approximately 10–11% of the world's proven oil reserves in 2002.[45] Additionally, a significant percentage of Iraq's oil fields were either unexplored or undiscovered. If Saddam would now sell his oil for euro instead of dollars, the European states would have an incentive to open trading to strengthen the value of their currency. If this happened, other OPEC states would face pressure to follow suit. The value of the dollar would fall, and Americans might face the possibility of rising interest rates and a weaker currency. In short, Saddam's decision posed the first serious threat to American hegemony since the end of the Cold War.

### 9/11 AND THE WAR FOR PERMANENT AMERICAN HEGEMONY

The 9/11 terrorist attacks provided the U.S. with the opportunity to deal with each of these security threats. Speaking in an interview in May 1998, prior to the attacks, bin Laden seemed to express belief that the violence in the U.S. homeland would compel the Americans to abandon their positions in the Middle East. His argument was based on (1) his observations of the U.S. withdrawal from Lebanon following the October 1983 barracks bombing and (2) the American withdrawal from Somalia following the perceived failure of Operation Gothic Serpent, otherwise known as "Black Hawk Down," in May 1993. In the interview, when discussing the withdrawal from Somalia, bin Laden stated,

> Our boys were shocked by the low morale of the American soldier and they realized that the American soldier was just a paper tiger. He was unable to endure the strikes that were dealt to his army, so he fled, and America had to stop all its bragging and all that noise it was making in the press after the Gulf War."[46]

While these arguments are directly from bin Laden, an alternative theory is that the terrorist leader was not speaking sincerely. Instead, his purpose behind the attack may have been to strategically provoke the U.S. into a larger confrontation in the Middle East. As part of this process, al Qaeda would decentralize and spread into various civilian populations within multiple states throughout the region. In doing so, al Qaeda hoped to provoke the U.S. into attacking these civilian populations indiscriminately. While this would certainly result in casualties for the terrorist group, it is a common practice for insurgencies to push their target governments into indiscriminate violence.[47] Doing so may compel civilian populations to turn to the terrorists for protection, even if the civilian population is not sympathetic to the terrorists' cause and does not necessarily share the terrorists' ideology. By triggering a violent American reaction, bin Laden's call to all Muslims to rise up against the apostate governments would be realized, which in turn would start a large revolution throughout the region that could bring about the second coming of the caliphate.

Regardless of bin Laden's true intentions, the terrorist attack did provoke a violent American response. The U.S. first sought to use its military power to dismantle al Qaeda in Afghanistan. This effort expanded contacts with many of the neighboring states, including Kazakhstan, Uzbekistan, and Tajikistan, which all provided a way for the U.S. to secure vital energy supplies from Central Asia and ensure that these commodities would continue to be traded in dollars. Further, Afghanistan contained vast deposits of minerals and rare earths. The invasion of Afghanistan therefore gave the U.S. an opportunity to both eliminate the threat to Saudi Arabia and denominate sales of Afghanistan's primary commodities in dollars.

Most importantly, while the U.S. sought to dismantle al Qaeda and sympathetic terrorist organizations, the 9/11 attacks also gave the U.S. the pretext to depose Saddam Hussein and remove the threat of the oil sales in euros as opposed to dollars. Immediately after the attack, American policymakers seemed to search for any reason to link the attacks to Saddam Hussein. Though very little evidence existed of a cooperative relationship between Saddam and al Qaeda, American officials openly suggested that Saddam could provide al Qaeda, or a group like al Qaeda, with nuclear material that might be used against American cities. Numerous administration officials claimed that the U.S. needed to wage preemptive war before it was too late.[48] Two years after 9/11, the U.S. initiated Operation Enduring Freedom to depose Saddam Hussein.

By the end of April 2003, with the fall of Baghdad, the U.S. had seemingly neutralized each of the threats to its dominance. The U.S. quickly deposed the Taliban, Saddam Hussein, and put Osama bin Laden on the run. The U.S. installed new regimes in both Afghanistan and Iraq that would reflect and protect American strategic interests. Most significantly, both states would now become critical partners in sustaining American domination over the world's energy market. However, in the new world where the dollar would have to compete with the euro, or possible other future currencies, the U.S. needed to cement the link between energy and dollars by gaining the cooperation of other key states with energy supplies and those states along the world's energy trading routes. Prior to the start of the Iraq war, the position of most states participating in the energy market was to default to the U.S.-led system of trading energy for dollars. With Saddam's adoption of the euro, and with bin Laden's rise, the willingness of these states to cooperate in the petrodollar system was no longer guaranteed, nor could it be taken for granted by the U.S. Consolidating the energy market under American control would therefore require the U.S. to both contain threats against cooperative suppliers and transit states, secure the westward and eastern trade routes from the Middle East, and deter any external challengers to the energy market.

To protect this infrastructure, the U.S. would need to cultivate its relationships with several of its old alliance partners, and many new ones, by extending its old deal with the Gulf states to many of its new partners. These states would agree to support the U.S.-created energy market by providing bases and free passage of American forces, and placing their surplus financial assets in U.S. treasuries, banks, and investment houses. In exchange, the U.S. would provide these states with permanent protection from all of their internal and external enemies, as it had done for the other members of OPEC. The U.S. justified this forward presence as necessary to fight terrorist groups that posed challenges to its new allies throughout the globe.

Figure 2.1 presents the U.S. State Department's intelligence assessment of al Qaeda's presence in November 2001 and illustrates how the threat of terrorism provided the U.S. with the opportunity

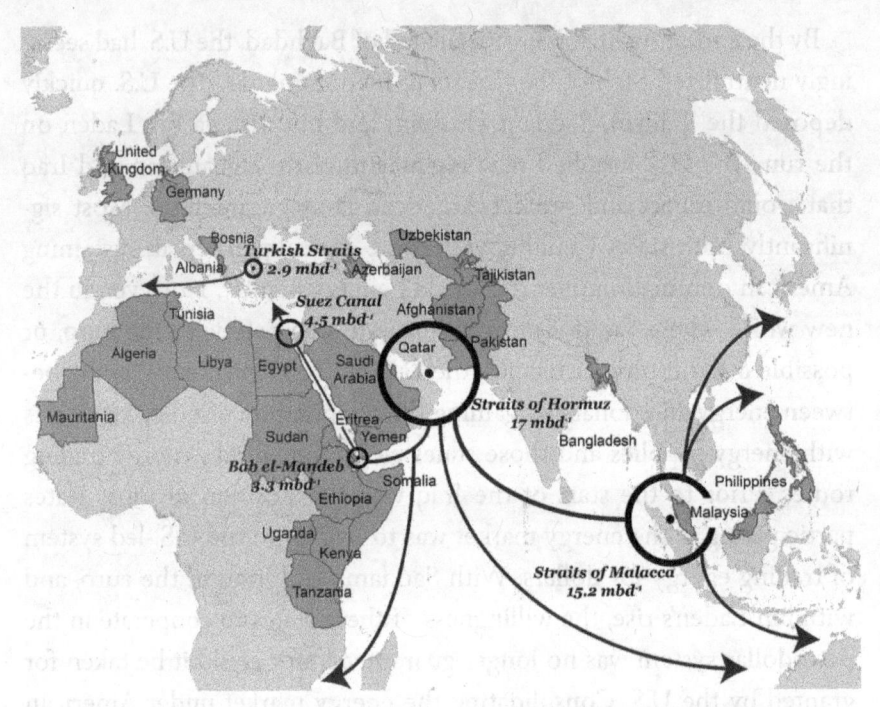

Figure 2.1. Trade Routes and Chokepoints for Global Energy and the Spread of al Qaeda.

Note. Shaded areas indicate declared al Qaeda presence. Data on energy trade routes and chokepoints are from U.S. Energy Information Administration (2017). Arrows represent sea routes for global energy sales. Circles represent chokepoints in the energy routes. Chokepoint names and volume passing through labeled in bold.

to permanently secure its hegemony over world energy markets. Following Operation Enduring Freedom, al Qaeda seemed to spread from Afghanistan throughout the former Soviet Republics and throughout North and East Africa. Notice the correlation between the states hosting al Qaeda and the routes of the energy trade. In the east, both Malaysia and Indonesia are identified as hosts of al Qaeda affiliates, including the Jemaah Islamiyah organization. Both states are at the gateway to the Strait of Malacca, where over 15% of the world's oil travels. This is the gateway to Asia for Middle Eastern oil. Dominating the energy market therefore requires cooperation from Malaysia, Indonesia, and the Philippines. Each of these states became willing partners in the war on terror. Malaysia's Mohammed Mahathir enthusiastically signed up for American initiatives to combat terror, despite years of anti-American rhetoric, creating the Southeast Asia

Regional Center for Counterterrorism (SEARCCT) to serve as a hub for the region's counterterror efforts. While Malaysia's al Qaeda cell did not appear terribly active, both Indonesia and the Philippines had active al Qaeda cells within their territory. Similarly, the government of Indonesia signed up to receive military aid to combat terrorist organizations within its territory. One possibility behind these developments is that both states felt a genuine sense of threat from terrorist groups. Indonesia suffered a terrorist attack in the resort city of Bali that killed over 200 tourists in October 2002; another attack targeted a Marriott hotel in Jakarta in August 2003. Including these high-profile incidents, Indonesia suffered 299 attacks resulting in 660 fatalities in the period 2000–2005.[49] For its part, the Philippines battled the Islamic separatist groups known as the Moro National Liberation Front (MNLF), the Moro Islamic Liberation Front (MILF), and the al Qaeda–linked Abu Sayyaf group. These conflicts in Mindanao resulted in 394 terrorist attacks and over one thousand deaths in the same period, 2000–2005.

At first glance, these numbers seem quite disturbing and signal that terrorism was indeed a security risk for these states, making it obvious that they would benefit from increased security cooperation with the U.S. However, let us put the damage caused by terrorism to each of these states in perspective. The Global Terrorism Database indicates that Malaysia suffered a grand total of two attacks in the period 2000–2005. While Indonesia and the Philippines suffered considerably more, the attacks in this entire period resulted in the death of .000003 of Indonesia's population, and .00001 of the Filipino population. Again, while each individual death is tragic in and of itself, and the optics of terror are very disturbing, it does not appear that terrorist groups in any of these countries posed a significant threat to the survival of these states. Yet, each of these states was very willing to cooperate with the U.S. in exchange for a security guarantee. An alternative interpretation is that both leaders accepted a security guarantee from the U.S. in exchange for cooperating with American energy initiatives, which would prove to be very lucrative for all the states involved. The states would agree to cooperate in keeping both the Strait of Malacca and sea lanes open so oil and gas could reach both China and Japan. This in turn would enable the U.S. to cement a critical role in the energy trade in the Pacific. While the resources from the U.S. could serve as a check against domestic enemies within both states, security ties with the U.S. would also be useful in guarding against the rising power of China in the future.

While the eastern routes from the Strait of Hormuz rely on transit through the Strait of Malacca, the westward routes from the Strait of Hormuz split in two directions. First, ships trading energy could enter the Red Sea using the opening at the Bab el-Mandeb Strait off the Yemeni coastline. This waterway is quite small: only about twenty miles between the city of Ras Menheli in Yemen to the city of Ras Siyyan in Djibouti. Yet, this waterway and the Suez Canal are the only links from the Indian Ocean to the Mediterranean Sea. The Red Sea route is critical to transporting Middle Eastern energy to Europe, given that the alternative route is to navigate around the African coast to the Cape of Good Hope, which would add substantial time and monetary cost. The protection of this entrance to the Red Sea is critical for maintaining the world's energy market and is why, despite the lack of resources within the country, the U.S. doubled down on its commitment to protecting the regime of Abdullah Saleh in Yemen. The Yemeni president faced multiple insurgencies against his regime in the early 2000s, including separatists in the south, opposition from the Shia Houthi sect, and al Qaeda–inspired militants. The U.S. viewed Yemen as a fractionalized society lacking both a national identity and a strong central government. To maintain security over Bab el-Mandeb, and to prevent the passageway from falling into the hands of either hostile militants or Iranian supported ones, the U.S. made Saleh a critical partner in the war on terror, a role the Yemeni president seemed to relish. The U.S. further doubled its efforts on the African side of Bab el-Mandeb. First, the U.S. gained permission from President Ismaïl Omar Guelleh to begin the Combined Joint Task Force–Horn of Africa program in Djibouti. As part of this effort, the U.S. built a military facility at Camp Lemonnier in Djibouti, giving the U.S. the ability to use its military power to protect the entrance to the Red Sea.

In addition to deepening its cooperation with Djibouti, the U.S. returned to Somalia, a country it had once abandoned. Although Somalia had seemingly long left the consciousness of American policymakers, the fact that Somalia bordered Bab el-Mandeb and had a growing presence of fighters sympathetic to al Qaeda raised alarms in Washington. Since intervention into Somalia was politically difficult, the U.S. relied on a strategy of providing military assistance to regional allies to combat Islamist groups in the Horn. These states included Ethiopia, Kenya, and Uganda. Together, these states would serve to contain any possibility of an Islamist group taking control of southern Somalia and would protect energy traffic through Bab el-Mandeb. In exchange, each of these states gained increased military assistance and cooperation from U.S. headquarters in Djibouti. The U.S. further ignored irregular democratic elections and human rights abuses of each of these countries in exchange for their cooperation. This effectively made cooperating with the U.S. a deal none of these states could refuse. With the cooperation of these countries, energy supplies could cross safely through Bab el-Mandeb to the Suez Canal, where Egypt's president Hosni Mubarak would guarantee their passage.

In addition to moving through the Red Sea, energy from the Middle East is also sent south down the African coast to the Cape of Good Hope. Securing these routes required the U.S. to cooperate with Kenya, Tanzania, and South Africa. Interestingly, each of these states had been a cooperative partner with the U.S. prior to 9/11. Al Qaeda famously attacked the American embassies in both Kenya and Tanzania in 1998, bringing it to global infamy. South Africa also remained a cooperative partner with the U.S., given its status as Africa's financial leader. Once around the Cape, energy supplies either travel west to Latin America or head northwest to the United States. An additional source of energy comes from Africa's west coast, where both Angola and Nigeria were becoming significant suppliers. The routes from these two suppliers transport energy north past Algeria to either the Mediterranean Sea or to northern Europe.

Taken together, these passages comprise the critical sea routes for the American-dominated energy market. Interestingly, although there were other large militant groups practicing terrorism elsewhere in the world, such as the Forces démocratiques de libération du Rwanda and the National Army for the Liberation of Uganda, as well as the Communist Party of Nepal, these groups were not on the State Department's 2002 list of designated foreign terrorist organizations.[50] The groups on the list were largely those in states that serve as key suppliers of global energy and those along the critical supply lines. The group of terrorists targeted by the U.S. would grow following the war on terror.

At the turn of the millennium, the future of governing world energy supplies was believed to be in Central Asia. The "Stans," or former Soviet republics, were becoming more prominent sources of oil, natural gas, and other rare earths key to powering the industry in the future. Further, numerous states dreamed of a "New Silk Road," or a land route connecting China and India with the European states. With the possibility of constructing such a critical land or pipeline route, along with seemingly limitless supplies in Central Asia, the supply of energy in the Stans represented a prize to whatever state could dominate it. After the invasion of Afghanistan, the U.S. found itself in a unique position to do reach for that prize. Despite some effort by Russia to resist the U.S. military's use of its former republics, the Stans were cooperative partners with U.S. efforts in Afghanistan. In exchange, the U.S. would guarantee the safety of these states, provide them with military aid, assist in developing their energy resources, and protect them from the possibility of Russian aggression. With the U.S. given the ability to exploit energy in these areas, and build the link between Central Asia and the East, the U.S. was in position to dominate the energy market in perpetuity. The war on terror compelled the U.S. to redouble its efforts to protect the current energy infrastructure, but it also gave the U.S. access to new supplies and partners both in the Middle East and Central Asia. Now, the task for the U.S. would be to guarantee the security of its new partners. This task would soon prove to be more difficult than the American policymakers originally expected.

# 3

# TERRORISM AND THE PROBLEM OF MORAL HAZARD

U.S. hegemony appeared unassailable in the spring of 2003. The U.S. had established friendly regimes in Afghanistan and Iraq and had secured the cooperation of the world's major producers of energy as well as the states comprising the key transit routes. The U.S. extended its guarantee to protect these host states from all internal and external enemies, so long as these hosts cooperated in the petrodollar system and recycled their profits back to U.S. markets. The new war on terror required the U.S. to guarantee the security of these host states while building them into reliable partners to protect the world's energy infrastructure. Yet, despite the security guarantees and enormous commitment of resources, terrorist violence in the American-backed host states became far worse following the end of Operations Enduring Freedom and Iraqi Freedom. Figure 3.1 demonstrates that both terrorist attacks and the number of fatalities from this violence in the affected regions of the Middle East, Asia, and Africa exponentially increased during the period 2002–2007. These data suggest that U.S. was failing to protect

*Monsters to Destroy: Understanding the War on Terror*. Navin A. Bapat, Oxford University Press (2019).
© Oxford University Press.
DOI: 10.1093/oso/9780190061456.001.0001

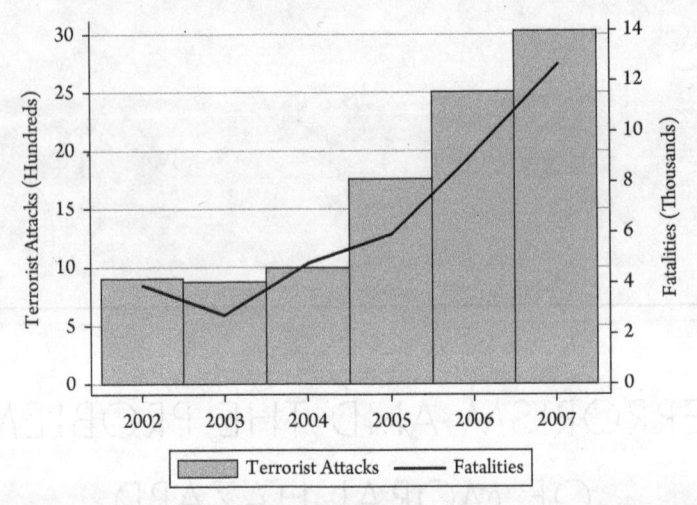

Figure 3.1. Terrorist Attacks and Fatalities from Terrorism in Middle East, Africa, and Asia, 2002–2007.
Note. Data from the Global Terrorism Database; see National Consortium for the Study of Terrorism and Responses to Terrorism (START). 2018. Global Terrorism Database [data file]m. Retrieved from https://www.start.umd.edu/gtd. Counts exclude attacks in North America, South America, Europe, and Oceania.

and secure the key host states that supplied energy and served as transit routes.

This chapter argues that this failure can be attributed to a moral hazard problem created by the U.S. strategy. Moral hazard refers to a situation where an individual, who would ordinarily avoid risk, gets some form of support that allows her to take these same risks that may produce adverse outcomes. In this case, since the host states had American protection, they were free to take the risk of engaging in increasingly corrupt behaviors, all while labeling their political opponents as "terrorists." Even though many of these groups were motivated by local grievances and showed little interest in the politics of energy, the U.S. was obligated to defend the hosts so long as the threat of "terrorism" existed. Further, since the U.S. would pay to defend hosts from all terrorist threats, but would reduce its military support if the threat of terrorism receded, the American strategy gave host states little incentive to disarm its terrorists. Instead, the hosts developed incentives to play up the threat of terrorism and demand U.S. protection. As a result, the host regimes, such as Afghanistan, Pakistan, Yemen, Egypt, and numerous others, grew increasingly corrupt, repressive, and unresponsive to their populations, leaving the U.S. to defend them from the growing terrorist threats in their territories.

However, despite this clear evidence that these hosts were exploiting the security arrangement, I argue that the U.S. continued to support these host states in order to protect its dominance over global energy markets. This protection enabled host leaders to ignore the demands of their local populations while continuing to recycle profits into American treasuries and financial institutions. Paradoxically, the increasing terrorist violence served the interests both of the U.S. and of the host leaders. It forced the U.S. to defend the host leaders, even as they refused to negotiate with their political opponents. Simultaneously, it made host leaders dependent on the U.S. for their security, which in turn supported their participation in the petrodollar system. In a sense, the threat of terrorism *benefited* the U.S. by giving it reason to provide protection, which in turn supported the host states' willingness to cooperate in the petrodollar system. To make this argument, let us first examine the security situation faced by the U.S. at the end of the Iraq war.

## SECURING THE GLOBAL ENERGY MARKET AND THE PROBLEM OF WEAK STATES

The security situation in most of the host states under the American security umbrella began to deteriorate shortly after the U.S. victory in Afghanistan. Both the Pakistani Taliban and various Kashmiri militant groups responded to Pervez Musharraf's renouncement of terrorism and rapprochement with India by staging numerous assassination attempts against the critical U.S. ally. American policymakers viewed the situation with considerable concern. Afghanistan was only accessible through Pakistan and some of the former Russian republics, which could be pressured at any time by the Russian leader Vladimir Putin to suspend cooperation with the U.S. It was therefore essential for the U.S. to protect Musharraf against these militant threats and keep him in power. Similar strains were emerging in other traditional American allies following the victory in Iraq. As the Sunni insurgency in Iraq grew, the Saudi monarchy faced an insurrection in its own territory from al Qaeda sympathizers. In May 2004, these terrorists staged a high-profile attack against the Khobar oil compounds. Similarly, in October 2004, al Qaeda–inspired terrorists attacked hotels in Egypt's Sinai resorts, killing thirty-one people and wounding over a hundred others. Both the Saudis and the Egyptians pledged to work even harder to fight al Qaeda and prevent it from recruiting their nationals for terrorist attacks. Similarly, Ali Abdullah Saleh of Yemen faced increasing attacks from militants affiliated with al Qaeda. Maintaining Yemen as an American ally allowed the U.S. uninterrupted access to the energy chokepoint of Bab el-Mandeb at the opening of the Red and Arabian seas, which was critical for the passage of goods from the Middle East to the Suez Canal en route to Europe. Saleh's government further faced a rising Houthi insurgency in the north following its effort to arrest the Zaydi sect leader Badreddin al-Houthi, a key opponent of the regime.

For the energy-market states serving as hosts to terrorists, the task of disarming these groups would be very difficult from both the military and political perspective. The ability of these states to project power throughout their territories was often limited by geographic terrain and poor infrastructure. These areas where the state's reach was limited were ripe for the growth of terrorists and insurgent movements.[1] For example, Pakistan's semiautonomous Federally Administered Tribal Areas (FATA) consists of a territory in the border region of the state, which is very mountainous and lacks a substantial road and rail infrastructure. The Pakistani government therefore faced considerable difficulties in conducting military operations in these borderlands. Similarly, while the Indonesian government can secure the main island of Java, the country consists of 200 million people and over 17,000 islands, with some of them well over 500 miles from the capital. The task of eliminating these terrorist groups, such as the Quetta Shura in Pakistan and Jemaah Islamiyah in Indonesia, from these territories was going to be exceptionally difficult for these host states, particularly since many of them were resource poor to begin with.

Yet, the George W. Bush administration argued that it could overcome these structural factors with greater U.S. economic and military support to hosts of terrorist groups. President Bush confidently claimed in a speech at the Virginia Military Institute in 2002:

> We know that true peace will only be achieved when we give the Afghan people the means to achieve their own aspirations. Peace will be achieved by helping Afghanistan develop its own stable government. Peace will be achieved by helping Afghanistan train and develop its own national army. And peace will be achieved through an education system for boys and girls, which works. We're working hard in Afghanistan. We're clearing minefields. We're rebuilding roads. We're improving medical care. And we will work to help Afghanistan to develop an economy that can feed its people without feeding the world's demand for drugs.[2]

A little over a year later, in his "Mission Accomplished" speech on the deck of the U.S.S. *Abraham Lincoln*, Bush similarly stated about Iraq:

> We will stand with the new leaders of Iraq as they establish a government of, by, and for the Iraqi people. The transition from dictatorship to democracy will take time, but it is worth every effort. Our coalition will stay until our work is done. And then we will leave—and we will leave behind a free Iraq.[3]

Bush's strategy was outlined in the State Department's release of the National Strategy for Combatting Terrorism in February of 2003.[4] The document stated that the U.S. would strengthen the capacity of weaker and reluctant host states to project power and fight terrorists throughout their territories by providing them with economic support, military aid, and, in some cases, large deployments of U.S. troops. Bush argued that in the post-9/11 world, the risk of terrorists gaining traction in weaker host states posed a security problem for all states in the international system. This was especially true in cases where these hosts had the material to produce nuclear weapons, such as Afghanistan, or already maintained a nuclear arsenal, such as Pakistan. The task of rebuilding the nonexistent governmental institutions of Afghanistan, and the task of securing and developing Iraq's dilapidated infrastructure, required

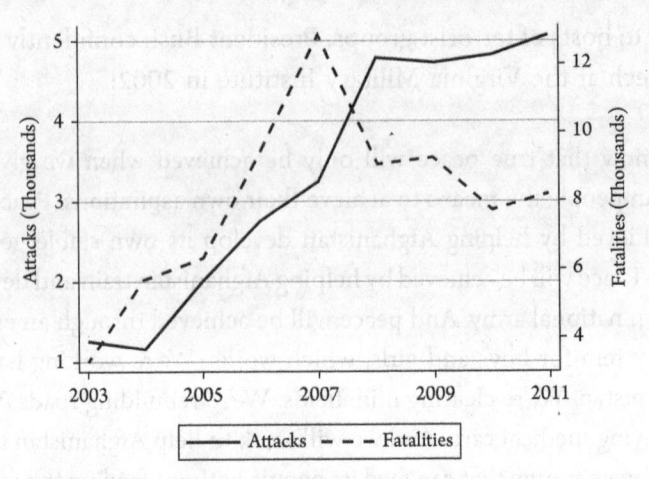

Figure 3.2. Terrorist Attacks and Fatalities in the Iraq War Period, 2003–2011.
Note. Includes both domestic and transnational attacks from the Global Terrorism Database; see National Consortium for the Study of Terrorism and Responses to Terrorism (START). 2018. Global Terrorism Database [data file]m. Retrieved from https://www.start.umd.edu/gtd.

a substantial financial and military commitment. The estimated cost soared during Bush's first term from a predicted $33.8 billion in fiscal years 2001 and 2002 to $94.1 billion in fiscal year 2004, and to $107.6 billion in fiscal year 2005.[5] The wars, coupled with the Bush tax cuts of 2001 and 2003, resulted in budget deficits of $377 billion in 2003 and $412 billion in 2004. The Bush administration argued that the U.S. needed to accept both the burden of building "democratic" regimes in Afghanistan and Iraq and the burden of defending other hosts from al Qaeda and its affiliates.

These arguments were supported by numerous academics who concluded that forcing weak states to fend for themselves would lead to the formation of terrorist groups. These groups would then acquire more deadly weapons, contribute to more terrorist attacks, and possibly contribute to wider interstate wars.[6] Many sophisticated data analyses supported the conclusion that failing states were favorable environments for the rise of terrorist and other militant groups.[7] The task of preventing such expansion was portrayed as a noble good that only the U.S. could provide and as a burden that the U.S. reluctantly needed to accept to fight the evil of terrorism.

However, by the end of the decade, the strategy of state building looked like an abject failure. Figure 3.2 demonstrates that despite

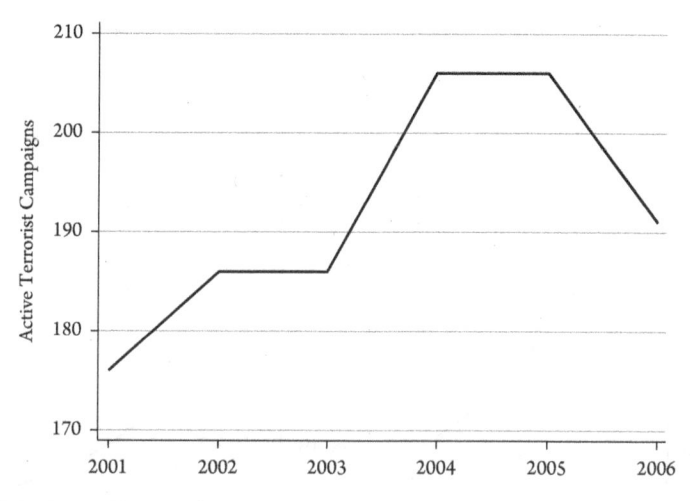

Figure 3.3. Active Terrorist Campaigns, 2001–2006.
Note. Data based on Jones and Libicki (2006), a study sponsored by the RAND Corporation.

billions of dollars spent, and several thousands of lives lost, American efforts could not prevent the rapid rise in terrorist attacks globally in the decade following the fall of Baghdad. Figure 3.3 further demonstrates that the number of active terrorist organizations throughout the world grew following the initiation of Operations Enduring Freedom and Iraqi Freedom. Despite the immense U.S. effort that went into strengthening the host states of the energy infrastructure, the result was more terrorist groups and more terrorist attacks.

Evidence suggests that the American strategy was undermining its own strategic objectives. The purpose of providing military assistance was to enable host states to defeat terrorists in their territory. To determine how effective U.S. military support was in achieving this objective, consider the relationship between American military aid and the duration of terrorist campaigns. We can determine the U.S. commitment of counterterrorism aid using the U.S. Overseas Loans and Grants Greenbook for 2008.[8] We can then determine if the provision of this aid contributed to a shortening of terrorist campaigns using a dataset from the RAND research organization that contains information on 184 terrorist campaigns against 48 states during the period 1997–2006.[9] Empirically, if the U.S. strategy was effective, the provision of military aid should *increase* a terrorist group's hazard of collapse.[10]

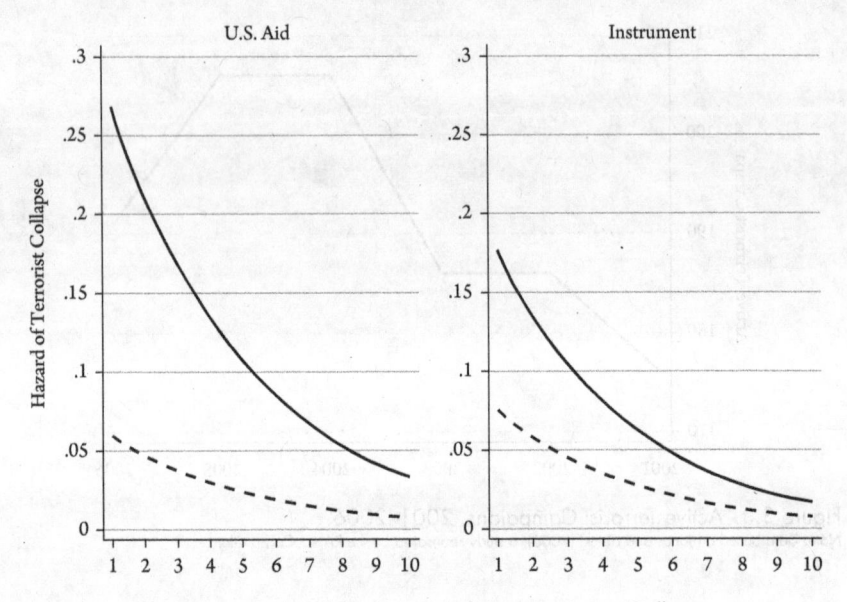

Figure 3.4. U.S. Military Aid and the Hazard of Terrorist Group Collapse.
Note. Solid line represents the rate at which terrorist groups collapse (in statistical terms, the "hazard") in cases with no military aid from the U.S.; dashed line represents the rate at which terrorist groups collapse in cases where the U.S. provides some level of antiterrorism support. Please see appendix for description of methodology and statistical results.

Disturbingly, Figure 3.4 demonstrates that U.S. military support had the exact opposite effect, in that the provision of aid increased the propensity of terrorist organizations to survive. We see that the rate at which terrorist groups collapse—that is, the "hazard," in statistical terms—is *lower* in countries where the U.S. provides military aid (dashed line) than in countries where the U.S. provides none (solid line). In other words, even though the U.S. provides military assistance to a state that is fighting terrorists, the probability that the group collapses in fact drops in proportion to that aid. These results demonstrate that U.S. assistance clearly did not facilitate the collapse of terrorist organizations and may have instead contributed to a prolonging of these violent campaigns.

We see that despite the heady predictions of the American foreign policy establishment, the American strategy ended up contributing to more terrorist attacks, more fatalities from terrorism, more terrorist groups, and a general prolonging of terrorist campaigns. What caused the U.S. strategy to fail so spectacularly?

## EXTERNAL MILITARY AID AND INTERNAL CONFLICT

To scholars of foreign aid, it is not particularly surprising that the U.S. encountered substantial difficulties. Numerous empirical studies demonstrate that foreign aid tends to make recipient states less democratic, more corrupt, and more prone to internal rebellion.[11] To be sure, some of these studies suffer from selection bias, meaning that donor states are only likely to provide military aid to recipient states that are relatively weaker and more prone to rebellion. Therefore, a simple analysis of whether military aid associates with political stability that does not account for these strategic incentives is likely to be biased. Nonetheless, within the pool of aid recipients, military support is notorious for creating disincentives for states to pursue sound economic policy.[12]

These empirical studies strongly suggest that if the goal of military assistance is to build functional states that would faithfully execute favorable policies, military aid often achieves the opposite. It is easy to point to the behavior of anti-Communist recipient countries during the Cold War, which often possessed some of the worst human rights records as defined by both Freedom House and Amnesty International.[13] If we apply these insights to the problem of transnational terrorism, we might expect that military aid itself may both increase terrorist activity and exacerbate the conditions that led to the formation of the group in the first place. If military aid increases the corruption of host states, and creates disincentives for recipient states to enact sound policies, this in turn may negatively affect economic growth. Given these patterns, it is very difficult to argue that American policy was based on sound reasoning, and far easier to conclude that the strategy was simply hubris.

However, let us consider an alternative explanation. In the academic literature, the success of antiterrorism policies is usually based on whether they result in a decrease in the number of terrorist attacks.[14] While this appears to be a reasonable and appropriate metric, the literature suggests that fluctuations in the count of terrorist attacks may have multiple interpretations. For example, although al Qaeda staged the most significant terrorist attacks in history on 9/11, al Qaeda would appear to be contained if we measure success solely by examining the number of terrorist events, given that it only produced one successful attack in 2001. On the other hand, a considerable literature suggests that terrorist violence may increase if a group is relatively weaker or on the verge of collapse.[15] However, if we use the number of attacks as the metric, we again see that a group that is dying may appear to be a significant threat, given that such a group might stage multiple attacks. These theoretical insights suggest that using the number of attacks as a metric for determining the success of U.S. counterterrorism strategy may be leading to flawed conclusions about the effectiveness of U.S. policies.

Let us consider an alternative measure of success. From the policymakers' perspective, the goal of military aid is not only to disarm a terrorist group but also to prevent the group from accomplishing its strategic objectives. Although many studies simply assume terrorists are interested in maximizing violence, micro-level and rational choice studies indicate that violence by itself is typically not the goal of these groups. Instead, these groups often have defined political aims and behave in a strategic, rational fashion to achieve them. The goals of terrorist groups span from seeking a change in a policy, to the overthrow of a central government, to the pursuit of secession. If this is true, the central goal of military aid might not be to prevent terrorists from engaging in violence but rather to prevent these groups from achieving their strategic objectives. For example, while military aid may contribute to an increase in terrorist violence, such assistance might convince host states to stand firm and refuse to negotiate with terrorist challengers. Additionally, military support may make it more difficult for terrorists to defeat the recipient state and increase the length of time the group must fight to accomplish its goals. Since most terrorist groups cannot sustain collective action for extended periods, simply keeping the terrorists at bay might lead to a situation where the group collapses on its own. This suggests that if we refocus attention away from the number of terrorist incidents, we may see that military aid is accomplishing U.S. strategic objectives, in that it is enabling recipient states to hold the line against terrorists and maintain a pro-American orientation.

This alternative concept of success is consistent with U.S. efforts to protect the hosts that were critical to the supply and transit of

TERRORISM AND THE PROBLEM OF MORAL HAZARD • 49

energy. Given this alternative definition, let us now analyze the logic of American strategy to examine both its relative effectiveness and its unintended consequences.

## THE LOGIC OF AMERICAN STRATEGY

We can use logical deduction to predict the effects of economic and military aid using Figure 3.5, which presents a stylized view of the decision-making of a state that is hosting a terrorist group. These host states can adopt one of three strategies in response to terrorist challengers. First, the host might choose to negotiate with the terrorists and

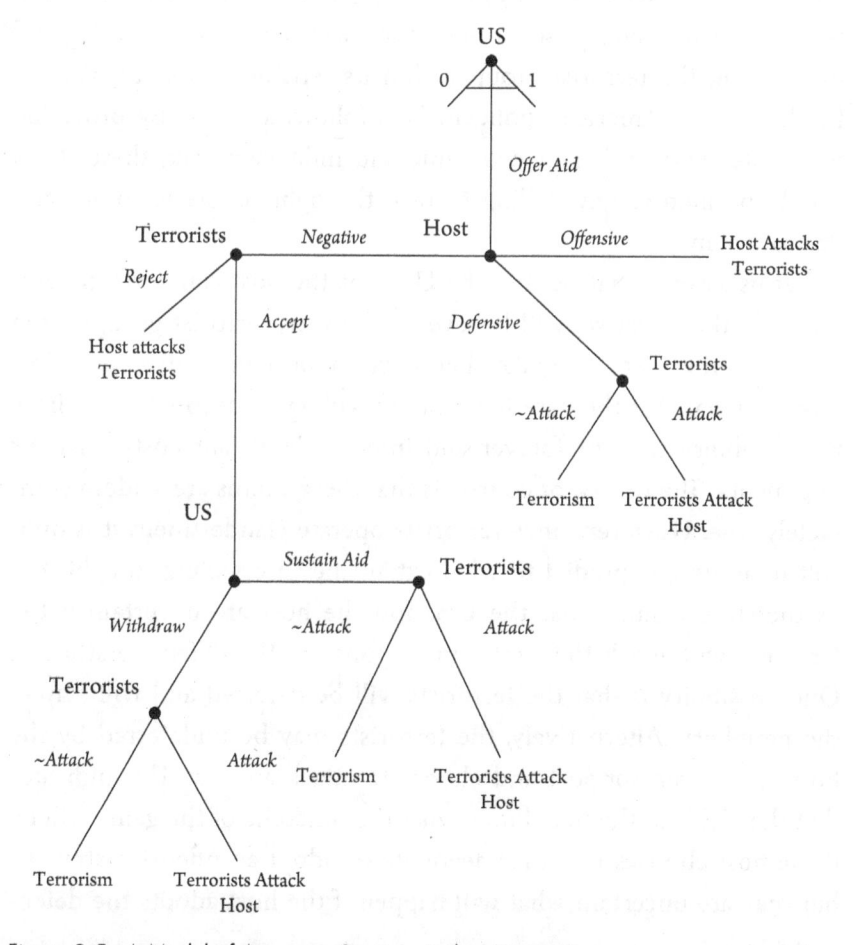

Figure 3.5. A Model of American Strategy in the War on Terror.
Note. A full presentation of the game diagrammed here and its equilibria are available in the mathematical appendix.

accommodate their views into the government's policies. This might antagonize the U.S., but based on studies in bargaining theory, it is the most efficient way to resolve the conflict. The economic and military aid from the U.S. increases the host's power in negotiation and therefore allows for a more favorable settlement. Alternatively, the host makes no concessions to the terrorists but encourages lower-level members of the terrorist groups to accept the host's sovereignty. The state further uses American military support to build defenses at the host's center, but it takes no offensive military actions to disarm the terrorists. This represents a gamble by the state that the terrorists will either be deterred from beginning a conventional campaign to oust the host government or will be defeated if they make such an attempt. The third option is for the host to engage in a military offensive aimed at disarming and dismantling the terrorist group within its territory. This appeared to be the goal of American policymakers following 9/11. By providing host states with sufficient economic and military power, these states should be increasingly willing to take the fight to the terrorists and destroy them.

Let us assume that neither the U.S. nor the host can perfectly predict how the terrorists will behave. To be sure, terrorist groups often go out of their way to make themselves appear unpredictable. Most groups signal that they are fanatical, unwilling to negotiate, and have the capability to fight forever and impose significant costs on their opponents. The reality, of course, is that these claims are seldom completely true. However, since terrorists operate clandestinely, it is difficult to accurately predict to what extent they are willing to fight. Let us therefore assume that the U.S. and the host are uncertain if the terrorists will attack the center in response to the defensive strategy. One possibility is that the terrorists will be deterred and will stay in the periphery. Alternatively, the terrorists may be undeterred by the host's American support and choose to attack anyway. This indicates that the U.S. and the host know what the outcome of the game will be if the host chooses to either negotiate or adopt an offensive strategy, but they are uncertain what will happen if the host adopts the defensive strategy.

## CASE 1. NEGOTIATION

Although negotiating with terrorists is often derided in the policy world, let us consider the value of such a decision. First, negotiation allows both the host and the terrorists to spare themselves the cost of a military encounter. Rather than wasting these resources on fighting, both the terrorists and the host should be better off striking some deal that reflects their balance of power and the likely outcome of a conflict. For example, suppose the host and the terrorists attempt to form a power-sharing agreement that divides seats in a legislature between the two sides. If the host has a 65% chance of defeating the terrorists in battle, an efficient settlement should grant the terrorists 35% of the seats in the legislature while keeping 65% of the seats for the host. Similarly, if the host only has a 25% of defeating the terrorists, it should grant the terrorists 75% of the seats and keep only 25% for itself. This deal reflects the balance of military power between the two sides, but it is advantageous since it saves the resources that would be lost from fighting.

Suppose the host makes an offer to the terrorists that reflects the balance of military power between the two sides. The terrorists then have the choice to accept, directly attack the host government to destabilize it at its center, or reject the deal. To be sure, the terrorists should prefer winning the conflict outright and seizing total control of the territory. However, fighting is costly, risky, and burns resources. Alternatively, the terrorists may stay in the periphery and hope for a better deal later as their capabilities improve. This requires the terrorists to accept nothing in the short term and risk that their capabilities will improve in the long term. This is certainly not a guarantee, as numerous terrorist groups fall victim to infighting, organizational dysfunction, mass defections, or police capture. Since the future is uncertain, and the terrorists instead are guaranteed to obtain some benefits through negotiation, *the terrorists are always better off accepting a negotiated settlement immediately.* The only reason terrorists can reject power-sharing deals that reflect the balance of power between their group and the host is if they are irrational. The popular literature often portrays terrorists as irrational, indicating that this explanation is plausible.[16] However, while individual terrorists may be irrational, the scientific literature strongly suggests the opposite about terrorist groups and their leadership.[17] These individuals appear strategic and rational in pursuing their policy goals. If this is true, continuing to fight is irrational, and strategic terrorist leaderships should accept power-sharing deals. In fact, they may often welcome such deals, particularly in cases where the host state is relatively weaker. For example, if the host only has 15% chance of defeating the terrorists in combat, a negotiated settlement would likely yield the group somewhere close to 85% of the spoils. In these cases, where the host state is weaker, terrorists therefore may gain substantially from negotiation.

We therefore see that negotiating with the terrorists is relatively easy if the host offers a settlement that accurately reflects the balance of power between the two sides. This should spare the host, the terrorists, and the civilians within the host's territory of the damage from internal conflict. However, while negotiation is valuable for both the host and the terrorists, it is not so for the U.S. Since the goal of the U.S. is to keep the terrorists out of power, *power-sharing agreements are not in the interest of the U.S., even though they are efficient.* Once the terrorists gain autonomy within the host's government, they may alter the status quo in a way that compromises U.S. interests within the host's territory. For example, suppose Saudi Arabia agreed to restrict the ability of American oil giants to exploit oil in the Ghawar oil field of the Eastern Province to appease Shi'a minority groups.[18] In theory, a deal is efficient. The Saudis obtain peace and the Shi'ites gain extra revenue. However, this deal would increase the price of crude for the U.S. and therefore force oil giants to raise oil prices, which would weaken the U.S. dollar. Even worse, if such a deal were to become permanent, or if Shi'ites demanded that the Saudi monarchy restrict U.S. firms' access to the Eastern Province, this would create a cascade that would significantly harm the American position in Saudi Arabia. We therefore see that while negotiation between host states and their terrorists may be the best way to resolve these conflicts, and that it spares losses in human life and resources, these deals may not be preferable to the U.S. These changes would further undermine the justification for continuing to provide military support to the Saudi kingdom in the first place. Therefore, once the terrorists alter the host's policies, the U.S. no longer derives a benefit from maintaining military cooperation. The U.S. will therefore respond to any deal with the terrorists by suspending military aid and cooperation with the host.

The strategy of negotiation therefore creates several risks for the host state. Since the U.S. is guaranteed to suspend its military support once the terrorists are given concessions, the power of the host relative to the terrorists will fall following the settlement. For example, in the case above, the U.S. would likely cut some of Saudi Arabia's military support should it negotiate with terrorists in Ghawar. As a result, the kingdom's power would precipitously decline relative to Shi'a militants in the Eastern Province. Should this power shift occur, the probability that the Shi'a militants could defeat the Saudi police and military forces would rapidly increase. This in turn would destabilize the original settlement between the Saudis and the Shi'a militias. For example, with U.S. support, the Saudis may have a 60% chance of disarming the Shi'a militias. An efficient negotiated settlement would divide control of the Eastern Province, allowing the Saudis to keep control of 60% of the territory while granting the Shi'a militants the remaining 40%. However, if the Saudis lose their American military support, the probability that the Saudis could disarm the Shi'a militias may fall to 30%. In this case, the original deal that split the territory is no longer stable. With the U.S. out of the picture, the Shi'a militants may no longer accept only 40% of the territory and may instead demand 70%. As a result, the militants may abrogate their commitments and begin an offensive against the kingdom to seize this additional territory.

We therefore see that negotiating creates a commitment problem and a substantial risk for host states. If the host with American support offers a deal that reflects the balance of power with its terrorists, but the U.S. will withdraw its support following this deal, the terrorists may be unable to credibly uphold the terms of the agreement. This problem becomes progressively worse if the host is critically dependent on the U.S., given that losing American support will create a larger power shift in favor of the terrorists. As a result, the more aid the U.S. provides, the less credible any deal is between the host state and the terrorist group.

By contrast, if the U.S. were to offer no military aid at all, and the host offered the terrorists a deal that reflected the actual balance of power between itself and the group, the negotiated settlement would be stable and the terrorists would fulfill it. Unfortunately for the U.S., such a deal would mean a loss of cooperation with the host and would undermine this state's cooperation in the American-supported petrodollar system.

### CASE 2. HOST ADOPTS DEFENSIVE TACTICS

Let us now consider the alternative strategy of adopting the defensive posture. In this case, the host makes no concessions to the terrorists but encourages lower-level members of the terrorist groups to accept its sovereignty. The host further uses American military support to build defenses at its center but takes no offensive military actions to disarm the terrorists. This represents a gamble by the host that the terrorists will either be deterred from attacking the host at its center or will be defeated if they do. If the terrorists do attack the center, however, they will be met by the host's American-supplied military. If the terrorists choose not to attack the center, they will stay in the country's periphery. Since the government does not attack them directly, it is possible that one or more factions vying for power will begin to compete and might possibly tear the movement apart.

In the absence of U.S. military assistance, hosts recognize that they are unlikely to prevail in a conflict with the group and should therefore prefer negotiating a power-sharing deal that allows them to hold onto some power versus none. Weaker hosts will therefore prefer negotiation if they receive no assistance from the U.S. However, if the U.S. bolsters a host's capability, a weaker host may prefer adopting the defensive posture over negotiating. If such a host adopts the defensive strategy, and the terrorists attack the center, the host has a greater chance of defeating the terrorists with American military support. If the terrorists instead choose not to attack the center, the leadership remains the sole sovereign over the territory. On the other hand, if the host negotiates, it would be forced to split the territory's benefits between its followers and those of the terrorists. We therefore see a key effect of the U.S. security guarantee: *American support undermines negotiation between host states and terrorist challengers.* Rather than negotiate, the provision of American support allows hosts to consolidate their power, keep the benefits of the territory for their followers, and demand that the terrorists surrender unconditionally.

As an example, consider the case of the U.S.-Yemeni relationship. In 2000, al Qaeda operatives based in Yemen launched an attack against the U.S.S. *Cole*. This attack was troubling in that it suggested that al Qaeda was willing to directly challenge the U.S. military and was undeterred by the significant presence of U.S. forces in the region. The U.S. responded by providing Yemen with greater military and economic support to fight al Qaeda. Yet, the terrorist group appeared stronger than ever in 2010, despite nearly a decade of American military support for Yemen. This would suggest that the policy of supporting Yemen against al Qaeda was a failure. However, let us consider the counterfactual. Since the Yemeni government is not a particularly stable state, and al Qaeda appears relatively stronger in Yemeni territory, an alternative strategy might have been for President Saleh to negotiate with al Qaeda. Such an agreement may have allowed al Qaeda to stage attacks from Yemeni territory so long as the group did not directly target Saleh or his government. On the other hand, since the U.S. provided Saleh with support, Yemen remained cooperative with the U.S. and refused to grant al Qaeda sanctuary. This case demonstrates that while U.S. military aid was unsuccessful at disarming al Qaeda, it was successful in keeping Yemen loyal to the U.S., and it may therefore be considered successful.

### CASE 3. HOST ATTEMPTS OFFENSIVE

We see that U.S. support gives hosts an incentive to avoid negotiation. Ideally, U.S support should encourage hosts to engage in an offensive to decisively end the conflict. However, since the host faces military costs in an offensive, but can avoid these by adopting a defensive strategy, the host should strictly prefer taking American aid while doing nothing to disarm their terrorists. In other words, from this perspective,

*U.S. military support should not only discourage hosts from negotiating, it should also discourage hosts from disarming their terrorists.* This demonstrates that military aid discourages negotiation, which accomplishes an American objective but discourages host regimes from fighting terrorism, which is seemingly antithetical to American strategic interests.

The model reveals a perverse incentive created by the war on terror. Although the U.S. was committed to defeating terrorists, it often found its host partners less enthusiastic, committed, and willing to take casualties. In some cases, the U.S. found that the hosts it was empowering appeared to be protecting their terrorist adversaries. We see a logic for why: disarming the terrorists is costly, but perpetually deterring them affords host leaders the chance to remain in power indefinitely with minimal risks and no cost.

Nowhere is this behavior more observable than in the case of Pakistan following 9/11. During Musharraf's rule, the U.S. supplied a substantial amount of economic and military support to Pakistan, with the intention of building Pakistan's capability to fight terrorism in its northern territories. This aid continued despite numerous reports that the aid was being used by Pakistan to bolster its military capacity against India and despite considerable intelligence that Musharraf was doing little to remove Taliban sympathizers from the Pakistani ISI (the national intelligence agency). At first glance, one might ask why the U.S. continues to supply Pakistan with military aid, given that there is no evidence that Pakistan is taking any action to disarm the Taliban. However, if the U.S. suspended military support to Pakistan, it is very likely that the government would reach some negotiated settlement with the Taliban that would allow the group free reign in the north. Such an agreement might also enable Pakistan to provide greater military support to the group so that it could protect its interests in a future Afghanistan, all while receiving a seemingly perpetual American annuity.

### WHY AMERICAN SUPPORT CONTINUES DESPITE HOST ABUSE

Given that the provision of military support discourages host states from fighting terrorists, an appropriate question is: why does the U.S.

continue this policy? To answer this question, we must consider what the outcome of failing to provide military support would be. According to the model, host states would likely respond to the loss of U.S. military support by negotiating with their terrorists. If this occurs, the terrorists will enter the host government, and American interests within the host are likely to be compromised. It is easy to imagine that if either Afghanistan or Pakistan destabilized, and a fundamentalist government took control of the territory, the incumbent presidential administration would be labeled as an incompetent foreign policy failure. One need only look at the reaction to the "loss of China" during the Truman administration and the punishment dealt to the Carter administration following Ayatollah Khomeini's takeover of Iran to imagine the political fallout from the destabilization of an American-supported host. In the cases of Afghanistan and Pakistan, the consequences may be far worse, given the ten-year commitment of American lives and treasure to the region. This fear of a political backlash, coupled with the relatively low cost of supplying military aid and the likelihood that the increased political violence will be confined to the host state's territory, makes it seem reasonable that any presidential administration would prefer continuing to provide military support to host states in the name of protecting American security and economic interests.

We can compare this dynamic to the political discourse during the Cold War. During this period, American policymakers were frequently charged with being "soft on Communism" or "Communist sympathizers" if they tolerated the presence of socialist movements within the governments of the newly independent states. This label was considered political suicide at the time, and it seemingly gave politicians an incentive to signal hawkish attitudes toward revolutionary movements in general. As a result, presidents from Truman to Reagan all exhibited a willingness to support autocratic regimes with abysmal records on human rights simply to prevent Communist insurgencies from gaining a place in the governments of their host states. In the present day, American politicians often signal a hard line toward Islamic movements to demonstrate their resolve against terrorism. This produces a situation where the U.S. appears willing to support clearly antidemocratic regimes to prevent Islamists from entering into the governments of these host states, solely to avoid the political punishment associated with "losing" states. This is particularly true of strategically important states, such as Pakistan and Saudi Arabia. In these cases, the model predicts that the U.S. will continue providing military support to host states, even if these host states would refuse to negotiate with terrorists without it. Unfortunately, this results in a prolonging of terrorist campaigns. If a host refused to compromise with terrorists but did not receive military aid, it is likely that some groups, particularly extremist ones with tastes for violence, might attack the host at the center—and would likely be disarmed as a result. However, American military support is likely to deter even these types of terrorists from attacking the center, thereby prolonging the terrorist campaign.

It is easy to argue that this type of U.S. response is reactionary and that it identifies non-elites in "terrorist" movements as more aggressive than they may truly be. After all, if a deal is possible between the host and a terrorist group, why couldn't the U.S. also strike a deal with the terrorists to protect its economic interests? Certainly, the terrorists might agree to protect the interests of the U.S. upon entering power, which in turn might give the U.S. more reason to restrain the host from increasing their repression. The problem with these guarantees on the part of the terrorists is that they are simply not credible. From a position of weakness, when the terrorists are outside of the government, they are likely to tell the U.S. exactly what it wants to hear. Once power is achieved, however, there is simply no guarantee that these terrorists will not ultimately undermine the position of American multinationals or compromise the dollar as the standard of exchange.[19] This suggests that if a revolution takes place in an American-supported host, it is very unlikely that the group that comes to power will continue to protect American interests.

Historically, the U.S. watched in several cases as politicians promising reform assumed control over the governments in host states, only to see these reformers fundamentally threaten American interests. For example, Jacobo Árbenz Guzmán was elected president of Guatemala in 1951 on a leftist platform of land reform, unionization, and minimum-wage laws.

Each of these reforms presented a threat to the traditional American dominance of Guatemalan politics. More specifically, these reforms threatened the economic interests of the U.S. Fruit Company, which effectively controlled 42% of Guatemala's land and maintained a near monopoly on Guatemala's infrastructure, all while being exempted from taxes. Once Árbenz took over the reins of power in Guatemala, nothing short of a coup could stop him from implementing these policies that were detrimental to both American and economic interests. This case demonstrates that there is a substantial risk to the U.S. when facing reformist leaders in that these individuals may compromise the strategic status quo that is disproportionately beneficial to the U.S.

To make matters worse, these leaders may often signal initially that they are willing to cooperate with the U.S. Take, for example, the behavior of Fidel Castro following the Cuban Revolution. After his initial victory, in a speech on July 17, 1959, announcing his takeover of the Cuban government Castro adamantly denied that he was a Communist. Castro stated, "I know the world thinks of us, we are Communists, and of course I have said very clear that we are not Communists, very clear." Following this declaration, many American policymakers believed that they could cooperate with Castro, particularly given that Castro's predecessor Fulgencio Bautista was quite repressive, corrupt, and embarrassing to the U.S. However, history reveals that Castro misrepresented his true intentions. Soon after, Castro embarked on numerous land reforms, which involved confiscating the private property of Americans—who owned about 75% of the island. Although Castro initially appeared willing to cooperate with the U.S., events soon proved otherwise. This demonstrates yet another U.S. concern with reformist leaders: even if they appear cooperative, it is unclear whether they will remain cooperative.

These problems may not stop within the borders of the state in conflict. Reformers may seek to encourage other non-elites in other states to rebel against the American-supported status quo. Consider the case of the Iranian Revolution of 1979. This revolt largely occurred in response to several of the Shah's economic reforms. To pacify the rebellion, the Shah initially made some concessions to the protestors. However, the fact that the Shah was willing to negotiate signaled to the dissident groups that his regime was weak. The protests therefore worsened, culminating with his expulsion at the hands of Ayatollah Khomeini. This was a critical blow to the U.S., as Iran had long been a key ally in the Middle East and sat atop the third-largest oil reserve in the world. Any action by Iran to price oil in another currency could potentially threaten the U.S. system of dominance. Although Saudi Arabia made up for the loss of Iran in the revolution, the conflict did not stop there. Khomeini appeared to actively support dissident groups throughout the Middle East to further destabilize American strategic interests. Iran further gave support to Shi'ites living within Saudi Arabia in the east, posing a critical threat to the petrodollar. Iran further provided some degree of inspiration to marginalized Shi'ites in Bahrain, which was home to the U.S. Fifth Fleet. Compromising the kingdom would destabilize the petrodollar, and compromising the home of the Fifth Fleet could prevent the U.S. from projecting its military power to provide the security guarantee needed to sustain the petrodollar system. In the case of the Iranian Revolution, radical change within the state not only threatened the position of American firms but also could potentially destabilize the entire petrodollar system.

Faced with this possibility, it is perhaps unsurprising that the U.S. remains committed to protecting the peg between the U.S. dollar and global energy trades from any and all militant challengers. Any rebellion in the world that may threaten this critical U.S. interest is viewed as a national security threat, but particularly those in the Middle East, given that these rebellions may threaten the system of petrodollar recycling that is critical to American hegemony. If a group nationalizes the holdings of multinationals, or indicates that it may stop accepting dollars altogether, a shock may occur in the global economic system that could potentially destabilize it. While one could argue that this is far-fetched and perhaps unlikely, the U.S. does not seem prepared to take this risk, given the potential for extreme consequences and the inability of dissident movements to credibly commit to restraining their ambitions and their revolutions.

Again, it is very easy to condemn the U.S. for this behavior. However, before doing so, it is essential to understand how much this benefits all

Americans. If investments in the U.S. lost their profitability relative to other markets, demand for dollars might decline. This would be particularly true if major revolutions in energy-producing states—such as Iran, Afghanistan, or Saudi Arabia—took place. If these regimes were to fall, and a new group took power and began pricing their energy products in a currency other than dollars, international demand for dollars would fall. This means that the U.S. would have to raise interest rates to gain access to capital to finance the budget deficit. Higher interest rates would also mean that ordinary Americans would face greater difficulties purchasing homes, cars, and other large-ticket items. At the same time, higher interest rates would force the U.S. government to either increase taxes to cover the payments, cut back on social programs, or both. These cutbacks would likely cause unemployment to spike while the dollar depreciates. In short, if the chain reaction that compromises American hegemony takes place, the U.S. economy would experience a correction that would harm the poor and middle classes in the U.S.

These consequences, and the political aftereffects of a potential economic downturn, make it a risk that no American president would dare take. If the choice is between risking negotiation versus simply supporting the regimes of host states and refusing to compromise with terrorists, it is clear what the optimal choice is. This is particularly true given America's preponderance in military power, and the reality that most of these rebel movements are likely to collapse relatively quickly. The fact that many of these groups are forced to resort to terrorist violence only reinforces the idea that they are weak and unable to consolidate territory. Therefore, we can understand the hard line that the U.S. draws against terrorism as largely an effort to prevent any changes to the lucrative status quo that preserves American political and financial hegemony.

### CASE EXAMPLES. NIGERIA AND HOSNI MUBARAK'S EGYPT

To illustrate these dynamics, let us consider the cases of two American-supported host states: Nigeria and Egypt. While Nigeria is a key global supplier of oil and an OPEC member, Egypt is home to the Suez Canal, one of the critical transit routes for energy supplies to reach markets in the West. The argument predicts that neither regime should have taken extensive steps to disarm the terrorists within their territory. These hosts would instead engage in corrupt and abusive behavior, all while using the threat of terrorist destabilization to force the U.S. into maintaining support. The argument would further predict that the U.S. would maintain support for these two regimes, despite their behavior, given that Nigeria is a key supplier of energy and Egypt is a critical transit state.

Let us first consider the case of Nigeria. The oil shocks of the 1970s, along with high levels of corruption in the Nigerian government, contributed to its fiscal crisis in the late 1970s. The IMF and other international institutions declared that the Nigerian state's economic policies created excessive government spending, enabled inefficient state-owned enterprises to survive, and fed high rates of inflation. The Nigerian government therefore needed to make structural reforms in its economic policies to continue receiving loans from the IMF. These reforms required Nigeria to balance its budget, stabilize the naira at a competitive exchange rate, divest itself of state-owned enterprises, and pursue export-led growth, particularly in its abundant energy sector. After seizing power in a coup, new president Badamasi Babangida began Nigeria's structural adjustment in 1986 by deregulating the agricultural market, doing away with price controls, and allowing Nigeria's currency to float on the market. Immediately, the value of the naira plummeted, effectively making Nigerians poorer relative to the rest of the world and less able to purchase goods from abroad. However, the fall of the naira made investment in Nigeria more attractive because of the consequent lower labor costs, and it made Nigerian exports more competitive on the world market. In 1999, the new Nigerian president Olusegun Obasanjo took steps to privatize state-owned oil companies to attract additional investment. Exports and foreign investment into Nigeria surged, which, according to supporters of structural reform, would have the effect of alleviating many of Nigeria's economic and political problems.[20]

These results did not materialize. By the late 1990s, the number of Nigerians living on less than $1 per day rose from approximately 28.9% to 70.2% of the working population, and the number of Nigerians living on less than $2 rose to over 90%. Because of weaker labor unions, industrialists in Nigeria had no need to increase employment or reinvest the profits in their factories. Instead, with lower taxation and relaxed regulation of financial sectors, Nigerian capital could simply transfer the excess profits into foreign investments, including investments in the U.S. The result of this system was that those in control of Nigeria's key export sectors, particularly oil, experienced considerable increases in wealth, whereas the larger portion of Nigeria's population found themselves with lower wages, fewer jobs, fewer safety protections, a vastly weakened social safety net, and an increasingly corrupt government incapable of responding to their basic needs.

The program of structural adjustment was met with mass protests. Nigeria saw numerous riots from former employees of state-owned enterprises, university students, and local businesses. The Nigerian government found itself in conflict with the Ogoni population in the southeast part of the Niger delta where its oil reserves were located. The Nigerian government asserted in 1979 that it had full ownership of all of Nigeria's territory and it could decide what compensation to award residents if it needed the land. The government's efforts to assert control of the territory and its oil wealth led to an insurrection involving the Movement for the Survival of the Ogoni People (MOSOP) in the early 1990s. The group demanded that oil companies that were beginning to invest in the area, including Shell and Chevron, negotiate with them on future drilling and compensate the people of the territory with some of the oil profits. Nigeria further faced unrest from the Ijaw Youth Council (IYC), which mobilized in the delta under what became known as Operation Climate Change. The organization attempted to bring attention to the environmental degradation in the Ijaw territories in the Niger delta. In response, the Nigerian military pushed into these regions and began a violent drive to pacify the territory. In one high-profile event, the Nigerian military attacked the village of Odi in the oil-rich Bayesla state on November 20, 1999, killing scores—or perhaps even many hundreds—of civilians.[21]

Despite these repressive actions, it is easy to see why the U.S. sided with the Nigerian government. U.S. was Nigeria's largest trading partner, and Nigeria was an OPEC state and a leading supplier of oil to the U.S. Although it certainly appears the U.S. could compel the Nigerian government into curbing its human rights abuses in the delta, let us consider the potential consequences of this decision. If the U.S. were to protect groups such as MOSOP and the IYC, along with others in the Niger delta, these groups would likely demand a greater share of Nigeria's oil profits. This in turn would make the trade less lucrative for both the Nigerian government and American multinationals. The second possibility that appears more dangerous for American strategic interests would occur if U.S. threats pushed Nigeria to increase its trade with China or the European Union. Either the E.U. or China (or both) could push Nigeria to begin pricing its oil in euros or renminbi (RMB), in violation of OPEC's system. The Nigerian government might have reason to comply with such a request if most of its trade shifted to these states. Nigeria's decision to take this action as one of Africa's leading oil producers might encourage other states to do the same. We therefore see that the simple act of opposing Nigeria's repression of dissident groups might lead to significant costs for the U.S., particularly with intense competition for markets from the E.U. and China. On the other hand, if the U.S. continued providing Nigeria with defense capabilities, the U.S. could minimize the risk of the rebellions in the delta while simultaneously encouraging Nigeria to continue the status quo policy of pricing oil in dollars. Although the U.S. has no ideological dispute with the groups in the delta, the need to protect the trade for energy in dollars causes the U.S. to enter into a conflict with Nigeria's militant groups, which the U.S. refers to as "terrorists."

By 2006, these groups coalesced into the Movement for the Emancipation of the Niger Delta (MEND) in 2006. The dispute between the Nigerian state and the MEND rebellion was settled in 2009 with a government amnesty. The Nigerian state offered cash payments to senior MEND leaders and job training for some of the fighters in their movement. This split caused some degree of infighting within MEND, ultimately eroding the movement and causing it to collapse soon after the amnesty. However, the government made no offer to restrict the behavior of multinationals, clean up the damage from oil spills, or compensate the Ogoni or the Ijaw peoples for the environmental damage. In short, the amnesty resembled more of an effort by senior leadership to "cash in" from rebellion, and it did nothing to shift the policies of Nigeria in a way that would undermine the profits made by multinationals in the region. While Nigeria held the line, local discontent and the risk of a new MEND rebellion remained high, justifying continued military support from Washington to the Nigerian state.

A similar story can be told about Hosni Mubarak's Egypt. Following the 1973 Yom Kippur War, President Anwar Sadat embarked on a program to improve Egypt's relations with the U.S. He began by expelling Soviet advisors from his territory. Sadat further announced that he would begin a series of economic reforms known as "Infitah," which encouraged privatization and the removal of the state's involvement in numerous sectors of the Egyptian economy. Sadat also took the very politically unpopular step of signing a peace treaty with Israel in 1979, which led to his assassination two years later. Subsequent to Sadat's death, Vice President Hosni Mubarak assumed the presidency; he expanded the Egyptian State Security Investigation Service to crack down on fundamentalist organizations that stood in the way of reform. Mubarak continued Sadat's program by deregulating state-owned enterprises and opening to foreign investment. Mubarak further initiated cutbacks in social services, coupled with decreases in taxation and emphasis on law and order. State-owned enterprises were typically auctioned off to Mubarak's political allies. The Egyptian currency plummeted, serving as a boon to capital in that it improved exports, and it improved tourism. Mubarak's families amassed billions and the military entered every aspect of the Egyptian economy. The top earners in Egypt's economy saw their share of the nation's wealth increase.

Yet, for most Egyptians, prices increased, wages fell, labor unions were suppressed, the health care system was dismantled, and income inequality increased. These falling living standards gave support to the claims of numerous groups that the regime was incredibly corrupt and hoarding the state's resources. In addition to the Muslim Brotherhood, rebel groups such as Al-Gama'a al-Islamiyya and Talaa'al al-Fateh emerged to protest the regime's corruption and began engaging in acts of violence to weaken and destabilize the regime. These attacks included six assassination attempts against Mubarak himself. Mubarak quickly denounced these groups as "terrorists" that threatened Egypt's economic progress. To fight these groups, Mubarak refused to suspend Egypt's emergency law, which allowed him to suspend democratic competition for the presidency and suppress his political opponents. Mubarak consistently declared that this repression was necessary to continue the program of reforms and suppress the threat of terrorism, which he equated with his domestic opponents.

Despite clear evidence of human rights abuses, Mubarak remained a critical U.S. ally and remained unchallenged until the Arab Spring of 2011. Consistently, the U.S. faced a choice of whether to restrain Mubarak's repression, and thereby enable opponents of the very lucrative gains from Egypt's reform, or whether to support Mubarak's dictatorial rule. The Iranian Revolution of 1979 remained in the minds of American policymakers, who were determined not to let another Middle Eastern ally fall to the forces of fundamentalism. While Iran was critical to the U.S. for its oil supply, Egypt was critical because of its control of the Suez Canal. Approximately 8% of world trade passes through the Suez Canal along with 5.5% of the world's oil output. If Egypt were to fall into the hands of the coalition of fundamentalists in the territory, these groups could potentially shut the canal down or begin a guerrilla campaign against Israel, both of which challenge American security interests. These consequences give the U.S. little choice but to keep dissident movements suppressed and appease the Egyptian regime, which for most of the period 1981–2010 involved ensuring that Mubarak remained in power.

## CONCLUSION

Since 9/11, American policymakers have advocated for developing the capacity of governments that host terrorist groups. This strategy has argued that if terrorists thrive in weak state environments, the solution is to build weak states into strong states so terrorists cannot function. This strategy of using military aid to fight terrorists created a series of perverse incentives for the host states of the energy market. Since the U.S. needed to guarantee the security of host states to protect the petrodollar system, and would increase military aid if host states faced viable terrorist threats, the hosts had no incentive to disarm their terrorists. The results seemingly speak for themselves: the policy of providing host states with military aid has led to increased terror attacks, fatalities from terrorism, terrorist groups, and prolonged terrorist campaigns. Yet, given the larger American strategic aim and lucrative nature of dominating the global energy market, it appears the U.S. was willing to accept these results. Even as terrorist violence escalated, the U.S. was paradoxically accomplishing its key strategic objective.

However, since U.S. strategy encouraged hosts to allow terrorist groups to survive, terrorist violence in each of these states soon began spiraling out of control. In addition to the catastrophic human damage caused by civil wars, the damage of these conflicts affected both the strategic and economic interests of the U.S. The escalating levels of terrorist violence in Iraq virtually shut down the country's ability to export petroleum. The loss of Iraqi oil had two consequences. First, the lack of revenue was making it impossible to rebuild the country or attract investment in the face of unremitting civil violence. Second, the loss of Iraqi oil was coming at a time where global supplies were strained and demand was increasing. Given the limited supply, the price of oil increased in the mid-2000s.

Figure 3.6 indicates that the price of Persian Gulf oil rose from $36.03 per barrel in January of 2005 to a high of $57.34 in August before falling to $48.77 in December. This rise represented a 35% increase in the price of oil throughout the year, and a 59% increase from December 2004. This was considerably higher than the 2.5% increase in the price of oil per barrel between 2002 and 2003, and the 12% increase from 2003 to 2004. This was the nightmare scenario for policymakers—the increase in oil prices indicated that the dollar was losing value to inflation. Additionally, although Afghanistan maintained considerable mineral

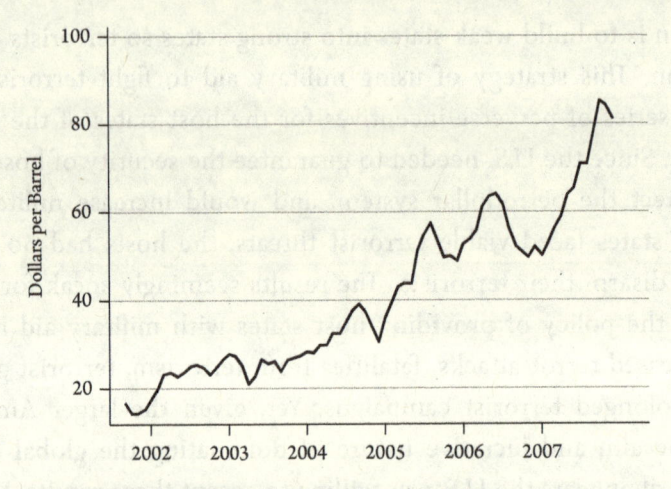

Figure 3.6. The Price of Persian Gulf Oil per Barrel in USD.
Note. Data shown here illustrating U.S. FOB costs of crude oil from Persian Gulf countries (in dollars per barrel) is from U.S. Energy Information Administration (2015).

riches and plans existed for constructing a pipeline to Central Asia, no development was possible because of the growing Taliban insurgency in Afghanistan and Pakistan. The inability to pursue reconstruction in Afghanistan indicated that the payoff to the U.S. for opening new markets in Central Asia was being lost. Although it was possible to write off these gains, the American security position in the Persian Gulf was also being diminished because of the inability of the U.S. to control the situation in Iraq and increasingly aggressive Iranian military activities supported by Ayatollah Khamenei and President Mahmoud Ahmadinejad.

By 2006, American policymakers seemed dead set on ending the Iraq war altogether and terminating U.S. involvement. This political mood placed the host states of the energy market in a precarious position. The hosts maintained control over their territories, even as their terrorists became stronger, as a result of American economic and military support. If this support were to end, the hosts would then be left to face much stronger terrorists that could become more aggressive. The growing doubt about the willingness and the ability of the U.S. to continue the war in Iraq was now creating a stark situation for the host states in the region. They could potentially face more powerful terrorists and desperately need U.S. help, but at their moment of need, the U.S. might be unwilling or unable to fulfill its security obligations. For the first time since the start of the war, the states of the energy market, and the terrorists fighting them, began planning for wars without the U.S. military.

# 4

# THREATENING ALLIES

Imagine an enemy that can't stand what we believe in, getting ahold of oil resources and taking a bunch of oil off the market in order to have an economic punishment. In other words, they say, you go ahead and do this, and if you don't, we'll punish you economically . . .

—President George W. Bush
September 15, 2006

I am not persuaded that 20,000 additional troops in Iraq is going to solve the sectarian violence there. In fact, I think it will do the reverse. I think it takes the pressure off the Iraqis to arrive at the sort of political accommodation that every observer believes is the ultimate solution to the problems we face there.

—Senator Barack Obama
January 10, 2007

The statements capture the essence of the problem. The U.S. needed to secure the host states in the energy market to maintain its financial dominance, but this protection enabled the host states to engage in corrupt and abusive practices, given that they could always rely on the Americans to defend them. Worse, since the U.S. would only expend resources to fight active terrorist groups, host leaders had an incentive

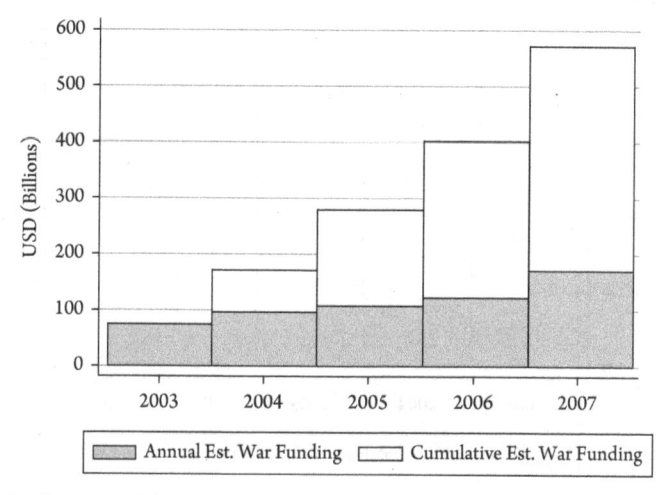

Figure 4.1. The Cost of the War on Terror (in Billion USD), 2002–2007.

to allow these terrorists to persist, all while engaging in behavior that strengthened the groups' popular appeal. Keeping these leaders in power supported energy trades in dollars, along with American control over their states' energy commodities, pipelines, transport systems, sea-lanes, and air space, all of which were essential to preserving U.S. financial dominance. As a result, the corruption of these leaders, and their inefficiency in fighting terrorism, was seen as a small price to pay in exchange for maintaining the petrodollar system.

However, by the mid-2000s, the terrorist campaigns in these states began escalating to insurgencies and full-scale civil wars.[1] While terrorism typically does not cause significant damage, civil wars are far deadlier. Figures 4.1 and 4.2 demonstrate that by 2007, the cumulative cost of the war exceeded half a trillion dollars and meanwhile the war had resulted in more American fatalities than the 9/11 attacks. These grim figures soon eroded confidence in the Bush administration's handling of the war. These figures further began to hurt the military's ability to replenish both the numbers and the quality of its recruits, particularly the Army and the Marine Corps.[2] This significant strain raised questions about whether the war was sustainable absent the reinstituting of the draft. On November 17, 2005, Representative John Murtha (D-PA) introduced a bill (H.J. Res. 73) to redeploy American forces and scale down their presence in Iraq. Murtha stated that with 80% of Iraqis

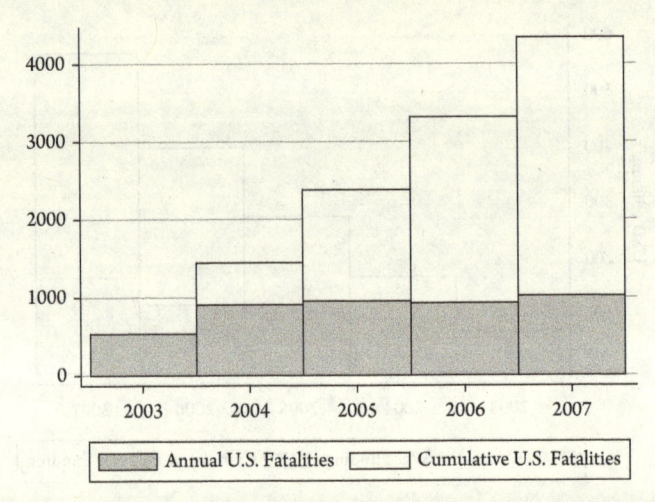

[Bar chart showing Annual U.S. Fatalities and Cumulative U.S. Fatalities from 2003 to 2007, with cumulative rising from about 500 in 2003 to over 4000 in 2007.]

Figure 4.2. The Increase in U.S. Fatalities in Afghanistan and Iraq, 2003–2007.

calling for the withdrawal of U.S. forces, and with 45% of Iraqis claiming that attacks on the U.S. were justified, the U.S. could no longer sustain its presence in Iraq. Support for Murtha's plan grew the following year after the bombing of the al Askari mosque in Samarra in February 2006. The bombing of one of the holiest sites in Shi'a Islam led to a rapid escalation of sectarian violence in Baghdad, with the number of monthly fatalities rising from the hundreds to the thousands. As the body counts worsened, Democratic challengers for the Republican-controlled House and Senate mobilized to end the war in Iraq, and perhaps the war on terror altogether.

Despite these pressures, Bush sought to assure the host states that the U.S. would fulfill its security obligations, regardless of the costs.[3] Privately, however, the administration recognized the pressure on the military and the turning of the political winds against the war. The strain on the military coupled with the increasing hostility of the American public to the mission suggested that if the Bush administration did not show some results quickly, the entire operation could become politically unsustainable. This in turn could force the Bush administration to reduce its level of support for Iraq, Afghanistan, or other host states in the energy market. Such a move would increase the risk that one of these regimes would destabilize at the hands of their insurgent challengers, which in turn would raise questions about the value of the American security guarantee. If this were to occur, it would weaken the value of U.S. protection, which in turn could undermine American domination of the world's energy markets and undermine the dollar. The stakes to the Bush administration could not be higher. The U.S. needed some concrete progress, or there was a chance that the American financial dominance would be jeopardized.

Faced with this risk, the administration began to ponder alternatives strategies to force the hosts to fight their terrorists while reducing the mounting American casualties and costs. Initially, the U.S. sought to guarantee the survival of the host regimes that governed the key territories necessary to maintain the peg between dollars and energy trades. Given the problem of moral hazard associated with this strategy, an alternative was developed whereby the U.S. would rely less on the host regimes and instead would recruit local groups, tribes, clans, or other forces within the host to secure the energy routes and supplies within these territories. These local, non-state actors would serve as proxy ground forces to protect territories critical to maintaining the global energy market. The U.S. could bolster the local capability using a smaller force consisting of drones, air power, and special forces. This strategy came to be known as a "light footprint," which focused only on the U.S. protecting its own interests within these territories by recruiting non-state actors within the host itself. The downside of this strategy, however, was that by empowering local non-state forces, the U.S. would be undermining the power of the host states it pledged to defend, and it would diminish the ability of the hosts to exercise sovereignty over their territory. This strategy was also certain to generate hostility from the host states, whose leaders could choose to break the peg between dollars and oil in retaliation.

In this chapter, I argue that the strain of the war on the military and the public backlash created a risk that the U.S. would be unable to indefinitely secure the host states of the energy market. This risk that the U.S. would scale back its military commitment to the host state, and would instead rely on non-state actors to protect the energy market, ultimately worked to compel the host states into fighting their terrorists. If the U.S. scaled back its security guarantee, the loss of U.S. support would rapidly weaken the host states relative to their terrorists, and it would leave them vulnerable to complete destabilization. This threat compelled several of the host states into actively fighting their terrorists, before they lost all American support. While this solved the moral hazard problem, it also created a negative consequence for the U.S., in that it weakened the strategic credibility of the American security guarantee. This in turn led host states to question whether or not they should continue to cooperate with the U.S. in maintaining the petrodollar system.

### SOLVING THE MORAL HAZARD PROBLEM

As the cost of the war on terror grew, particularly in the mid-2000s, the key question for the U.S. was how to compel the host states into disarming the terrorists in their territories. Let us again conceptualize the U.S. as a principal seeking to contain terrorist groups worldwide. To do so, the U.S. outsources the task to the leaders of host states where terrorists operate, who serve as agents of American policy. The problem, however, is that if these agents recognize that they will only continue to be paid if the conflict with terrorists continues, they will have no incentive to fully defeat or disarm their terrorists. Instead, they will accept the payments and continue to demand more to fight the terrorists. The U.S., as a principal, must therefore find some way to manipulate the incentives of the host states such that they prefer to disarm their terrorists.[4]

The solutions offered by the principal-agent literature focus on monitoring the behavior of agents[5] and sanctioning those agents that either cannot or will not perform tasks.[6] Applied to the war on terror, the prescription is that the U.S. should take considerable steps to monitor the behavior of host states, provide extra compensation to those hosts that perform well, and punish hosts that fail to disarm their terrorists. Let us consider the effectiveness of each of these policies. First, it seems to make clear sense that the U.S. should watch and regulate what the host does with the support provided. Keeping a close eye on the behavior of the host would not only allow the U.S. to identify those individuals that abuse the system but also allows the U.S. to provide extra compensation for good counterterrorism cooperation. If a host does a good job of suppressing its terrorists, the U.S. would continue to fulfill its security guarantee. On the other hand, the U.S. could sanction those hosts that are less cooperative. These threats could potentially remove a host's incentive to protect terrorists by imposing punitive costs should moral hazard occur. The threat of these costs might encourage host states to take the task of fighting terrorism seriously, thereby removing the incentive to abuse cooperation.

However, the imposition of punitive sanctions may also produce unintended consequences.[7] If we assume that the conflict between a host and a terrorist organization can be represented as a bargaining model, we would expect that the two sides should prefer some negotiated settlement to continued conflict. However, if a third party imposes sanctions, the third party may alter the expectations of the host and the terrorist group, which may incentivize one of the sides to continue the conflict. By imposing sanctions that restrict trade or investment, the sender creates a set of market imperfections that may disrupt the normal workings of the host's economy.[8] This may undermine the ability of the host to use its resources, harm its tax base, or generate hostility toward the regime, all of which would decrease the host's ability to engage in counterterrorism efforts. Simultaneously, since the host state's economy is weakened as a result of the ongoing conflict, it might become more vulnerable to destabilization at the hands of the terrorists, thereby causing the host to acquiesce or concede. If the terrorists observe the dwindling of the host's capacity under sanctions, they may believe that they are less vulnerable to the host's repression and therefore refuse to negotiate. We would therefore expect that sanctions that undermine a state's economic and military power would make it more difficult for host states to defeat their terrorist challengers.[9] This suggests that the punishment from sanctions may be counterproductive in fighting terrorist groups.

This highlights the conundrum: to compel hosts to fight terrorists, the U.S. needs to be able to punish abusive hosts. However, reducing support to abusive hosts could substantially increase the chance of a terrorist victory, which could harm the U.S. control over the global energy market, and ultimately its power. This problem is analogous to many other forms of coercion, such as blackmail, extortion, or the threat to wage war.[10] In the last case, states threaten others with mutually harmful conflict if their adversary does not yield to a settlement more favorable to the threatening state. The key aspect of using this coercion is that the threat to follow through must be credible, even though the act of starting an inefficient conflict appears irrational. In the case of the war on terror, the Bush administration needed to convince other hosts that it would punish them if they failed to take concrete steps to disarm their terrorists. The problem, however, was that this threat seemed utterly unbelievable. President Bush's political capital and legacy rested on his ability to win the war.[11] If this was true, and any reduction in support would weaken the ability of hosts to fight their terrorists, how could Bush credibly sanction the host states and undermine his own foreign policy objectives, despite the moral hazard problem?

### MAKING THREATS CREDIBLE

In situations where an individual cannot credibly follow through on a threat, one possible solution is to leave the execution of the threat to chance. In other words, if the Bush administration could not credibly cut off any of the hosts, perhaps it needed to rely on another agent that would indeed execute this policy. The Bush administration found such an agent in the form of the American public. The election season of 2006 indicated that the public was angry about both the inability of the Bush administration to win the war, the spiraling costs, and the mounting casualties. Growing public support for antiwar candidates indicated that the public was pushing for an end to the unlimited and unconditional support for host states in their fight against terrorists.

Although electorates often ignore international relations, citizens do tend to use retrospective voting to evaluate the performance of their leaders in high-profile examples of foreign policy.[12] If leaders fail to produce success in these high-profile cases, publics may view leaders as incompetent and seek to replace them. Since wars are certainly high profile, and since the outcome of battles and the conduct of war are public information, citizens can determine whether their leaders are performing well or performing poorly. Citizens do use this information in times of war to determine whether to replace their leaders.

The public's interpretation of the goals, costs, and probability of eventual success is often informed by two sources. First, citizens may turn to simplified indicators of performance, such as evaluating casualties.[13] A large literature suggests that citizens view casualties as negative, but they do also compare the level of casualties to the perceived goal of the military operation and the probability of eventual success. Second, the public may take cues from foreign policy elites.[14] Many of these elites focused on the goal of protecting the U.S. homeland from terrorist attacks, minimizing casualties, and preventing terrorists from gaining a safe haven. Few analysts discussed the economic implications of the destabilization of host states in the energy market. Even fewer discussed the need for the U.S. to fulfill its security obligation publicly. Although voting publics tend to punish incumbents who do not fulfill their treaty obligations, the U.S. agreements to defend Saudi Arabia and the other OPEC states were never formalized, nor were they public.[15] Since these agreements were private, and since these agreements were largely concluded in the 1970s, the memories of American elites of these agreements quickly faded, particularly when facing the difficulties of the war on terror. Elites were therefore increasingly willing to portray the war as unnecessary, counterproductive, and perhaps worsening the conditions leading to terrorism by giving host states a blank check.

In 2006, despite the risk that the OPEC states could break the peg between oil and dollars, the Democratic congressional leaders publicly denounced the war and increased the pressure on the Bush administration to redeploy from Iraq, or perhaps end the war on terror altogether. Since Congress traditionally defers to the executive in times of war, one could argue that these statements could be dismissed as cheap talk. However, while Congress sometimes refuses to constrain the president in foreign policy, there are numerous instances in which the legislative branch has asserted itself in international affairs.[16] For example, in 1973, the Democratically controlled Congress terminated appropriations for the war in Indochina and later refused the Ford administration's request for an extra $300 million in 1975 to fend off North Vietnam's advance. This decision to restrict funding was made even as the Nixon and Ford administrations charged that these decisions were enabling the growth of global Communism, weakening the U.S., and leaving a moral stain on the country for abandoning its allies. Although these drastic actions by Congress are relatively rare, Congress also suspended U.S. military support for operations in Angola and Nicaragua. For hosts in the war on terror, the rhetoric of Congress was therefore something to be taken seriously, particularly given the challenge posed by the growing insurgencies in their territories. The uncertain nature of congressional behavior, and the new threats to cut funding for the war on terror in response to the public's backlash, represented a tool that left "something to chance."[17] The day after the election, Bush declared adamantly that the U.S. would never simply abandon Iraq, Afghanistan, or any of its allies, despite the results. Bush stated in his press conference:

> I know there's a lot of speculation on what the election means for the battle we're waging in Iraq. I recognize that many Americans voted last night to register their displeasure with the lack of progress being made there. Yet I also believe most Americans and leaders here in Washington from both political parties understand we cannot accept defeat.[18]

Despite Bush's determination, antiwar Democrats now controlled the purse to supply the war effort. Since these antiwar Democrats only answered to their constituents, and not the U.S. at large, they could credibly undermine the security guarantee by reducing the available funds to the military, invoking the War Powers Resolution, or adopting some other sanction of the presidency. Therefore, regardless of Bush's determination to continue the war, the administration would be unable to fully guarantee the security of the host states if the Democrats sought to tie his hands.

Intuitively, we would think that these constraints would undermine the Bush administration's prosecution of the war. Strategically, however, the antiwar sentiment of the new Congress *strengthened* Bush's bargaining power against the hosts by allowing him to credibly threaten to abrogate the U.S. security guarantee. The Bush administration's domestic weakness soon turned into a source of bargaining power. In one famous instant, Secretary of State Condoleezza Rice visited Iraq to conduct a thorough review of the situation. As part of this review, Rice visited Baghdad to discuss the situation with both Shi'a and Sunni leaders. After her discussion with Shi'a leader Abdul Aziz al-Hakim, the secretary of state declared:

> Americans are not going to stay with you if you're asking us to be in the middle of your centuries-old fights. And so what is going to happen is we're going to leave, because we won't be able to stay, and within six months you'll all be swinging from lampposts.[19]

Rice's message was clear. While the Bush administration was publicly stating that it would stay the course and maintain the U.S. commitment to Iraq, it was privately signaling to the Iraqi government that it could not sustain this commitment indefinitely. If the leaders were unable to create the conditions to pacify their state prior to the U.S. exit, the government of Nouri al-Maliki would have to face his rivals in the Shi'a militias and the al Qaeda–dominated Sunni insurgency alone. Yet, from Maliki's perspective, there was reason to doubt that the Bush administration would follow through with Rice's threat. The central justification for participating in the U.S. energy market was that the U.S. could guarantee the security of these states. Would the U.S. really abandon Iraq and undermine its allies' confidence, knowing this could weaken its own energy market and its currency? Would the U.S. really be willing to forego control of close to a tenth of the world's crude oil reserves? The most likely beneficiary of a U.S. withdrawal would be Iran, who appeared determined to weaken American hegemony in the Gulf. Would the U.S. really allow Iran to have such enormous control over the Gulf's oil?

These consequences suggest that Maliki had good reason to be skeptical that the U.S. would completely abandon Iraq. However, while the U.S. may not have been able to choose a complete withdrawal over continuing to subsidize Maliki, there was an alternative option. Faced with growing military conflicts in Iraq, Afghanistan, and elsewhere, numerous officials privately began to express concern that these large commitments would at some point break the armed forces.[20] The U.S. would possibly soon face a situation where it could not maintain such a large force in conflict, and more importantly, it would be unable to replace its forces due to shortfalls in recruiting. Yet, these planners recognized that a complete withdrawal from the territories of the host states would likely lead to an increase in violence, undermine U.S. credibility, and possible create instability in the larger global energy market.

The administration therefore faced competing pressures. On one hand, public and congressional pressure to reduce the military commitment was growing. On the other hand, the administration needed to secure the global energy market to protect the petrodollar. To address both demands, military planners came up with an alternative option known as the "light footprint." This plan slightly resembled Murtha's redeployment plan, except that it allowed for a larger residual force to remain in the territories of host states. These forces would seek cooperation with local actors within the host. The U.S. would supply arms and money to these groups, tribes, clans, warlords.[21] The locals would further be supported by a small contingent of military and special forces, and they would be supported by American airpower. In exchange, these local actors would assist the U.S. in establishing secure zones within the state's borders, and perhaps securing key territories to support the global supply chain for energy. For example, rather than empower Maliki in Iraq, the U.S. could cut side deals with the Kurds to secure access to their oilfields while empowering the Kurdish militia group known Peshmerga, translating to "those who face death," to provide security. While some in the administration viewed this strategy as a cheaper and perhaps more sustainable possibility than indefinitely securing host governments, it did have one drawback. Adopting a strategy that empowered local forces would all but guarantee that a host government would never fully consolidate and secure its territory.[22] U.S. support would instead be used to bolster forces that might eventually challenge for control of the host state, or would, at the very least, resist efforts by the host to exercise sovereignty. This option retained U.S. influence, but would ultimately weaken the host and its ability to control its own territory.

This suggests that while the U.S. remained committed and willing to fight for the peg between dollars and energy, violence in Iraq could become so bad that it might ultimately bypass Maliki's government. During his strategy review in 2006, Bush began questioning whether Maliki and his government were totally dysfunctional, and whether the U.S. should continue supporting him.[23] Similarly, in the strategy discussions leading up to the Iraq surge, Secretary of State Rice and her State Department confidant Philip Zelikow claimed that Maliki was "playing us for a sucker" and that the U.S., "needed to cut deals as necessary with these local bases of power."[24] As with Iraq, the threat of U.S. retrenchment loomed over the other host states in the system. Like Maliki, the other host leaders could observe that Bush's ability to mobilize the American public for the war was rapidly waning, the U.S. military was strained, and there was a distinct possibility that U.S. support would not be endless. Instead, the U.S. could choose to scale back its support and focus narrowly on protecting its own interests in preserving the peg between dollars and energy by working with local forces, such as militias in Afghanistan and the Alliance for the Restoration of Peace and Counterterrorism in southern Somalia. Given that some of these actors were either rivals or potential competitors, the possibility that the U.S. could shift to this alternative strategy altered the behavior of the host states and their willingness to fight their terrorists. To illustrate how, let us again turn to the logic behind the decision-making.

## OVERCOMING MORAL HAZARD

Figure 4.3 again presents the model of U.S. support for host states against terrorists. Recall, the central goal of the host leadership is to remain in power, whereas the goal of the U.S. is to keep the terrorists out of power. Both the U.S. and the host were uncertain about the terrorists' willingness to attack and destabilize the center. Facing this risk of conflict, the most efficient strategy for the host is to cut a deal with the terrorists, accommodate their demands, and share power. However,

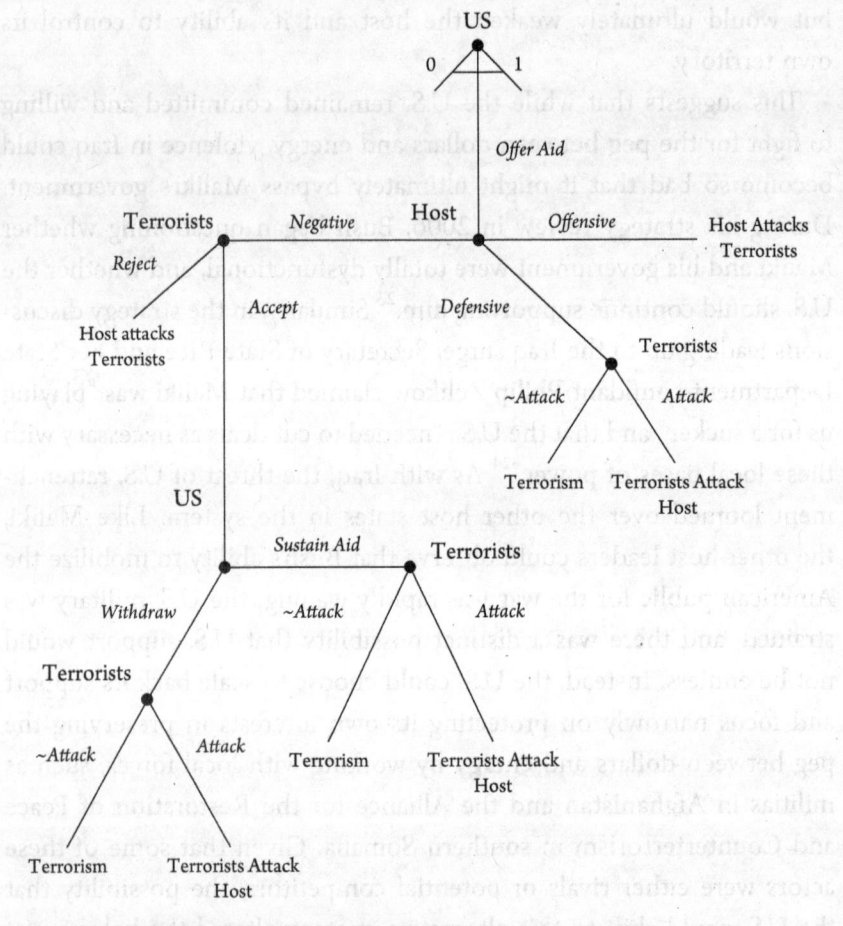

Figure 4.3. A Model of American Strategy in the War on Terror
Note. A full presentation of the game and its equilibria are available in the mathematical appendix. This version of the game assumes that the U.S. pays an increasing cost to support host states if the game continues, which represents the strain on the military and the political backlash in the U.S. against continuing the war.

these power-sharing deals threatened the host's cooperation in the petrodollar system. Therefore, to prevent the host from negotiating, the U.S. supplied the host leadership with sufficient economic and military aid to bolster their ability to fight the terrorists. This exogenous assistance allowed the host to reject negotiation, but encouraged the host to allow the terrorists to exist in the periphery to avoid the costs of a direct military encounter.

Previously, we assumed that the U.S. guarantee was credible. In this version of the model, let us assume that at some moment in time, the economic and political cost of the war may become so large that the

U.S. will be unable to fully guarantee the security of the host's leadership. At this point, the U.S. will either (1) cut the host off from aid completely or (2) reduce the level of support it provides and adopt a policy of working with local actors. This version of the model examines the strategic behavior of the host prior to the U.S. decision to alter its strategy of arming the host's leadership and national government.

Let us consider the host's behavior if the U.S. decides to reduce or terminate its support to the host. With less American support, adopting the defensive strategy and refusing to negotiate will likely result in an all-out assault by the terrorists, which may well succeed. The best option available to the host in this case is to negotiate with the terrorists. However, if the host waits to negotiate until after the U.S. reduces or eliminates its support, the terms of the power-sharing deal will shift even more in favor of the terrorists. Since the terrorists have been growing in the periphery, the ability of these groups to destabilize the center has improved in the second round from the first.[25] Nonetheless, since the host lacks sufficient U.S. assistance, it may have no choice but to offer a power-sharing agreement to end the war.

The third option is to engage in an offensive against the terrorists to wipe them out of as much of the territory as possible. The hosts that are most incentivized to adopt the offensive strategy are the very weakest ones, who seem the least capable of mounting these offensive operations. Since these hosts are so weak, the cost to the U.S. for keeping these regimes in power is likely quite high. This indicates that the probability that the U.S. shifts to working with local forces is also higher. If this is true, refusing to attack the terrorists immediately poses a considerable risk to the host state. If the host does not use its power immediately, it may lose it in the following round. This will compel the host to negotiate with the terrorists. The problem, however, is that negotiation is not terribly appealing due to the weakness of these states. If they strike a deal, it will reflect the true balance of power on the ground, which is not in their favor. However, when the host makes these decisions, it is receiving U.S. economic and military aid. In the present moment, these hosts are much stronger militarily due to American support. If these hosts continue to ignore their terrorists, there is a real risk that the U.S. will shift its strategy while the insurgency strengthens. This ultimately will leave the hosts trapped in an unfavorable peace deal. However, if these hosts have the advantage of American weaponry now, but will lose it in the future, these hosts can alternatively use their military power now to engage in an offensive and wipe their enemies out. At the very least, such an offensive may stalemate the conflict and lock in a settlement that is preferable to one that would be negotiated based on the current balance of power.

We therefore see that while American support for host states in their fight against terrorist groups encourages abuse, threatening to reduce and reallocate this support may compel host states into aggressive proactive measures to disarm their groups. The logic behind this insight is akin to the dynamics of the commitment problem identified in international relations. If a host can use American military support to temporarily deter a more powerful insurgency from attacking, but the U.S. is unlikely to continue providing this military support for much longer, the host can use the aid or lose it. Rather than accept a power-sharing deal on poor terms, and rather than risk an even worse deal if it loses American support, the host state can use its American support to wipe out the terrorists. Paradoxically, host states are more likely to cooperate with American strategic objectives when both they and the U.S. are at their weakest. In these cases, where the risk that the U.S. will shift to local forces is at its highest, host states have an incentive to use their American support to seize as much territory back from the insurgency as they can, before their level of support is reduced or cut. The model therefore demonstrates that in the war on terror, providing host states with strength encourages a weak response to terrorists, while forcing hosts to face their weakness yields desperation and compels them to disarm their terrorists immediately. To illustrate this hypothesis, let us examine the behavior of Iraq and Afghanistan when U.S. operations in both of those places were on the brink of failure.

### THE IRAQ AND AFGHAN SURGES

To demonstrate that causal mechanism, the historical record must demonstrate evidence that both Prime Minister Maliki of Iraq and President

Hamid Karzai of Afghanistan feared the possibility of losing their significant levels of American military support, and that this fear motivated both leaders to allow for increased offensive operations against their respective insurgencies. Let us first consider the case of Prime Minister Maliki in Iraq.

## Iraq and the Surge, 2006–2008

Maliki was aware in early 2006 that his government faced extensive peril. From the beginning of his tenure, the Iraqi prime minister resisted calls for an increase in American forces in Iraq. Instead, Maliki appeared to press in the opposite direction by calling for a reduction in forces short of a complete withdrawal. Maliki further resisted efforts to crack down on the Mahdi Army, a key Shi'a militia led by a cleric named Muqtada al Sadr. Sadr's ethnic cleansing of Sunni neighborhoods gained him considerable support within Maliki's ruling coalition. This popularity led Maliki to frequently interfere in American operations against the Mahdi Army.[26] Further, although Shi'a militias penetrated the Iraqi Army and were stealing arms and supplies, Maliki showed little interest in rooting out corruption in the national armed forces. In short, Maliki appeared perfectly content to allow terrorism to exist so long as he had American protection.

However, the general escalation of violence throughout 2006, and increasing calls for a redeployment of U.S. forces from Iraq, shifted Maliki's behavior. In an October conversation with Bush, Maliki expressed concern about a possible U.S. plan that would withdraw American troops if Iraq failed to reduce the level of violence in two months, and about the possibility that the U.S. would agree to a plan that split Iraq along sectarian lines.[27] In his conversation with Bush, Maliki signaled his commitment to both fighting the militias and adopting the American strategy to combat Sunni insurgents. This new commitment was met with some skepticism from the Bush administration. The prime minister was often seen as a protector of Sadr's militias and terribly weak in terms of combating al Qaeda. Bush therefore insisted that Maliki accept a larger troop presence (which he had opposed), commit his own forces to the offensive against Sadr and the militias (which he was often reluctant to do), and require that his forces avoid targeting Sunnis indiscriminately. Surprisingly, Maliki agreed to each of the demands, even as Sadr's political allies demanded that Maliki reject cooperation with Bush.[28] If Maliki's previous positions were more reflective of his ruling coalition's preferences, his acceptance of American terms suggests that he appreciated the gravity of his situation. It also suggested that he knew that he could not afford to lose American protection if he hoped to survive politically.

The reasons for Maliki's fear were clear, as his government's power was largely confined to Baghdad's American-protected Green Zone. Outside the Green Zone, violence in Baghdad was spiraling out of control. To put it in perspective, Baghdad averaged 637 monthly civilian fatalities from January 2004 to January 2006. After the al Askari bombing, the average monthly civilian fatalities in Baghdad increased by 140%, to 1,525 per month.[29] (See Figure 4.4.) The emerging Battle of Baghdad pitted the Sunni insurgency against Sadr's Mahdi Army. The orientation of the Sunni insurgency shifted after the capture of Saddam Hussein in late 2003. The old Ba'athists were displaced by a coalition of Sunnis that viewed Iraq's Shi'ites with hostility. The first group was the al Qaeda–aligned Salafists, which saw the Shi'ites as

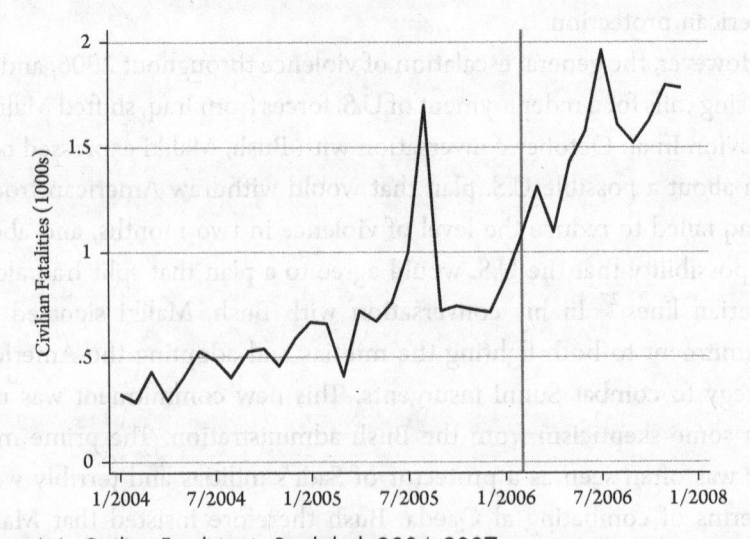

Figure 4.4. Civilian Fatalities in Baghdad, 2004–2007.
Note. Solid line represents the bombing of the al Askari mosque, beginning the sectarian Sunni-Shia conflict.
Source: https://www.iraqbodycount.org/

apostates. The second group consisted of former Saddam loyalists and Ba'athist officers who deeply feared Iranian influence in Iraq. The Mahdi Army responded to the bombing with a campaign of violence aimed at purging Sunnis from Baghdad's neighborhoods. The Mahdi Army also infiltrated the Iraqi Army, allowing Sadr's soldiers to skim and steal military equipment and supplies to further their fight. Politicians within the Iraqi state protected Sadr, whose public supporters applauded his activities and relied on him for security. Sadr gradually assumed control of neighborhoods away from a rival Shi'a militia known as the Badr Organization. However, in the process, the Mahdi Army became looser and less under Sadr's control. The organization fragmented into more factions, and many sought to establish their own fiefdoms in Baghdad's neighborhoods.[30]

Both the Sunni insurgency and the Mahdi Army posed significant challenges to Maliki's government. On one hand, the al Qaeda–led Sunni insurgency was desperate to restore its domination over Iraq and return the Shi'ites to their subservient position. On the other hand, Sadr's Mahdi Army was engaging in acts of vigilante violence that were undermining Maliki's place as the sovereign of Iraq and monopolist of force. To make matters worse, Sadr was popular with Maliki's supporters, which compelled Maliki to protect him and his organization. Sadr's growing popularity, and his alleged ties to Iran, meant that he could eventually emerge as a challenger to Maliki's rule. The Mahdi Army was armed with American supplies and were unlikely to be defeated. Al Qaeda in Iraq further had little hope of seizing control of the Green Zone and forcibly expelling the Americans. By the middle of 2006, the majority of Sunni insurgent leaders recognized that they were losing the war with the Shi'a militias and that their prospects for retaking control of Iraq were diminishing rapidly. As a last resort, al Qaeda could only engage in spectacular acts of violence in hopes of causing the Americans to withdraw.

The positive news was that these al Qaeda actions, and the diminishing chance of victory over the Shi'a militias, caused several of the Sunni insurgents to reach out to the Americans by mid-2006.[31] The movement by the Sunni insurgent leaders to suspend violence against the Shi'ites, and instead focus on disarming the al Qaeda terrorists in

Anbar, came to be known as the "Anbar Awakening." By forming what became known as "Awakening Councils," the Sunnis agreed to cease their efforts to destabilize the Iraqi state and they furthermore agreed to fight al Qaeda in exchange for bribes and protection. Interestingly, the Awakening Councils did not demand any place in the Iraqi state, as they knew that they were unlikely to get anything from Maliki. They were willing to fight Sunni extremists, so long as the U.S. would protect them from Sadr and other Shi'a militias. The problem, however, was that the Americans seemed to lack sufficient numbers to protect them from reprisals, which forced the Sunnis to continue fighting.

The surge of American forces therefore gave Maliki his best chance to disarm Sadr while simultaneously offering the Awakening Councils protection from their al Qaeda compatriots.[32] Rather than trying to build the capacity of the Iraqi forces, the strategy was now to use American forces to fight and clear Baghdad of Maliki's adversaries, both Sunni insurgents and Shi'a militias. The effectiveness of the surge, and the survival of Maliki's government, required him to authorize the U.S. to go on the offensive. President Bush stated clearly that Maliki needed to authorize all raids against Sadr and cease any efforts to restrict American activities. If not, the American public would demand a withdrawal, and the U.S. would be unable to sustain its position. Maliki agreed to all the U.S. demands.

President Bush announced the surge operation in January 2007. In response, Senate Majority Leader Harry Reid (D-NV) and Senator Russ Feingold (D-WI) developed a proposed bill to cut off funding for the entire Iraq operation by March 2008. Although the proposal failed, bipartisan support seemed to be growing for ending U.S. operations. Even Senate Minority Leader Mitch McConnell (R-KY), a stalwart supporter of the Bush administration, stated, "The Iraqi government, it strikes me, needs to understand that they're running out of time to get their part of the job done."[33] This bipartisan opposition signaled clearly that the U.S. and the Iraqis did not have much time to subdue both al Qaeda and Sadr. If results did not materialize quickly, a strong possibility existed that the U.S. would be forced to withdraw, leaving Maliki at the mercy of his adversaries.

The first surge operation, known as Operation Enforcing the Law, began in February 2007 with U.S. forces moving into the Sunni Doura district. In March, American forces entered Sadr City to clear the area of the Mahdi Army. Initially, the troop surge seemed to worsen violence and produce an increasing level of terrorist attacks.[34] In April, Sadr called on his forces to stop attacking Iraqi security forces and concentrate on the Americans.

However, a remarkable turn took place in August when Sadr ordered the Mahdi Army to suspend its operations as American force levels peaked.[35] (See Figure 4.5.) It is unclear exactly why Sadr made this choice. One possibility is that most of the neighborhoods were already cleared of Sunnis, so the Mahdi Army was victorious. However, another of Sadr's long-standing goals was to expel the Americans from the territory. On this front, Sadr was clearly unsuccessful. The Mahdi Army was unable to defeat the Americans in Baghdad and was unable to force an American withdrawal. Sadr was further unable to depose Maliki and seize control of Iraq for himself. Although violence sporadically

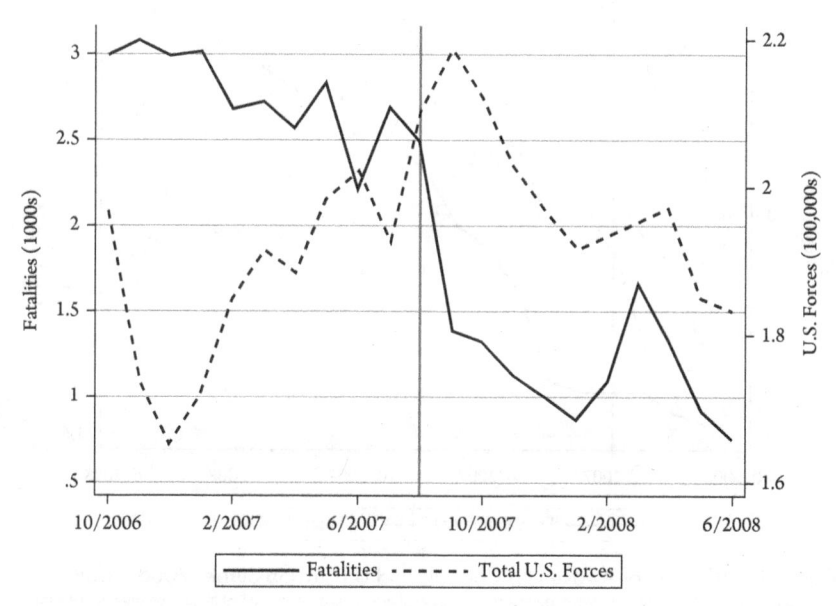

Figure 4.5. Violence in Iraq and Size of U.S. Troop Surge, October 2006–June 2008.
Note. Data on U.S. force size from Belasco (2009). Solid line marks Muqtada al Sadr's declaration that the Mahdi Army would stand down in August 2007.

continued with rogue factions, the Mahdi Army quickly ceased its operations. In a remarkable turnaround, the fatalities in Baghdad fell to their lowest levels in years.

Similarly, the back of the Sunni insurgency broke when al Qaeda was chased out of Baghdad, and the Sunni population in Anbar turned on the organization. Figure 4.6 demonstrates that the number of Awakening Councils opposing al Qaeda grew markedly after the beginning of Operation Enforcing the Law in February.[36] The collapse of the Sunni insurgency, along with the stand-down order of Sadr, indicated that the effort to push outside of the Green Zone was achieving success. Maliki appeared to defeat both his key Shia and Sunni rivals with U.S. support, and he was on his way to consolidating control over Iraq. This feat was remarkable, given that only a few months earlier, the U.S. seemed ready to leave and Maliki's government appeared to be at death's door.[37]

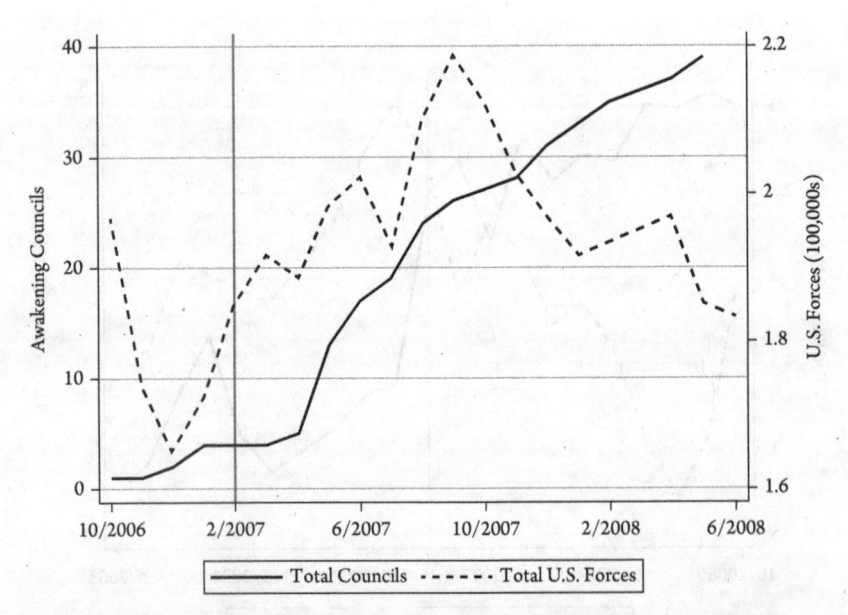

Figure 4.6. Growth of Awakening Councils and U.S. Troop Surge, 2006–2008.
Note: Solid line marks the start of Operation Enforcing the Law (Fardh al Qanoon), the first major operation of the surge strategy.
Source: Data from Stephen Biddle, Jeffrey A. Friedman, and Jacob N. Shapiro. 2012. Testing the Surge: Why Did Violence Decline in Iraq in 2007? *International Security* 37(1): 7–40, pp. 30–31.

Despite these victories, Democrats in Congress continued to proclaim the surge a failure as the U.S. headed for presidential elections in 2008. With the Democrats actively campaigning against the war, and Bush's popularity remaining at very low levels, Maliki faced a risk that a new Democratic president would suspend all support to his government. It was therefore paramount for Maliki to show results so that American operations could continue—and to neutralize his enemies in case it did not. In this environment, Maliki ordered the beginning of Operation Charge of Knights in Basra in March 2008. This operation aimed to use Iraq's American-backed forces to wipe out Sadr and the Mahdi Army. The operation was bold, given that no Iraqi government had defeated an Iranian-supported militia to this point, and Sadr maintained a substantial fighting force and considerable popularity. Yet, Maliki was determined to follow through with the operation, because in his words, "There will be no Iraq in six months."[38] Although Charge of Knights began poorly, the operation soon achieved success, as the Mahdi Army was chased out of Baghdad with American assistance. Quickly, Maliki pivoted to attack the Mahdi Army's position in Sadr City in Baghdad. In a coordinated effort, Maliki and the U.S. defeated the Mahdi Army and placed Sadr City under Maliki's control.[39] For the first time in months, the Iraqi prime minister was seen as a true sovereign and leader of Iraq, with unchallenged military power.

Consistent with the explanation, we see that Maliki's victory stemmed from an impending commitment problem. With American support, Maliki could remain in power indefinitely and was therefore content to allow the status quo of violence. When faced with the possibility that his power would collapse as the result of a drawdown in U.S. support, Maliki became much more aggressive in his fight against the Sunni and Shia insurgencies. If Maliki did not use his American backers immediately, he risked losing them altogether, and he would be left to face the wrath of the Sunnis and Sadr on his own. This commitment problem therefore solved the Iraqi moral hazard problem and compelled the Iraqis to cooperate.

In addition to the possibility of weakening against Sadr, Maliki had reason to fear that if he did not deliver results, the Americans would turn to the Sunni militias in Anbar known as Awakening Councils, or the Kurds in the north, or both, as alternative, local partners. The Awakening Councils were seen as critical pieces to defeating al Qaeda in Anbar. In exchange for Awakening Council assistance, the U.S. guaranteed protection and arms for the Sunni sheiks. The U.S. further agreed to protect the Sunnis from both the Shi'a militias and Maliki's government. Since the program was so successful, few in the U.S. wanted to suspend cooperation with the Sunni militias. However, the cooperation between the U.S. and these militias raised the possibility that the U.S. would favor the Sunnis over Maliki's Shi'a government. If that were to occur, some of the American assistance flowing to Maliki could end up in the hands of the Sunnis in Anbar. These Sunnis would then use this support to permanently prevent Maliki from establishing full sovereignty over Iraq. Maliki was therefore forced to deliver results by disarming Sadr immediately, or face the possibility that the U.S. would shift support to the Sunnis. The strategy appeared to be successful. The U.S. granted Maliki's government oversight of the 51,000 armed Sunnis in the militias in 2008. This ensured that the group's ability to challenge Maliki would be minimized, which in turn allowed Maliki's government to establish sovereignty over the territory.

Maliki's second worry was that the U.S. would also turn to its Kurdish allies as local partners. The U.S. had maintained substantial ties to the Kurds in the north since the first Gulf War. This created a fear that the U.S. would become more open to Kurdish independence if Baghdad continued to be dysfunctional. Although the Kurdish parties traditionally supported Maliki's Dawa Party, and supported him in his fight with Sadr, the Iraqi prime minister had considerable reason to be wary of the Kurds and their intentions. A key dispute between the Kurds and Baghdad was the status of several key oil-producing cities, particularly the city of Kirkuk. The Kurds claimed that Kirkuk should be part of their territory, as along with other cities in the Diyala and Ninveveh provinces. To make matters worse, the Kurdish Peshmerga remained armed and operational, and enjoyed substantial military ties to the U.S. This suggested that if Iraq were to collapse, the first ally the U.S. could turn to would be the Peshmerga. This relationship could produce a situation where the Peshmerga could become increasingly aggressive in asserting Kurdish territorial claims. Additionally, the Kurds refused to renounce the possibility that they would one day declare independence. If they did so, a substantial part of Iraq's oil revenue would be lost. Moreover, the coalition that kept the Shi'ites in power would be weakened, and the door could be opened to yet another conflict between Sunnis and Shi'ites if the Kurds declared independence. Given that the U.S. maintained long ties with the Kurds, it was unclear if the U.S. would push back against these aspirations for independence if Maliki failed to demonstrate the viability of his Iraq. For each of these reasons, failure to deliver results in disarming both the terrorists and militias was a significant and grave risk for the Maliki government.

These risks subsided once Maliki's adversaries were neutralized. Once these risks faded away, Maliki's motivations and incentive to cooperate with the Americans followed. Maliki's political coalition remained hostile to the U.S. and continued to push for an American withdrawal. These Shi'a-dominated political figures shared greater ideological similarities with Iran than with the U.S., and they were instructed by the legendary Iranian commander Qasem Soleimani to oppose a continued American presence in the country.[40] Since the Iraqis faced a greatly reduced threat from both al Qaeda and Sadr, Maliki became less willing to maintain cooperation with the U.S. Success seemingly exacerbated Maliki's worst instincts, as he began a campaign of repression against the Sunnis and solidified his power with kickbacks and favors to his political allies. These actions would soon come back to haunt Maliki, when the opportunity for the Sunnis to rise up came again following the Arab Spring in 2011. The waning threat of terrorism had ended the need for the two states to maintain the high level of military cooperation, for the time being.

## The Afghan Surge, 2009–2012

As Iraq's conflicts settled, the Taliban insurgency in Afghanistan was ramping up its level of violence. Throughout 2008, Taliban groups made considerable gains in the southern and eastern parts of the country, and established total control in parts of the Helmand, Kandahar, Paktika, and Khost provinces. Figure 4.7 demonstrates that the Taliban were

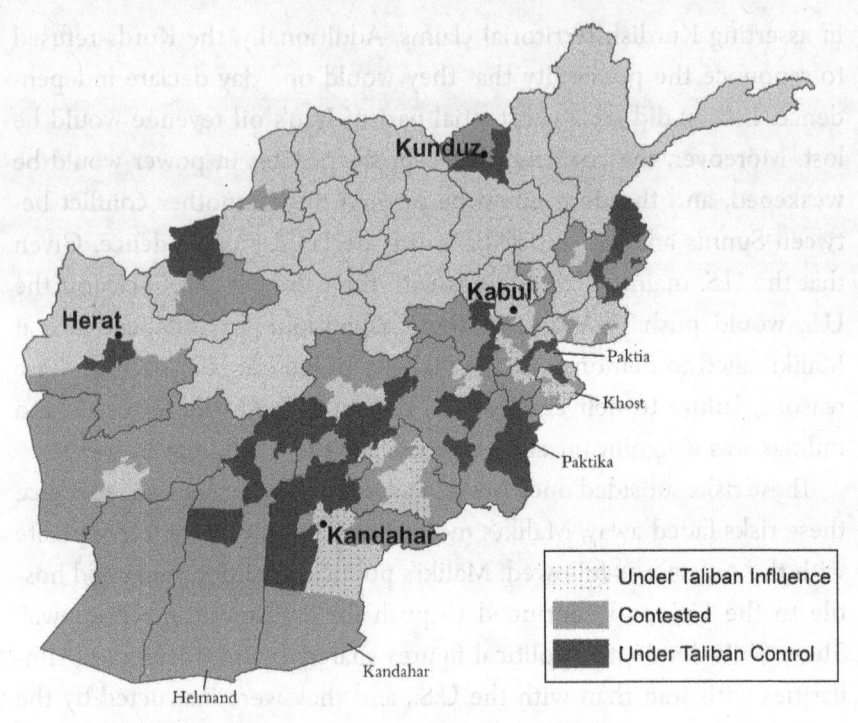

Figure 4.7. Estimated Taliban Control over Afghanistan, 2009.
Note. Data adapted from Roggio (2009).

contesting control of the entire Pakistani border, which would place the group in position to destabilize International Security Assistance Force (ISAF) supply lines. Attacks surged against American convoys along Highway 1, the key roadway linking all of Afghanistan's major cities. The loss of control over this road, and over the routes through Pakistan, would leave the air corridor through Russia as the sole resupply route for ISAF. Supplying Afghanistan solely by air would be difficult both because of the difficulty of transportation and because access depended on the cooperation of Russia. ISAF's position was therefore becoming very precarious, and possibly untenable.

Yet, Karzai made little effort to reverse the Taliban's momentum and win back support among his population. In a 2008 brief, U.S. analysts declared that Karzai "was at the center of the governing challenge."[41] Although Karzai often decried the collateral damage caused by American operations, and professed his willingness to negotiate with the Taliban, these statements were driven by his desire to appeal to his ruling coalition. A 2009 diplomatic cable by Ambassador Karl Eikenberry went even further by declaring that "President Karzai is not an adequate strategic partner." Although the Bush administration chose to ignore these behaviors and focus on maintaining cooperation, the new Obama administration appeared less willing to hand Karzai a blank check.[42] In a notable incident, Vice President–elect Joseph Biden led a bipartisan delegation to Afghanistan in late 2008 to meet with Karzai. At the dinner, Biden emphasized to Karzai that his government needed to work to reduce corruption if it hoped to continue receiving U.S. assistance. Karzai responded by blaming the U.S. and citing errant airstrikes. In a break with diplomatic protocol, Biden stormed out of the dinner and claimed that the remarks "were beneath" the Afghan president. President-elect Obama seemed to share Biden's diffidence toward Karzai and continued to publicly chastise the Afghan leader for corruption in the government.[43] Despite his considerable dependence on the U.S. to stay in power, Karzai remained defiant. In an election against Karzai's rival Abdullah Abdullah, Karzai loyalists used bribes, threats of violence, ballot rigging, and other forms of fraud to produce a victory for the incumbent Afghan president. Karzai refused to accept any evidence that the vote had been tainted. He quickly began to view the Obama administration as an adversary and continued his demonization of his American protectors.

As the frustration of the Obama administration with Karzai grew, the military situation in 2009 in Afghanistan continued to deteriorate. The U.S. sent 20,000 additional troops into the eastern part of the country to fend off growing instability. Taliban fighters from the south further began infiltrating and staging terrorist attacks in Kabul. The Taliban's grip of Helmand and Kandahar continued to tighten, which raised the possibility that ISAF's position would soon become untenable. In response, General Stanley McChrystal recommended a robust counterinsurgency strategy that would increase the level of U.S. troops in Afghanistan, similar to the strategy adopted by General David Petraeus in Iraq. The goal of the Afghan surge was to directly challenge the Taliban, take control of the villages within Taliban territory, and subsequently remain in these areas to help the villages develop. The presence of infantry would decrease coalition reliance on airstrikes, which tended to be more damaging and less accurate. Over time, the steady presence of U.S. forces would enable the local population to assist in building an intelligence network, which could then be used to keep the Taliban at bay.

Upon receiving the recommendation, Obama stated, "We have a government with a serious dependency issue. If I'm Karzai, this looks great to me, because I don't have to do anything. It's unacceptable."[44] Consistent with Obama's criticism, Vice President Biden offered a plan resembling the light footprint strategy. Biden's plan was predicated on the belief that Karzai was far too corrupt, making it impossible for the U.S. to save him. His plan would instead decrease U.S. forces and focus only on attacking al Qaeda targets and preventing their camps from resurfacing. Since there were only an estimated 300 al Qaeda fighters remaining in Afghanistan, this strategy could rely on unmanned drones and special forces to focus on hunting the terrorists in Afghanistan and the border region. This plan to limit U.S. objectives and work with local partners became known as 'Counterterrorism Plus.' The idea won support from Ambassador Eikenberry, who suggested that U.S. support for Karzai was fueling his inaction. In opposition to the McChrystal plan, Eikenberry stated in now-famous cable:Karzai continues to shun responsibility for any sovereign burden, whether defense, governance, or development. He and much of his circle do not want the U.S. to leave and are only too happy to see us invest further.

Karzai soon recognized Obama's loss of faith in both leadership capability and with the entire Afghan operation by mid-2009. To hedge against the possibility that the U.S. would shift to Biden's "counterterrorism plus" plan, Karzai offered repeatedly to negotiate with the Taliban. Karzai allegedly stated in a closed-door meeting with Afghan political figures that he would join the Taliban if the U.S. continued to pressure him to reform.[45] Yet, the Taliban refused to negotiate with Karzai so long as American forces remained in Afghanistan. The Taliban's rejection of negotiation was likely driven by three facts on the ground. First, the presence of the U.S. military was artificially improving Karzai's power, which would force the Taliban to strike a deal whose terms did not reflect their strength relative to Karzai's government. Second, the Taliban's position was continuing to improve as they seized more territory in the south and east, and as both active and passive support from Pakistan continued to grow. Third, with the public weary of the decade-long war, the U.S. appeared to be on the cusp of withdrawing. These factors likely led the Taliban to believe that there was no reason to settle since the war's momentum seemed favorable.

Karzai therefore found himself almost completely isolated. The Taliban did not want to talk, and his American protectors appeared eager to abandon him. Since the loss of American forces would spell almost certain doom for his government, Karzai publicly voiced support for the surge and insisted that he would work to clean up corruption in Afghanistan.[46] Although there is little evidence that the Obama administration believed that Karzai's governance would improve, the president authorized the surge of 33,000 troops to Afghanistan to stave off his defeat.[47] Karzai agreed to allow General McChrystal to pursue counterinsurgency tactics in Helmand and Kandahar to break the Taliban's hold over the south.

However, the Obama administration insisted on imposing a timetable on the surge's operations and creating a deadline for withdrawing the additional forces. In his speech at West Point announcing the surge, Obama stated that "the days of providing a blank check are over" and that "after 18 months, our troops will begin to come home."[48] Immediately, hawks in the U.S. derided the president for setting the deadline; they argued that it sent a message that the American commitment to success was not ironclad. Strategically, however, Obama's reason for setting the deadline was to send a decisive signal to Karzai that the next year was his last shot, and that he needed to become more serious about combating the Taliban. If he didn't, the political pressure for the U.S. to leave would become impossible to ignore, and he would be left to fight the Taliban on his own.

The first part of the strategy expanded attacks against al Qaeda and Taliban strongholds in Pakistan. These strikes aimed to kill key leaders in both al Qaeda and the Taliban, thereby disrupting the ability of the former to plot attacks and the latter to continue making territorial gains.

Figure 4.8 demonstrates that American drone strikes into Pakistani territory increased in the first year of the Obama administration, and they rapidly escalated in 2010 as U.S. forces grew in Afghanistan. The bulk of these strikes took place in North Waziristan, which was long a headquarters for the Taliban Quetta Shura. According to one account, while the drone attacks killed marginal numbers of fighters, it also increased infighting within the Taliban to discover where the U.S. was acquiring its intelligence.[49] The increasing number of strikes therefore did disrupt the Taliban's ability to further its campaign in Afghanistan and significantly degraded the al Qaeda core in the region.

The results of the ground war were more mixed. Figure 4.9 indicates that the ground operations of the Afghan surge seemed less effective at disrupting the ongoing insurgency. We see that since 2004, ISAF fatalities had been steadily rising in both Helmand and Kandahar, the two key hotbeds of Taliban activity. The solid line represents the decision to pursue General McChrystal's counterinsurgency. In 2010, the first year of the strategy's implementation, ISAF fatalities rose to their highest

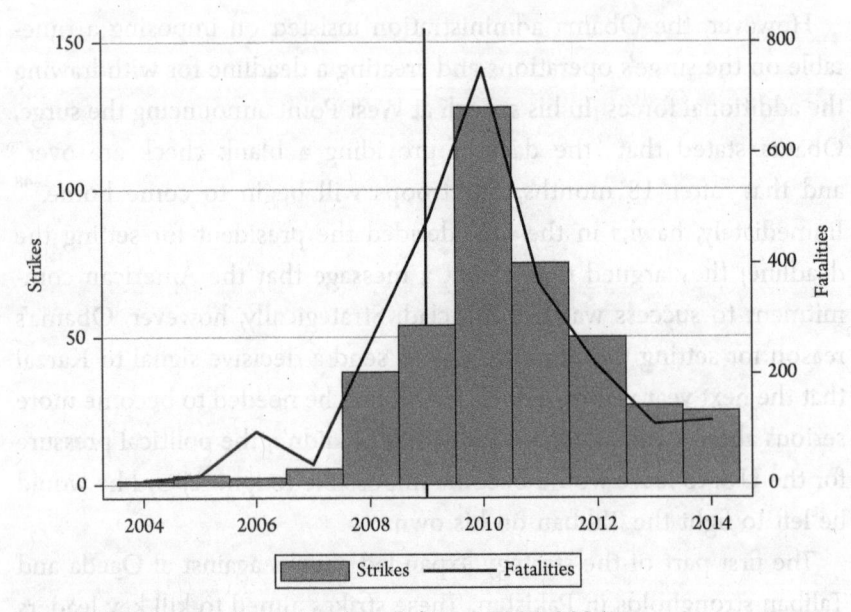

Figure 4.8. American Drone Attacks in Pakistan, 2004–2014.
Note. Solid line in 2009 represents the Obama administration's approval of surge.
Source: Data from New America Foundation, Available at: https://www.newamerica.org/in-depth/americas-counterterrorism-wars/pakistan/

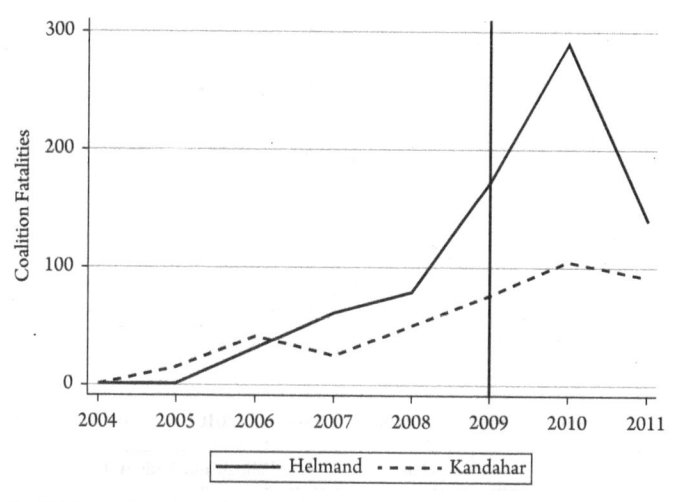

Figure 4.9. ISAF Coalition Fatalities in Helmand and Kandahar Provinces, 2004–2011.
Note. Solid line represents the start of the Afghan surge.
Source: http://icasualties.org/chart/Chart

levels in both Helmand and Kandahar. This pattern is somewhat predictable, since ISAF suffered more fatalities as it engaged in more offensive operations. However, these casualty numbers declined considerably in Helmand and slightly in Kandahar in 2011. These numbers seemed to offer some hope that perhaps the ground strategy, in conjunction with the air war over Pakistan, may have been yielding some signs of success.

American policymakers were perhaps even more encouraged by the data in Figure 4.10, which plots the fatalities of Afghan government supporters and Taliban supporters over time. As in Figure 4.10, we see that the decision to begin the surge in 2009 did not seem to appreciably alter the trend of increasing Taliban fatalities and steady Afghan government fatalities. However, we can see that following 2011, the number of Taliban killed falls slightly. This could suggest a positive sign that the surge strategy was working.

U.S. politicians and military planners have remained skeptical of body counts as measures of success since the Vietnam War, and for good reason. Such data tells us something about the trends in conflict, but does not appear to conclusively answer the question of whether the offensive was working. With the data in mind, we can get a better

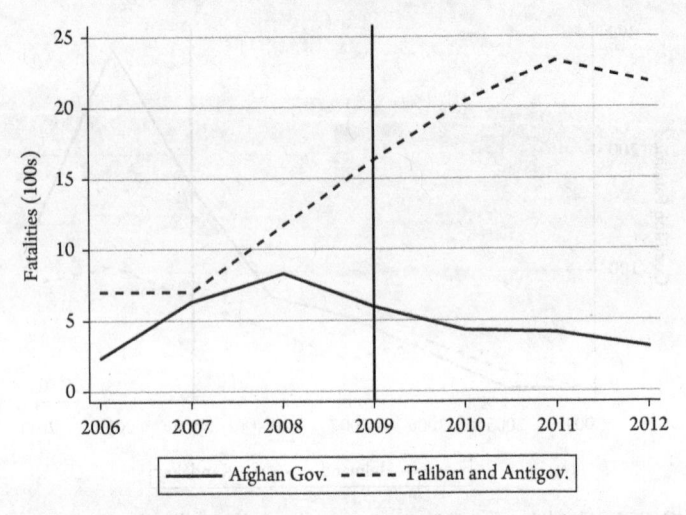

Figure 4.10. Pro-Government and Anti-Government Fatalities in Afghanistan, 2006–2012.

sense using descriptive accounts. In March 2011, the United Nations reported that the number of districts under Taliban control was falling and that the Afghan security forces were improving in their capabilities. Yet, the report also noted that the Taliban were increasing their hold over other previously uncontested districts.[50] Other analyses revealed similar assessments: the U.S. offensive into the south was diminishing the Taliban's control over Helmand and Kandahar, but these gains were very fragile and could be reversed if the Afghan government did not consolidate them.

These gains would soon reverse following the execution of Operation Neptune Spear, which resulted in the death of Osama bin Laden in Abbottabad on May 2, 2011. President Obama stated in a speech late that evening, "We can say to those families who have lost loved ones to al Qaeda's terror: justice has been done.[51]" While this moment was cathartic for many Americans, this operation seemed to remove Americans' concerns about the future of Afghanistan. The U.S. had invaded almost ten years earlier to bring the terrorist leader to justice. Now that this objective was achieved, it would be difficult for the U.S. to justify continuing to spend billions of dollars in Afghanistan, particularly when unemployment in the U.S. the same year was at 9.1%

and the budget deficit was over 8% of GDP. Further, the fact that bin Laden's compound was less than a mile from the Pakistani Military Academy at Kakul, known as the country's West Point, raised alarm among policymakers that Pakistan was a duplicitous ally. Military intelligence officials long suspected that in addition to bin Laden, Pakistan was protecting the Quetta Shura and the Haqqani networks, both Taliban groups the U.S. was trying to destroy.

Bin Laden's death was a watershed. With the terrorist leader dead, both the public and political leaders in both parties became unwilling to continue subsidizing the Afghan regime. The Obama administration was no longer compelled to fully guarantee Karzai's stability, which allowed the drawdown in surge troops to continue until 2012. In a discussion with his foreign policy team in 2015 President Obama stated, "The fever in this room has finally broken. We're no longer in nation-building mode."[52] Instead, the U.S. would turn to local allies as part of Biden's "counterterrorism plus." It would provide a minimal number of troops to mitigate the risk that the Taliban would return, but it would not provide the massive amount needed to ensure the survival of the Afghan regime. In May 2012, the U.S. signed the "Enduring Partnership between the Islamic Republic of Afghanistan and the United States of America." This agreement designated Afghanistan as a major non-NATO ally and provided for a bilateral security agreement where eventually less than 10,000 U.S. forces would remain. The size of this force would make the task of deposing the government in Kabul difficult for the Taliban, but it did not provide the U.S. with the capability to disarm the insurgency. Further, the U.S. signaled its willingness to negotiate with Taliban officials, though the group continued to hold out for perhaps better terms in the future.

Although Karzai's presidential term would end in 2014, and he was not permitted to run again by Afghanistan's constitution, he did not go quietly. Karzai suspended talks with the U.S. over the bilateral security agreement in 2013 due to the American plan to negotiate with the Taliban. Later in the year, Karzai announced that he would refuse to sign the bilateral security agreement. White House Press Secretary James Carney then stated that a failure to sign the agreement would make it "impossible for the United States and our allies to plan for a presence post-2014."[53] Faced with the threat of a complete American withdrawal, the Loya Jirga, which was the assembly in Afghanistan tasked with critical decisions, signaled its support for the agreement. The agreement was signed on September 30, 2014, the day after the new president Ashraf Ghani assumed power from Karzai. Although in following years the Taliban insurgency continued, and the Afghan state did not appear close to consolidating its territory, the Obama administration decided that this situation is "Afghan good enough."[54]

## CONCLUSION: THE EURO CHALLENGE FADES AND THE SECURITY GUARANTEE UNRAVELS

The early experiences of Afghanistan and Iraq, along with worsening terrorism in Pakistan, Yemen, Saudi Arabia, and Central and Southeast Asia, signaled to U.S. policymakers that the security guarantee created what economists refer to as a moral hazard problem. If the U.S. promised to defend hosts from any terrorist challenger with its own blood and treasure, host leaders were happy to allow the U.S. to fulfill its obligations. While host leaders used the American security umbrella to avoid the task of fighting terrorists, the groups were growing in power. This growth made the task of containing rebellions more difficult, costly, and bloody for the United States. By the late 2000s, the American public began clamoring for an end to the wars in Iraq and Afghanistan. The public had little understanding or knowledge of the petrodollar or the financial incentives for the U.S. to continue protecting the states of the energy market. Instead, the U.S. public saw rising fatality rates and ever-increasing cost for no discernable gain. This raised the pressure on American leaders to end its involvement in foreign wars and restrict the use of the U.S. military in combating terrorism in the future.

Although this new strain of isolationism could be interpreted as a weakness, the threat of losing American protection forced host states to finally use their military support to disarm the terrorists in their countries. While these states were invulnerable with American support, they would be forced to face the powerful insurgencies in their territories alone if the U.S. retrenched. These conflicts promised that the hosts would face one of two unpalatable options. The hosts would either be forcibly deposed from power or would have to strike unfavorable deals to survive. Faced with this possibility, the U.S. surprisingly gained greater cooperation in conflicts that appeared to be lost. The success of the Iraqi government in defeating the Sunni insurgency and disarming Muqtada al Sadr were impressive. Much of the U.S. defense establishment attributed this success to the COIN (counterinsurgency) strategy advocated by General Petraeus, which required larger commitments of American forces to combat terrorist and insurgent challengers.[55]

However, two events effectively halted the willingness and ability of the U.S. to pay for such large-scale operations. The first one was the global financial crisis of 2008, which began on September 15 with the collapse of the Lehman Brothers investment bank. This event, which came to be known as the Great Recession, triggered a collapse in the stock market, as indexed by the drop in the Dow Jones Industrial Average shown in Figure 4.11. The collapse prompted Treasury Secretary Hank Paulson and Federal Reserve Chairman Ben Bernanke to inject capital into the major U.S. financial institutions and reduce interest rates to close to 0%. The Dow Jones lost almost half of its value by March 2009.

The data from Figure 4.12 demonstrates that the U.S. began shedding hundreds of thousands of jobs per month, and unemployment in the U.S. soon reached over 10%. These devastating financial conditions increased the U.S. budget deficit from $458 billion in 2008 to $1.4 trillion in 2009—an increase of 208%. To combat this deep and growing recession, the Obama administration enacted a $787 billion fiscal stimulus known as the American Recovery and Investment Act. This large increase in federal spending, coupled with the trillion-dollar cost of sustaining the war on terror, raised questions throughout international markets about the financial strength of the U.S. Global worries about U.S. deficit spending, along with general weakness in the economy, were now forcing the U.S. to cut back on large expenditures. This new reality changed the state of the world for the U.S. military in fighting the war on terror. Previously, the U.S. could use its power to guarantee the security of the host states. Following the Great Recession, the U.S. could not

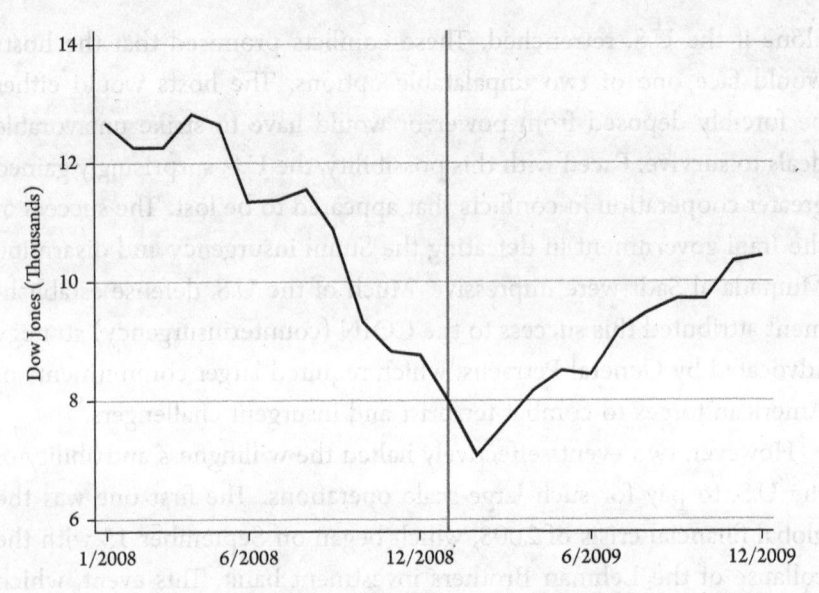

Figure 4.11. The Dow Jones Industrial Average and the Financial Crisis of 2008.
Note. Solid line indicates transition from George W. Bush to Barack Obama in January 2009.

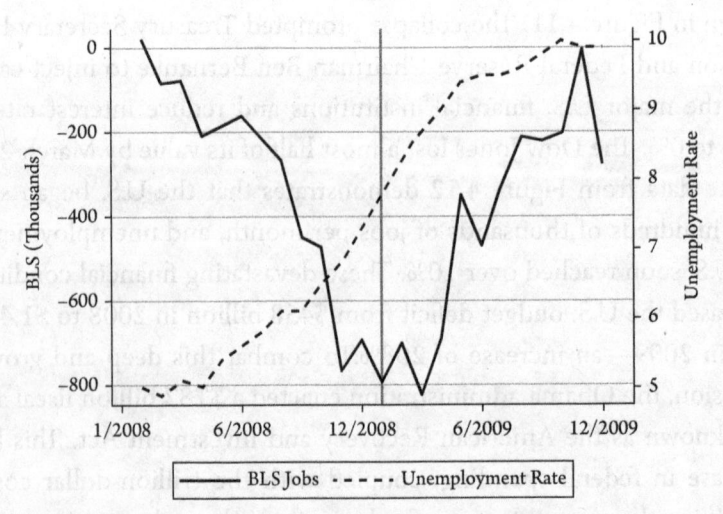

Figure 4.12. Job Losses and Rising Unemployment in the Wake of the Financial Crisis, January 2008–December 2009.
Note. Data from the U.S. Bureau of Labor and Statistics. Solid line indicates transition from George W. Bush to Barack Obama in January 2009.

sustain these large operations for extended periods. The danger was that if the U.S. could not provide the hosts with security, it would abrogate the deal that allowed for petrodollar recycling. In a time of significant government borrowing, and credit freezes throughout the U.S., it was even more essential for the U.S. to protect this system so that international capital could continue returning to American markets.

Yet, even as the U.S. seemed to be losing its status as protector of the global energy market, a second event strengthened the American grip over the world financial system: the European sovereign debt crisis.[56] As the financial crisis spread in 2009, several European countries found themselves unable to refinance their loans or repay their creditors. This raised the risk that these states would default, which in turn created the risk that financial contagion would spread to the other core European lenders, particularly Germany. This problem was particularly acute in Greece, which had long underreported the extent of its financial problems. Beginning in 2010, the EU offered Greece a series of monetary bailouts, but only under the condition that Greece adopt "austerity" policies. The austerity measures involved a significant reduction of government spending and greater emphasis on collecting tax revenues. In a time of recession, these actions seemed to worsen the short-term economic pain Greeks were experiencing, leading to higher unemployment rates and economic stagnation.[57] The EU demanded similar conditions for the other peripheral states that faced the risk of default, leading to substantial increases in unemployment. This process was particularly painful for the younger population. Unemployment rates in Greece, Spain, and Italy reached over 40% in 2015.[58]

The depth of the European sovereign debt crisis significantly shook the confidence and the popularity of the EU. On one hand, leftist movements such as Greece's Syriza demanded an end to austerity measures. On the other, rightist movements argued that the EU's freedom of movement was threatening the sovereignty of the member states and their culture. Although the movement to end Greek participation ("Grexit") in the EU failed, the British public voted in favor of leaving the EU ("Brexit") in 2016. This success emboldened other nationalist movements throughout the continent, which also demanded an end to the EU. This political and economic instability made it very unlikely that the EU could challenge the dollar in world finance in the foreseeable future.

The fading of the euro as a potential competitor to the dollar represented a key moment in the war. As it occurred, the euro seemed to lose its ability to replace the dollar in the sale of global energy products. States and investors were flocking to U.S. treasuries and American commercial banks, which seemed relatively safer than other assets. If the motivation for the war began to protect American financial dominance, and the euro was losing its status as a competitor, the task of protecting the place of the dollar in the short term was essentially complete. The fact that much of the world continued to purchase U.S. securities in a time of financial turmoil indicated that the dollar's place was secure, and the exorbitant privilege enjoyed by Americans would hold, once the U.S. pulled itself out of the recession. This meant that the host states in the energy market were losing their ability to threaten to denominate their sales in an alternative to the dollar. As a result, the U.S. effectively became free from the host states' threat to undermine the peg between dollars and energy sales. With growing economic and human costs from the war, this shift allowed the U.S. to move completely to the light footprint strategy and punish ineffective host leaders by reducing or cutting their military assistance.

This newfound willingness to reduce aid to the host states was observable throughout the Arab Spring. The first challenge surfaced in December 2010, when a Tunisian named Mohammad Bouazizi immolated himself in front of a Sidi Bouzid police department. Bouazizi's act was intended to protest the police's demand for bribes that prevented him from continuing his work as a street vendor. Within hours, hundreds of other Tunisians joined the protests against the state, triggering widespread unrest in the capital city. With the situation spiraling out of control, President Ben Ali fled Tunisia on January 14, 2011, to find sanctuary in Saudi Arabia, ending his twenty-three-year reign as undisputed ruler of the North African state. Although Ben Ali was a consistent U.S. ally against terrorist groups, his loss did not seem significant to the U.S. Consequently, the Obama administration took no action to keep Ben Ali in power, embraced the revolution, and called for democratic reform in Tunisia.

Although Tunisia was a partner in counterterrorism, Ben Ali's regime was not seen as a critical loss for the U.S. Days later, however, the key U.S. ally of Egypt, home to the Suez Canal chokepoint, began facing its own insurrection. A year earlier, in June 2009, Obama had made a speech in Cairo called "A New Beginning." The speech represented an attempt by the new president to repair relations with the Arab world that were damaged by the events of the Iraq war, particularly reports that American soldiers wantonly killed and tortured Muslims. In the speech at Cairo University, Obama stated:

> So let me be clear: no system of government can or should be imposed upon one nation by any other. That does not lessen my commitment, however, to governments that reflect the will of the people. Each nation gives life to this principle in its own way, grounded in the traditions of its own people. America does not presume to know what is best for everyone, just as we would not presume to pick the outcome of a peaceful election. But I do have an unyielding belief that all people yearn for certain things: the ability to speak your mind and have a say in how you are governed; confidence in the rule of law and the equal administration of justice; government that is transparent and doesn't steal from the people; the freedom to live as you choose. Those are not just American ideas, they are human rights, and that is why we will support them everywhere.[59]

The speech was received very positively among individuals in the Arab world. However, the rhetoric emphasizing better governance and greater freedom perhaps created the impression that he was no longer interested in preserving the survival of the Arab states indefinitely. While this may have been true for states that were more marginal to U.S security interests, such as Tunisia, it did not appear to be true for critical regimes such as Mubarak's Egypt. The survival of Mubarak was critical for three reasons. First, Mubarak consistently cooperated with the U.S. in keeping the energy trade route through the

Suez Canal open. Second, Egypt remained a key point of access for the U.S. to project power into the Middle East. Third, Mubarak was essential to keeping peace with Israel and fending off anti-American militants within Egyptian territory. For each of these reasons, President Obama quickly lent his support to Mubarak as protests began in Egypt on January 25, 2011. Mubarak quickly attempted to subdue the protests by declaring curfews and eliminating Internet access to halt the collaboration of various opposition groups that were rising up. When these actions failed, Mubarak attempted to pacify the rebellion by reshuffling his cabinet and promising reforms. Yet, these steps failed to stop the protests, and clashes began to break out between the opposition groups and the police forces. These events suggested that if Mubarak were to survive, he would need to either surrender control of the state or break the back of the opposition with force.

Most of Obama's advisors recommended adopting a strategy that would allow Mubarak's government to survive, even if the Egyptian leader stepped down. Yet, on February 1, Obama informed Mubarak that his rule "must end now." For his part, Mubarak seemed stunned, and told the president, "You don't understand this part of the world. You're young." However, Obama signaled that the U.S. would no longer protect Mubarak and demanded the longtime Egyptian leader stop down. Instead, the Obama administration pushed for an orderly transition in Egypt and ultimately accepted the rise of Muslim Brotherhood leader Mohamed Morsi as the rightful leader of the state. While cooperating with Morsi, Obama continued to provide funding to the Egyptian military to ensure that the U.S. continued to protect its access to the Suez Canal and maintained its alliance with the armed forces. These relationships seemingly would secure Egypt's place in the global energy market, regardless of the political turmoil in Cairo.

The decision to abandon Mubarak represented a clear break from the American security commitment to provide security to the host states of the energy market in exchange for their cooperation. The decision by the Obama administration raised the question: had the experiences of Afghanistan and Iraq, along with the financial crisis, weakened the

U.S. to such an extent that it could no longer be counted upon? If this were the case, each host would need to prepare for a potential future without the U.S. Each state would therefore need to begin planning for a more unilateral foreign policy, which would involve using force to protect its resources and strategic interests.

# 5

# HEGEMONIC DECLINE AND THE ESCALATION OF VIOLENCE

You left the Egyptians, you turned your back on the Egyptians, and they won't forget that.[1]

—General Abdel Fatteh el-Sisi
August 3, 2013

It is a concerning factor for us if America pulls back. America has changed, we have changed, and definitely we need to realign and readjust our understandings of each other.[2]

—Saudi Prince Turki al Faisal
April 18, 2016

The long experience of war in Afghanistan and Iraq, coupled with the financial crisis and the fading of the euro challenge, ended the ability of the U.S. to provide indefinite security for the key host states of the energy market. However, even as American support faded, the terrorist campaigns and insurgencies that took hold in the post-9/11 era continued, increasing the security risk to those host states. The leaders of the host states now faced two commitment problems. First, the host leaders faced the possibility that the U.S. would abandon them, which in turn would leave them vulnerable to the terrorists they long cultivated. These terrorists were now far more powerful than they were previously, having seized territory and gained foreign support. If the U.S. abandoned any one of the hosts, they would find themselves unable to defend their territories needed to harness their natural resources, and the trade routes on which this trade depended, from rivals seeking to steal their markets. Second, the loss of American support could encourage the rivals of host states to become more aggressive. These rivals could begin challenging the hosts by either increasing their support to terrorists in an effort to destabilize their rivals or by engaging in conventional operations to "stabilize" areas to rid them from terrorist influence. These justifications could be used opportunistically by rivals in an effort to undermine the ability of hosts to draw resources, thereby permanently weakening these states.

In this chapter, I argue that the fading of the U.S. security guarantee led to an increase in violence throughout the energy market states. If the U.S. was unable to protect them, the host states became vulnerable to military challenges by their rivals. As a result, several of the host states began initiating conflicts to eliminate their internal and external rivals immediately, before they lost American support entirely. However, because the U.S. was now adopting a strategy where it worked with local partners to protect its energy interests, rather than working with host governments, these efforts often escalated into larger, longer, and more deadly international conflicts. To illustrate this dynamic, the following chapter examines the rebellion in Yemen and the conflicts in both Syria and Iraq—involving the U.S., Bashar al Assad, Iran, Russia, Turkey, Saudi Arabia, and Qatar, along with the Free Syrian Army, al Nusra, and the Islamic State (ISIS). The chapter concludes by arguing that this escalation indicates that many of the host states once allied with the U.S. now seem to doubt the value of the security guarantee. This may lead to a future where these hosts seek alternative security commitments, initiate their own wars to secure their resources and defend their territories, and become unwilling to participate in the petrodollar system.

## THE U.S. SECURITY GUARANTEE LOSES CREDIBILITY

The Obama campaign trumpeted the president's record in the war on terror during his reelection campaign in 2012. Osama bin Laden was dead, the Afghan surge had stalemated the Taliban's advance toward Kabul, and the last U.S. combat forces had left Iraq on December 18, 2011, having defeated both the Mahdi Army and al Qaeda. The president achieved yet another success by eliminating the Libyan leader Muammar Qaddafi and Qaddafi's challenge to the petrodollar system. Two years earlier, Qaddafi had announced a proposal to denominate North African oil sales in a new currency known as the African gold dinar, which would be backed by Libya's substantial gold reserves. The gold dinar threatened to replace the French-supported West African CFA franc as the unit of exchange in North Africa, and it challenged the tie between energy and the U.S. dollar.[3] The insurrection in Libya during the Arab Spring offered both the French and the U.S. cover to eliminate this challenge to both of their strategic interests. The U.S., the French, and the British opened an air campaign to halt the advance of the Libyan army toward the rebel stronghold of Benghazi.[4] Although the bombing was justified as a way of stopping Qaddafi's forces from committing a mass atrocity, the air support enabled the rebel forces to capture Tripoli in October.[5] The allies quickly devolved political power to the local National Transitional Council of Libya in an effort to avoid creating another chronically dependent regime, like Afghanistan and Iraq. For a short time, Operation Odyssey Dawn appeared successful. Obama's adoption of the light footprint strategy seemed to be paying dividends, as it gave the U.S. the ability to fight terrorists while avoiding the moral hazard problem associated with the security guarantee.

Despite this illusion of success, Figure 5.1 demonstrates that the light footprint strategy associated with an unraveling of the security situation in 2011, when numerous insurgencies and terrorist campaigns began following the onset of the Arab Spring.[6] A key catalyst for the growth of these militant organizations was the beginning of the Syrian civil war. Initially, the Obama administration expected that the Assad regime would crumble quickly, as was the case with Mubarak in Egypt. However, by July 2011, it became clear that the Free Syrian Army (FSA)

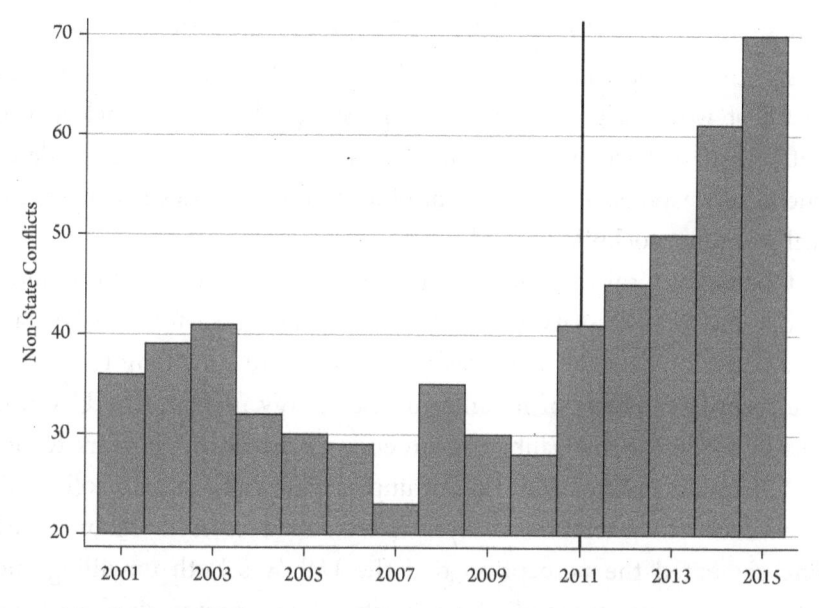

Figure 5.1. The Spread of Militant Violence in the Developing World, 2001–2015. Note. Data on non-state conflicts obtained from Nils Petter Gleditsch, Peter Wallensteen, Mikael Eriksson, Margareta Sollenberg, and Håvard Strand. 2002. Armed conflict 1946–2001: A new dataset. *Journal of Peace Research* 39(5): 615–637; Therése Patterson and Kristine Eck. 2018. Organized Violence, 1989–2017. *Journal of Peace Research* 55(4): 535–547. Solid line represents 2011, which is the start of the Arab Spring.

lacked the capability to topple Assad's regime. Most of Obama's foreign policy team favored intervening on behalf of the FSA with air support. The president, however, was both skeptical that the FSA could defeat Assad and concerned about dragging the U.S. into an open-ended conflict. Despite his refusal to intervene, Obama demanded that Assad step down and warned the Syrian leader against using any weapons of mass destruction against the rebels. The president stated on August 20, 2012:

> We have been very clear to the Assad regime, but also to other players on the ground, that a red line for us is we start seeing a whole bunch of chemical weapons moving around or being utilized. That would change my calculus. That would change my equation.[7]

In what appeared to be a direct repudiation of Obama, reports surfaced on March 19, 2013, that the Syrians had indeed used chemical weapons. Yet, Obama again refused to attack Syria unless he received congressional authorization. The president's hesitancy was driven by the potential second-order effects of intervention. If the U.S. deposed Assad, this action could lock the U.S. into another long and costly conflict that would sap its power. The president therefore struck a deal with Russian President Vladimir Putin to remove Assad's stockpile of chemical weapons. The agreement obligated Syria to destroy its chemical weapons stockpile by mid-2014.

Obama's refusal to attack Syria created a shock for the host states under the U.S. security umbrella. This behavior seemed to be part of a pattern where the U.S. was either unable or unwilling to protect the security interests of its allies in the energy market. The U.S. was unable to defeat the Taliban insurgency decisively, took years to defeat al Qaeda in Iraq, and did nothing as Mubarak's regime collapsed. The failure to intervene in Syria after Assad crossed Obama's red line cemented the perception that the U.S. was both unwilling and incapable of guaranteeing the security of the energy market. Even the Saudis, who represented the linchpin in the petrodollar system, stated that the kingdom was far too dependent on the U.S. for its security, and that it needed to consider a "major shift."[8] The Saudi ambassador Adel al-Jubeir stated further that the U.S. refusal to intervene meant that "Iran is the new great power of the Middle East, and the U.S. is the old."[9] Jordan's King Abdullah followed with a similar sentiment by stating, "I think I believe in American power more than Obama does."[10]

These quotes illustrate that while the light footprint strategy may have led to some tactical successes, it was also contributing to a general loss of faith in American credibility among the hosts states of the energy market. The host states seemed to face a new reality where U.S. support was not ironclad and the U.S. might or might not protect their internal security and external interests. Clearly, if the U.S. was willing to sit by and watch Mubarak fall, and if the U.S. was willing to reverse course in Syria and not protect Arab interests, there was a positive probability the U.S. could not be counted on when any of the states needed American support. As a result, the host states began reaching the conclusion that they would need to provide for their own security from internal adversaries, and they would face new threats

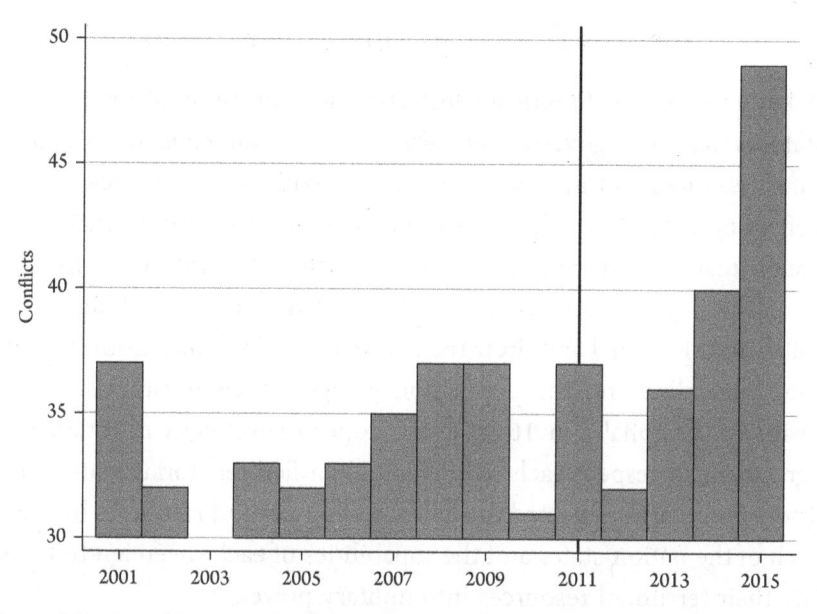

Figure 5.2. Armed Interstate Conflicts, 2001–2015
Note. Data obtained from Gleditsch et al. 2002, Patterson and Eck. 2018. Solid line represents the start of the Arab Spring.

from rival states. Theoretically we might expect the hosts, after losing the support of their American ally, to open negotiation with their insurgencies and make political concessions to terminate these wars. However, according to Figure 5.2, the loss of faith in the U.S. during the Arab Spring coincided with an *increase* in interstate conflict.[11] In some cases, such as Saudi Arabia's bombing campaign in Yemen and Turkey's invasion of northern Syria, hosts intervened in other states with their conventional militaries to destroy perceived terrorist threats. In other cases, such as Qatari and Egyptian support for Khalifa Haftar in Libya, the states used non-state proxies to fight terrorists in foreign territories. This new interventionism led to a significant increase in violence and fatalities, and it created several seemingly intractable conflicts in Syria, Iraq, and Yemen.

This raises the question: did the perceived loss of U.S. reliability lead to this escalation of interstate violence? To explain this pattern, let us first examine why the host states saw the loss of U.S. support as posing such a significant threat to their security, and why war seemed to be the optimal response to their new sense of insecurity.

## HOST POWER AND THE THREAT OF TERRORISM

A key reason why American protection was so essential for the host states is that these governments often suffered from considerable structural weakness and internal dysfunction, rendering them incapable of defending themselves. The Western ideal of a state assumes that a sovereign maintains a monopoly on legitimate force within its internationally recognized territorial boundaries.[12] The European states largely followed this model and drew their power to field armies from the land they controlled and the population living in their territories. At the Peace of Westphalia in 1648, the European sovereigns negotiated an agreement to respect each sovereign's identified territorial boundaries. These boundaries reflected the balance of power and resources between each of the nation-states and the capabilities of each sovereign to translate their territorial resources into military power.[13]

However, this process of state formation did not occur in the colonized regions of Asia, Africa, and the Middle East. Instead of drawing their resources from the territories under their control, the colonial governments relied on external assistance coming from their ruling European powers.[14] The resulting boundaries following decolonization therefore did not reflect the ability of sovereigns to control their territories, draw upon resources, and transform these resources into military power and protection. Instead, the boundaries reflected the balance of power between the European colonial powers and their ability to project power into each of these regions. As a result, most of the states in the developing world are structurally weak and depend on external powers for support.[15]

To gain this external protection, leaders in newly independent countries came to rely on the extraction and sale of natural resources, especially oil. This reliance on primary commodities created economic distortions and negative externalities.[16] Empirically, the lucrative nature of oil and other primary commodities often encourages poor governance, and the presence of natural resources is also a known correlate of civil war.[17] These states often became completely dependent on their resource exports, which allows leaders to reward their followers with the most lucrative of jobs. As a result, these states became structurally weak, internally dysfunctional, and vulnerable to civil conflicts.

After the 9/11 terrorist attacks, the U.S. promised permanent protection to many of these states in exchange for economic cooperation. American support secured control over the host states' capitals, key territories within their state, and transit routes to market their commodities. However, terrorist challengers continued to exist in the peripheral areas of the host states' territories where the central governments did not maintain a substantial presence. Although U.S. protection made it impossible for these terrorists to defeat their hosts in a direct military confrontation, these groups were more successful at gaining influence in local pockets of territory, such as neighborhoods, villages, or towns.[18] Like mafia groups and street gangs, the groups compelled civilians in these peripheral areas to cooperate with their antigovernment efforts. Since the governments often lacked a substantial presence in these areas, terrorists used threats of punishment to force civilians to cease paying taxes to the state and begin paying tribute to the group. This produced a dual benefit for the non-state groups: they increased the resources at their disposal while simultaneously depriving the government of these same resources.

Over time, if enough territories fall into their hands, the terrorists may significantly shift the balance of power away from the host in their favor.[19] Control over a population allows the group to improve its economic and military capabilities by taxing and drafting from local civilians. This tactic further harms the government by depriving it of these civilians' labor and tax revenues. While the loss of most territories will not result in significant damage, the loss of strategic territories, such as a strait or a mountain peak, may result in significant shifts in power from the government to the insurgency. In that sense, the military power of both the host state and the terrorists is dependent on the territory they both control. Similarly, if the terrorists seize control of a critical economic resource, such as a vital waterway or oil well, the loss of this revenue may be crippling to the host government, while rapidly increasing the power of the rebels. Taken together, this suggests that if a terrorist group persists in the periphery, and if this group expands its influence into valuable territories, the group may precipitously strengthen while the host's power may collapse rapidly.[20]

Fortunately for the host states, the transition from landless terrorists to insurgents tends to take place in areas of marginal strategic and economic value.[21] For example, while the militant Pakistani TTP (Tehrik-i Taliban Pakistan) is quite active in the FATA region, the Pakistani state does not critically depend on this region for its tax revenue or to support its military. Therefore, even if terrorists transitioned in these areas, the damage was limited. Yet, this damage increased over time, given that gaining some territorial control increased the ability of insurgencies to spread into other localities. For example, although the Taliban was significantly weakened after Operation Enduring Freedom in 2001, it soon began infiltrating Afghanistan from the FATA region. Slowly but surely, these groups infiltrated numerous Afghan villages and towns and began exercising coercive influences over local populations. By using coercive threats against the population in southern and eastern Afghanistan, the Taliban transitioned from a collection of terrorists into a larger, wider insurgency. The Taliban's influence over key passageways in and out of Afghanistan, particularly in the areas near the critical Highway 1, gave it the power to destabilize the central government in Kabul.

This use of terrorism at the local level can be understood theoretically as a form of "salami tactic," where terrorists slowly destabilize small pieces of territory that ultimately lead to significant losses for the government.[22] Although no one village was critical to Kabul, each village that fell under the Taliban's control strengthened the group and enabled the Taliban to subsequently challenge more critical territories. The collective loss of these villages and territories undermined Kabul's power by sapping its tax revenues, its population, and its resources. This demonstrates that terrorism at the local level can weaken the state at the macro-level. In some cases, where terrorists destabilize critical territories, the power of the state may weaken precipitously.

To further illustrate this dynamic, consider the case of India and Pakistan in their dispute over Kashmir. The conflict began when Pakistani-supported militants crossed the Line of Control (LoC) to seize the city of Kargil. Kargil is a strategic point in the conflict because of its key location on the high points of the Himalayas, making it critical for the defense of Siachen Glacier. The Indian Army therefore viewed it as imperative to clear this area of Pakistani militants and reclaim its control, given that the loss of Kargil would significantly strengthen Pakistan's ability to project power into Kashmir. In the case of Israel's conflict with Hezbollah, the heart of the dispute is territorial control over the Shebaa Farms region. The Israeli government refuses to cede the Shebaa Farms region to Lebanon, despite ongoing Hezbollah violence, for two reasons. First, losing the Farms would make Israel's cities more vulnerable to rocket attacks. Second, and perhaps more important, losing Shebaa Farms could threaten Israel's limited supply of fresh water. These cases demonstrate the key problem: if terrorists can destabilize government control over its territories at the micro-level, but government power is contingent upon its control of these territories, terrorist destabilization can rapidly collapse the state's power.

For the host states, the last line of defense against such a collapse was the U.S. security guarantee. Even if terrorists transitioned to insurgencies and grew progressively stronger, none of them would be able to win a direct conflict against the U.S. military. The problem in the early 2010s, however, was that the U.S. no longer appeared willing to pay the enormous cost to defend these corrupt and weak regimes. Since the insurgencies were strengthening in the period of U.S. protection, the sudden loss of American support was a recipe for disaster. In addition to forcing the host states to face more powerful insurgencies in their territory, the withdrawal of American protection also threatened to radically shift the regional balance of power. As a result, host states would face a heightened risk of external conflict as well as destabilization from within.

## PREDATORY AND PREVENTIVE CONFLICT

To examine how rapid power shifts created by terrorist destabilization can contribute to external conflict, let us consider two hypothetical states. State A is a host state facing a threat from a terrorist group that is beginning to seize territory, while State B is a rival neighbor. Should the terrorists in A seize a strategic piece of territory, such as an oil well, the terrorists will weaken A's ability to convert its resources into capital. With this loss in revenue, A may be unable to maintain the balance of power between itself and B. Therefore, terrorist activity may alter the balance of power between A and B.[23] While A previously could contain B's military aggression, the shift in power may weaken A's future power to such an extent that B can now prevail in a conflict. If A takes no action, this loss in military power on account of terrorist activity will lead to a weaker bargaining position relative to B, and leave it vulnerable in the future. Upon observing that terrorist activity is sapping A's power, B may have an incentive to exploit its opponent's weakness and initiate foreign policy challenges. If the loss in power caused by terrorist activity is sufficiently large, there is a possibility that B may initiate conflict to exploit A's weakness, or that A may preemptively strike B to prevent it from doing so.

If the growth of an insurgency weakened a state's hold on its territory, or weakened its power by compromising the transit routes needed to exchange resources for capital, rival states will have an incentive to take advantage of the instability caused by terrorist activity. This predatory behavior may manifest itself in two ways. First, if terrorist activity holds the potential to weaken host states, rivals would have an incentive to support terrorist groups in order to gain coercive bargaining power.[24] Granting such weapons, resources, and political recognition can significantly improve the terrorists' capability to spread into additional territories and weaken host states further.[25] However, the key drawback in this relationship is the well-known problem that foreign support for terrorists often creates moral hazard.[26] Since the sponsor is subsidizing the cost of conflict, the group may lose its incentive to terminate its violent campaign. Instead, the group can continue fighting at a reduced cost while the sponsor bears the full costs of the violence, which are considerable in many cases.[27] Even if the group remains willing to terminate the violence, a second potential adverse consequence is that sponsorship may empower the group to the extent that it may undermine the sponsor's ability to conduct foreign policy. A classic example of this behavior occurred after Jordan's support of the Palestine Liberation Organization, which ultimately plotted to overthrow the monarchy of Jordan's King Hussein. In this case, support for the PLO was ultimately counterproductive in that it saddled Jordan with the cost of Israeli airstrikes and created an internal threat to its regime. However, even if the terrorists do not fully comply with the sponsor's wishes, their ability to take territory could weaken their rival. Therefore, even if some blowback occurs, or if terrorists began to act on their own agenda, terrorist activity still accomplishes the sponsor's goal of weakening its rival.

To illustrate, consider the example of Saudi Arabia. About half of the kingdom's total production is drawn from the Ghawar oil field in the Eastern Province. The Eastern Province is also home to a substantial population of Shi'a Muslims, many of whom are antagonistic to the strict Wahhabism of the royal family. This opposition led to the growth of dissident groups in the Eastern Province. While some of these groups, such as Saudi Hezbollah, appear openly aligned with Iran, others are calling for independence for the Eastern Province. Both scenarios are nightmarish for the kingdom. If the Saudis' control of the Ghawar oil field were to destabilize, the kingdom would lose its biggest source of revenue and potentially place its other oil fields in jeopardy. Given the importance of oil to the kingdom's economy, Saudi power is critically dependent on keeping control of the Ghawar oil field. Therefore, even if Shi'a terror groups are only successful locally, the destabilization of the Eastern Province could create a cascading effect that could undermine Saudi control of the entire territory, or encourage Iran to further meddle in the territory. This loss might also embolden rival Iran to challenge Saudi influence throughout the Middle East. Therefore, Iran seems to have an incentive to support terrorist activity in this region. Doing so forces the Saudis to spend resources defending its territory, which detracts from their ability to challenge Iran's foreign policy adventurism elsewhere.

An alternative, and perhaps complementary, strategy for rival states is to follow up their support for terrorists with a conventional military intervention.[28] The rival may initiate conflict under the guise of humanitarian intervention, restoring order, stopping state failure, or protecting its minorities. Rivals are only likely to engage in this behavior if they have something to gain from seizing control of their opponent's territory. These conventional interventions are more likely to occur under two conditions. First, conventional intervention is more likely if the rival is dependent on natural resources for its own economy.[29] Second, rivals are only likely to initiate violence in response to terrorism if their adversary's territory is strategically or economically valuable.

Let us consider some secondary implications of predatory conflict. Since 9/11, numerous studies have made the claim that weak or failing states were both hubs of terrorist activity and causes of international conflict. The upshot of these assertions was that it was necessary to transform these ungoverned spaces into stronger ones using a combination of military intervention and state building. The argument is that since these failed states create opportunities for terrorism, and the sovereign cannot reassert control of the territory, it is the responsibility of some outside actor to assume control and provide stability in the territory. That is, the weakness of the state facing the terrorists may provide a policy and moral justification for external powers to initiate conflict with the government in the name of fighting terror. However, these rationalizations may be potentially self-serving. The theory and the dynamics underpinning predatory conflicts point to terrorists as potentially destabilizing, thereby validating third-party intervention. But the theory does not dictate from whence such groups may garner support. It remains entirely consistent with the theory that the very country intending to invade a neighbor because of terrorist activity may be supporting the group in whose name the intervention is justified. The necessity of external intervention to confront strong terrorists may incentivize rival states to support terrorism, weaken a neighboring government, and thereby ultimately provide an opportunity for the rival states to justify their own intervention as a remedy for the chaos within their neighbor's borders. Terrorism may therefore afford rival states a reason to initiate aggressive wars to fight the very terrorists they may allow to operate from their own territories.

To illustrate, consider Rwanda's intervention into the Democratic Republic of the Congo, which represents a clear case of such a predatory war. At the end of the first war in the Congo in 1997, Rwanda occupied much of the eastern part of the country, an area full of mineral riches. Newly installed DRC President Laurent Kabila soon demanded that all foreign troops leave Congolese territory and return to their homelands. However, the Rwandan government argued that the Hutu extremist group known as the Democratic Forces for the Liberation of Rwanda (FDLR) was still active in the eastern part of the DRC and needed to be disarmed. Given that Kabila had just assumed power and lacked popular support in the territory, it was quite clear that he did not possess the capability to disarm the FDLR. This weakness justified Rwanda's continued presence and reinvasion of the territory, particularly given Rwandan leader Paul Kagame's references to the past massacres of Tutsis at the hands of Hutu. In addition to continuing the fight against Hutu extremists, the Rwandan occupation afforded Rwanda the added benefit of access to the eastern Congo's diamonds, coltan, and other mineral deposits. Fighting terrorism in the eastern Congo proved quite lucrative, and the presence of Hutu terrorists is what had given Rwanda the pretext to wage war.

For targets of predatory conflict, terrorist destabilization may therefore pose a critical threat to the survival of host states. The loss of control over key territories may permanently weaken the host's ability to support itself or field its military. If terrorists compromise a host's ability to procure and monetize its natural resources for its own security, the host might initiate attacks against terrorists within its rival to defend itself.[30] An interesting implication of this argument is that the *initiation of a "war on terror" is not necessarily aimed at disarming terrorists*. Instead, the more limited goal is simply to prevent the terrorists from undermining or seizing control over particularly valuable areas. Attacks on terrorist sanctuaries may represent efforts to disrupt the group's supply chain or attack its commanders, all with the intention of preventing the group from consolidating territorial gains that may threaten the state's security.[31]

### THE HOUTHI INSURGENCY IN YEMEN

To illustrate how the rise of interstate conflicts in the energy market was driven by fears of losing American support in the face of challenges from predatory challenges, let us first consider the case of the Houthi insurgency in Yemen. Like other host leaders, Ali Abdullah

Saleh used the American assistance to bribe his political allies and to augment his personal wealth. Even worse, Saleh periodically used American aid to bribe fighters aligned with al Qaeda in the Arabian Peninsula (AQAP) into attacking his political challengers in the Houthi movement to the north. Although Saleh seemed perfectly content with this arrangement, the growth of the Arab Spring in 2011 radically altered the political situation. Saleh claimed that protests were part of an Iranian effort to topple his government. His invocation of Iranian aggression was intended to compel the Americans into continuing support for his regime. However, the Obama administration believed that Saleh was abusing American assistance and was unwilling to come to his assistance. After a terrorist attack forced Saleh to leave the country for medical treatment, the longtime Yemeni leader was forced to cede power to his vice president, Abdrabbuh Mansur Hadi, in February 2012.

The Obama administration claimed that Hadi would be a cooperative partner in the fight against AQAP.[32] Figure 5.3 demonstrates that drone strikes against AQAP increased sharply in 2012. Hadi, however, soon faced a more significant challenge from the Houthi ethnic group in the northern part of the country. The Houthi were a group of Zaydi Shi'ites who primarily resided in the northwestern part of Yemen, along the Saudi border. Both the U.S. and the Saudis were long concerned about Iranian agitation among this Zaydi population. Saleh himself had charged that the Houthis were Iranian puppets and that Iranians were interested in supporting the Houthis to depose him from power.

Figure 5.4. demonstrates that despite Hadi's increasing cooperation with the U.S., the number of terror attacks and fatalities from the violence in Yemen increased exponentially in the period 2012–2015. Hadi's government faced an existential crisis in August 2014, when the Houthi began large-scaled organized protests in response to rising fuel prices. After Hadi seemingly took no action to address the demands, the Houthi began a military offensive from the north toward the major southern cities. These offensives achieved remarkable success, as the Houthi soon swept into capital city of Sana'a a month later, in September 2014. The insurgency soon jailed Hadi in the presidential

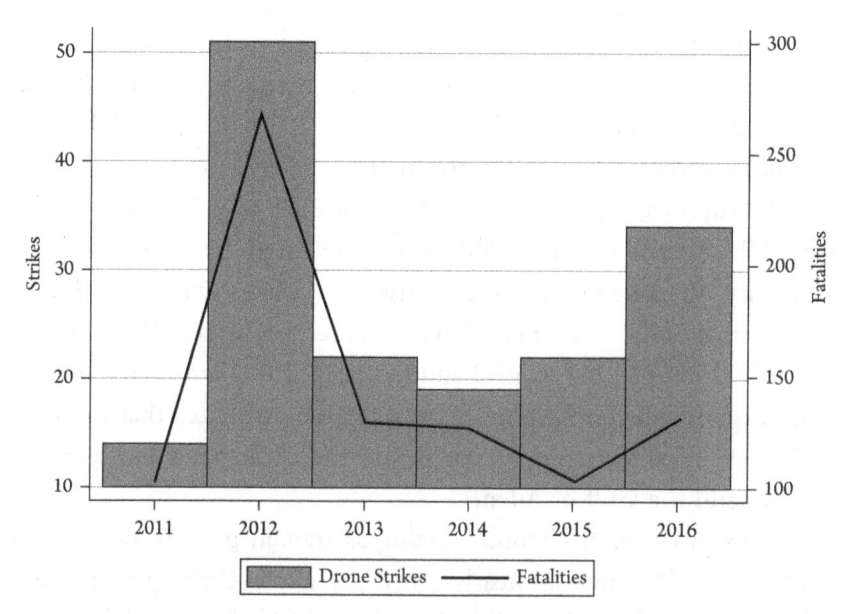

Figure 5.3. Drone Strikes in Yemen, 2008–2016.
Note. Data from Serle and Purkiss (2017).

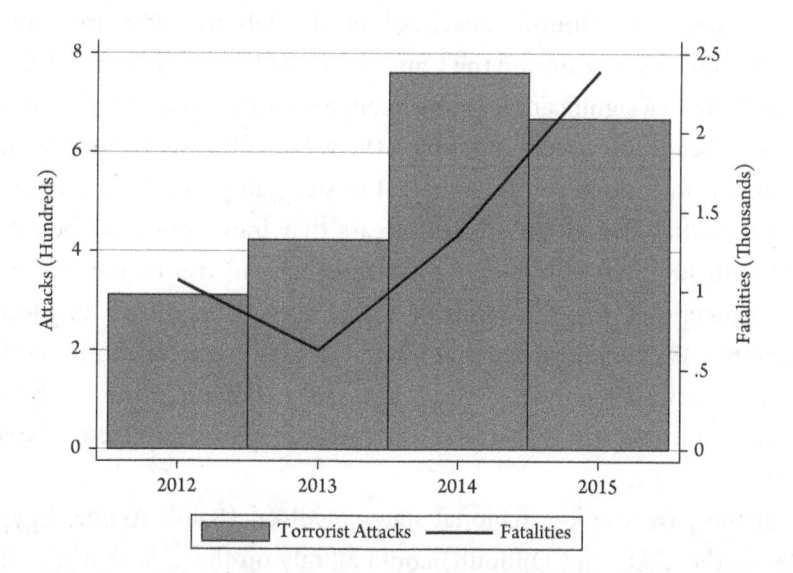

Figure 5.4. Terrorist Attacks and Fatalities in Yemen, 2012–2015.
Note. Data from the National Consortium for the Study of Terrorism and Responses to Terrorism (START). (2018). Global Terrorism Database [Data file]. Retrieved from https://www.start.umd.edu/gtd.

palace, though the Yemeni leader later escaped and fled south to the coastal city of Aden. The Houthi maintained their momentum. Fighting broke out at the airport in Aden in March 2015, indicating that the Houthi were on the verge of capturing the city.

These successes added to suspicions that Iran was the driving force behind the Houthi rebellion. Although Iran denied the accusations, the possibility of Iranian involvement raised the stakes when the Houthi took control of the bases near Bab el-Mandeb on March 31. Two days later, the Houthi seized control and militarized the Perim and Greater Hanish islands in the Red Sea. Figure 5.5 demonstrates that these islands created de facto aircraft carriers at the chokepoint between the Red Sea and the Gulf of Aden.

The potential for the Houthi, acting as Iranian proxies, now posed a critical security threat to nearly every U.S. ally in the region. By consolidating control of this chokepoint, where 3.8% of the world's energy passed, the Houthi could strangle all energy shipments and sea traffic to Europe. If the Houthi closed Bab el-Mandeb, the alternative route would move energy around the Cape of Good Hope, which would likely contribute to a significant increase in energy costs. Moreover, the loss of the Red Sea route would undermine the value of the Suez Canal, which in turn would significantly damage the struggling Egyptian economy. The potential closure raised Saudi fears that Iran would not be satisfied with just Bab el-Mandeb and would instead use its control over this chokepoint and the Strait of Hormuz to collapse the kingdom's economy. We therefore see that while the Houthis were motivated by the dysfunctional Yemeni government, their rebellion in the south had significant implications for the security of the region as well as the larger petrodollar system.

In the past, the key regional states involved (Saudi Arabia, Egypt, Oman, the UAE, and Djibouti) could all rely on the U.S. to rectify the situation. However, Obama's previous hesitance in assisting Mubarak and Saleh, and his refusal to respond to Assad's crossing of the red line, raised considerable doubt that the U.S. would act. Obama's ongoing negotiations with the Iranians over their nuclear weapons development further raised concerns that the president might even welcome

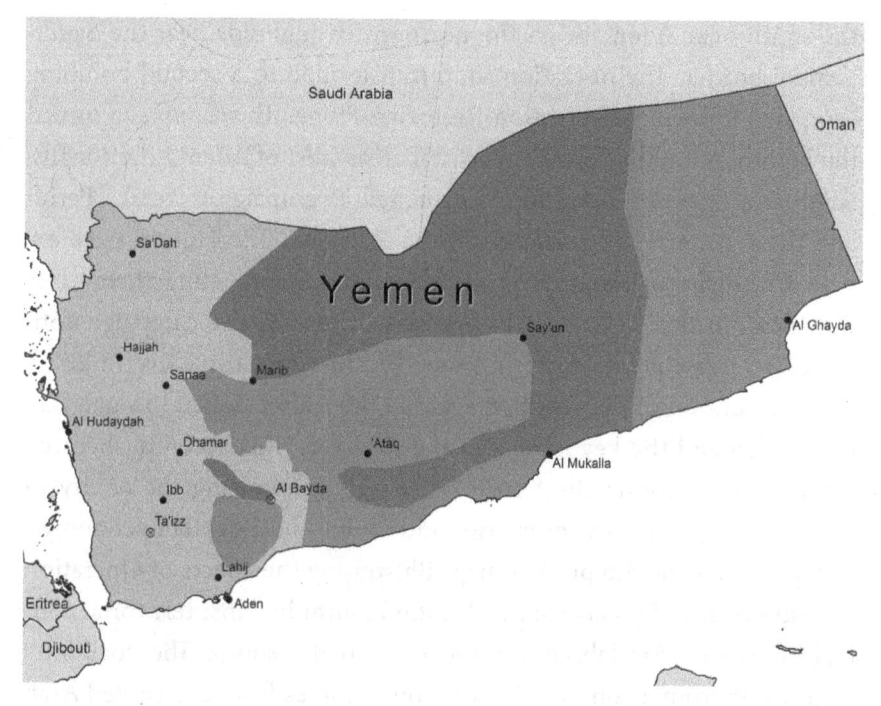

Figure 5.5. Civil War in Yemen.
Note. Data from Martin-Vézian, Centanni, and Djukic (2016). Dark gray areas indicate control by Hadi loyalists, medium gray areas are contested territory, and light shaded areas indicate Houthi control.

a Houthi takeover of Yemen, particularly since the Houthi were willing to fight AQAP. In this new environment, where U.S. commitments were no longer credible, these states needed to take some action on their own. Fortunately for them, each of these states maintained significant American military weapons and support. The Obama administration also initially signaled that it would supply a military operation to defeat the Houthi.[33] The problem was that none of the states could be sure if this support would last, particularly since Obama seemed more interested in concluding a deal with Iran. The states would therefore need to act swiftly to eliminate the threat, before they lost all American support for the operation.

On March 21, King Salman of Saudi Arabia announced the start of Operation Decisive Storm. This operation was led by the Saudi military, though it received logistical support from the U.S. The campaign involved significant aerial bombardment of Houthi military positions in the south near Aden and in the northern strongholds near the Saudi-Yemeni border. The operation soon transitioned to a second bombing campaign known as Operation Restoring Hope. This campaign forced the Houthi out of the southern coastal areas west of Aden. Additionally, Saudi and Egyptian naval forces launched a campaign to retake Perim and the Greater Hanish islands in the Red Sea. The Houthi were expelled from both islands by December 2015, eliminating their bases of control in the critical sea passageway. Although the campaign continued in subsequent years, and the Houthi were still active in 2019, the intervention of the coalition secured the transit points through Bab el-Mandeb and the key islands in the Red Sea. This accomplished the objective of securing the transit of energy, minimizing the ability of Iran to disrupt the flow of energy, and saving the Egyptian economy.

Figures 5.5 and 5.6 present maps illustrating the effects of Operation Decisive Storm. By February 2017, the Houthi had lost territorial control of Bab el-Mandeb, and other areas in the south. The coalition's gains came from a combination of ground forces from the United Arab Emirates (UAE) and the extensive aerial bombardment of the Houthis' positions.

Although the overall war in Yemen appears terribly costly and inefficient, the Saudis, UAE, Egyptians, and other coalition partners all viewed the loss of Bab el-Mandeb as catastrophic and were willing to do anything to secure it. Since each of the states feared that the Iranians would use the Houthis in a predatory fashion, and that there was a possibility that the U.S. would be unable to guarantee Yemen's security, the states initiated a very violent war. As a result, tens of thousands of Yemenis have died and the fight to keep Bab el-Mandeb and the coastal areas shows no sign of letting up.

### THE SYRIAN CIVIL WAR

A common explanation for the civil conflict in Syria is that it is driven by historic animosity between the Shi'a and Sunni branches of Islam. The more detailed reasoning behind that assessment is as follows: The Syrian government is ruled by the Alawites and a coalition of other

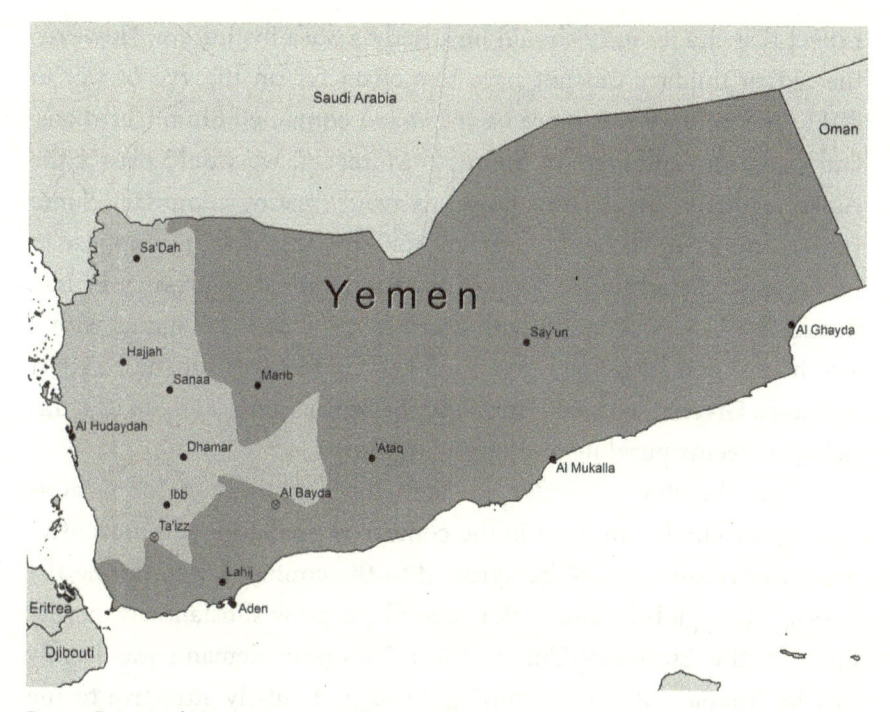

Figure 5.6. Civil War in Yemen, February 2017.
Note. Map from the European Council of Foreign Relations (2017). Dark shaded areas indicate areas controlled by Hadi loyalists and other anti-Houthi forces; light shaded areas indicate territories controlled by Houthi forces.

Shi'ites, whereas Sunnis are the majority in Syria's population. Because the minority hold control over the government, the Alawites reward their Shi'a allies with better political, economic, and societal privileges in comparison to the majority Sunnis. While this system is unsustainable in that the minority is receiving a disproportionate share of benefits compared to the majority, the Assad regime is sustained by external patrons, such as Russia and Iran. This colonial setup grants the external power substantial sway over the Syrian government, though the minority can subjugate the majority with external help. In this situation, the causal driver behind conflict is the commitment problem, where Shi'ites cannot share power with the Sunnis for fear of losing their limited control of the government.[34]

Although this explanation has some truth to it, it also has several observable anomalies. Theoretically, the most important institution for the survival of the Shi'a is the armed forces. We would therefore expect that the military should be strictly a Shi'a institution. However, the Syrian military did not have this character on the eve of war in 2011. The military was more balanced and contained Shi'a, Christians, and significant numbers of Sunnis.[35] Moreover, we would expect the Assad regime to do all in its power to avoid creating competing Sunni power centers in the polity. Again, however, this does not appear to be the case. Assad fueled support for the Ba'athist insurgency in Iraq during the U.S. occupation with arms; he provided the Sunnis with a safe haven; and he helped organized key conferences for the Ba'athist militants. Given the historic animosity between Sunnis and Shi'ites, this behavior seems puzzling and utterly irrational.

Let us therefore consider an alternative explanation for what is driving the conflict in Syria in the context of predatory and preventive wars over resources. The background to the conflict began during the 2000s, when global demand for natural gas grew substantially, particularly in the European Union (E.U.). European demand was largely met by Russia.[36] Russia's natural gas was particularly attractive to the E.U. due to Russia's proximity to Europe, and the ability of Russia to deliver natural gas supplies using pipelines. Unlike oil, transporting natural gas by sea or land requires liquefaction, which is an expensive process.[37] Natural gas can be transported more easily and inexpensively through a pipeline. The Russians maintained two key pipelines heading to Europe, which facilitated the ease of the transactions. These revenues accounted for 70% of Russia's natural gas income and were essential for Russian economic growth.

However, the Europeans increasingly voiced concern about their overreliance on Vladimir Putin's Russia as a source for energy.[38] Putin was known to harbor global ambitions of restoring Russian influence to the days of the Cold War. Putin was also known to squeeze supplies of energy to coerce neighbors into friendlier foreign policies. These risks pushed the Europeans to search for ways to diversify their natural gas supplies. The E.U. therefore needed to locate a supply that could reach their territory inexpensively, and preferably through pipelines. Until the late 2000s, the largest suppliers capable of delivering natural gas to Europe through pipelines were Russia and Iran. In 2009, Qatar began developing a proposal to create a pipeline linking its natural gas supplies to Turkey. Qatar maintained the third-largest supply of natural gas in the world, but it was forced to liquefy most of its gas to sell eastward. The Qataris therefore sought to construct a pipeline linking their supply to Turkey, which is well-positioned to move the gas across the Bosporus to continental Europe. For the Europeans, Qatar represented an attractive alternative to Putin's Russia, since it maintained a reliable reputation and was under the protection of the U.S. For his part, the Turkish leader Recep Tayyip Erdogan was very enthusiastic about the project, as it would make Turkey an energy hub for transactions into the E.U.[39] Turkey's emergence as the key transit point to the E.U. would likely be a financial windfall.

Two possible routes existed for the proposed Qatari-Turkish pipeline, as shown on the map in Figure 5.7. The first route would move through Saudi, Kuwaiti, and Iraqi territory and eventually pass through eastern Turkey. This plan presented three obstacles. First, the Saudis objected to placing any pipeline in Kuwaiti territory. Second, part of the pipeline would move through the Shi'a region of southern Iraq, where Iran's influence was strong. Since Iran was a competitor to Qatar in the natural gas market, the line would be vulnerable to sabotage at the hands of Iranian-supported militias. Third, the pipeline would then traverse through northern Iraq and eastern Syria, home to the Kurdish population. Given his concern with Kurdish separatism, Erdogan likely was not in favor of leaving the pipeline vulnerable to Kurdish activity. For these reasons, the route through Iraq did not seem like a prudent option.

The alternative route would move Qatari gas across northern Saudi Arabia and through the eastern part of Syria. This route was advantageous in that it bypassed the potential for Iranian and Kurdish sabotage. This route would allow the Qataris to sell their natural gas to the E.U., while the Saudis could minimize Iran's monetization of its natural gas, and the Turks could become an energy hub for Europe. The problem was that it required cooperation from Bashar al Assad. In 2009, discussions with Assad over the proposed Qatari-Turkish pipeline did not move forward.[40] Assad seemed to understand that

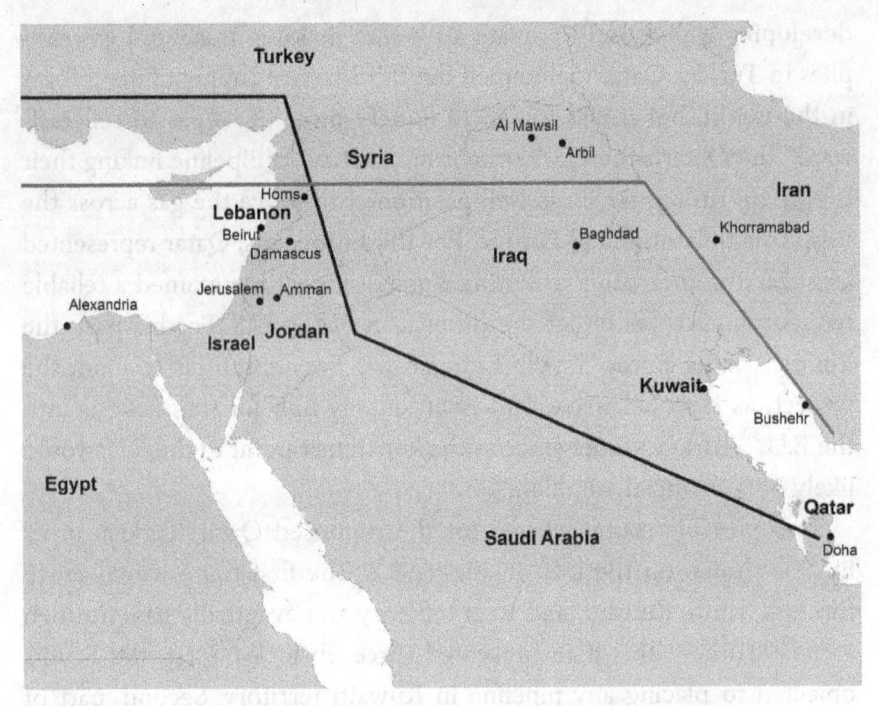

Figure 5.7. Proposed Natural Gas Pipelines from the Middle East to the European Market.
Note. Black line represents proposed Qatar-Turkey pipeline; gray line represents Iran-Iraq-Syria pipeline. Data for proposed pipelines from Austin (2015).

the opening of Qatari natural gas would undermine Russia's coercive power over Europe. Since Putin presumably preferred to maintain this power, Assad refused construction on the pipeline. Instead, discussions began over the construction of an alternative pipeline from Iran's Pars gas field across Iraq through Syria, which would bypass Turkey entirely on its way to the Mediterranean Sea. The Russians voiced no objection to sales from Iran, believing that their security arrangements with the Islamic Republic would prevent significant competition.

Although this strategy protected Russia's exports, the unrest in Syria following the Arab Spring created a new threat to Russia's hold on the European market. Since the CIA began destabilization efforts against Assad during the Iraq war, and since the U.S. had a vested interest in promoting Qatari gas over Russian gas, each of the interested parties mistakenly believed the U.S. would intervene on behalf of the rebels. Obama's refusal to intervene created a series of significant problems for the key U.S. allies in the region. For the Qataris, the loss of the potential pipeline meant that the European markets would either remain in the hands of the Russians or, worse, transition to the Iranians in the coming decade. While this loss would not be devastating to the Qataris, the fact that Iran stood to gain from natural gas sales to Europe threatened to increase Iranian power relative to the Saudis. The Saudis envisioned a future where the Iranians would become flooded with European capital, especially as the use of natural gas increased relative to oil. This would afford Iran the ability to challenge Saudi dominance in the region, and perhaps eventually in the Strait of Hormuz and the Saudi Eastern Province itself. The Saudis therefore saw the potential opening of the Iran-Iraq-Syria pipeline as an existential threat. For Erdogan, the opening of an Iran-Iraq-Syria pipeline meant that a pipeline would not pass through Turkish territory, scuttling his ambition to become the hub of global energy trades to Europe. It would further ensure that Turkey would remain dependent on Russia to satisfy its own demand for natural gas.

Facing these threats to their economic and political security, both Turkey and Qatar initiated a predatory war to seize control of the territory needed for the Qatari-Turkish pipeline. The Qataris and the Turks provided financing and resources to the Muslim Brotherhood in Syria, hoping that this organization could seize power from Assad. If it succeeded, the two states would have a friendly regime in Damascus that would facilitate the project going forward. With a wealthy foreign backer in Qatar, and access to resources to the north from Turkish territory, the Muslim Brotherhood gradually transitioned into the Free Syrian Army (FSA) and took the lead in fighting Assad's regime.

For two years, the FSA failed to topple Assad. However, Assad's use of chemical weapons against the FSA again raised hopes for an American intervention. Once Obama refused to do so, it became clear that if the Saudis, Turks, and Qataris wanted to depose Assad, they would need to do so largely on their own. Led by Bandar bin Sultan (Prince Bandar), the Saudis responded by shifting resources from the Muslim Brotherhood and the FSA to the jihadist movements in Syria, including those aligned with al Nusra and ISIS.[41] While financial responsibility shifted from the Qataris to the Saudis, Turkey remained the port of entry for foreign fighters, facilitating the movement of jihadist groups across the border into Syrian territory.

Facing this predatory war from the Saudis and the Turks, both the Russians and the Iranians again escalated their military support for Assad. While the Russians increased their military aid, the Iranians deployed their paramilitary forces and Revolutionary Guard units to fight in Syria. Additionally, the Iranians ordered Hezbollah to begin operations in the south to defend Assad. This preventive war aimed to ensure that Assad stayed in power and that construction on the Qatari-Turkish pipeline never got underway. If it did, the Russians would lose their monopoly over the Europeans, and the Iranians would lose all their market share to the Qataris. However, the Saudis maintained an additional weapon. As they did in the first Afghan War, the Saudis chose in September 2014 to use its oil weapon and flood the market with crude, pushing the price of oil down to $35 per barrel from $50 per barrel. This strategy was aimed at undermining Russian and Iranian's financial ability to continue the war.[42]

From the perspective of the Saudis and the Turks, the spread of ISIS appeared to be a significant success. Assad's position deteriorated in early part of 2015. By the middle of the year, ISIS seized control of the key eastern city of Palmyra, which was a central link in the pathway for the Qatari-Turkish pipeline. ISIS and other rebel groups were also on the doorstep of Aleppo, which was the last key city for the pipeline in the west, before it would reach the Turkish border. Figure 5.8 illustrates that with these two centers, along with the eastern half of the country, the territory needed to complete the Qatari-Turkish pipeline would be in the hands of the rebels. Although the spread of ISIS throughout these territories and into Iraq was a substantial embarrassment for the Obama administration, the Saudi-Turkish predatory war was on the verge of success.

However, the war would soon turn in favor of Assad as a result of American and Russian military interventions. The advance of ISIS into Iraq, along with its rejection of the recognized territories of the state system in the Middle East, prompted the Obama administration to

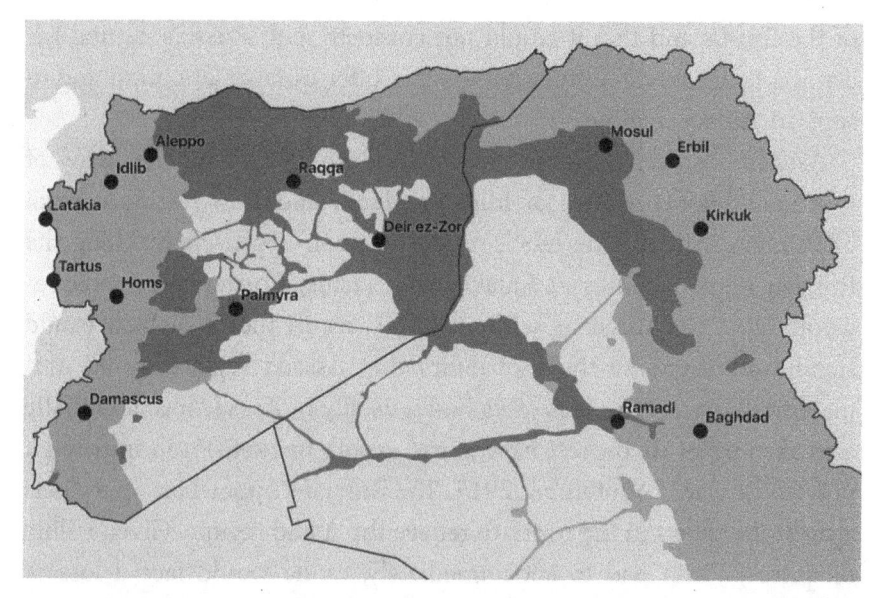

Figure 5.8. Area under Islamic State of Iraq and Syria (ISIS) control, January 2015.
Note. Dark shaded areas indicate ISIS control, light shaded areas indicate other population centers, very light shaded areas represent sparsely populated territories. Estimated territorial control from the IHS Conflict Monitor; see Lister (2016).

intervene on behalf of the Shi'a-led Iraqi government. The U.S. committed itself to protecting the Iraqi state once it toppled Saddam Hussein, and it was unwilling to allow Iraq's substantial oil reserves to fall into the hands of ISIS. After taking control of Mosul, ISIS began to encroach on the oil-rich Kurdish capital of Erbil. The U.S. further maintained substantial ties to the autonomous Kurdish region in the north of Iraq and was unwilling to allow the Peshmerga to collapse. The Obama administration therefore began an intervention to push ISIS out of Iraq and back toward the eastern part of Syria.

The success of ISIS also posed a fundamental security threat to the Russians, given that the group's conquests could eventually allow for the potential construction of the Qatari-Turkish pipeline. The pipeline could potentially break European dependence on Russia, weakening Russian cash reserves as well as its key source of coercive power in international affairs. To assuage Russian concerns, the Saudi intelligence chief, Prince Bandar, met with Vladimir Putin on July 31, 2013. Bandar signaled to the Russians that if Assad collapsed, the new regime to take control of Syrian territory would be "completely" under the control of the Saudis and that it would not compete with Russia's natural gas exports to Europe.[43] Putin rejected this offer in favor of continuing to support Assad's regime.

Assad's position continued to worsen into 2015, with the Army of Conquest taking control of Idlib in March and ISIS seizing control of Palmyra in May. The rebels' offensive soon began encroaching the Russian naval facilities at Latakia and Tartus. Losing these facilities would leave the Russians without any bases in theater, which would significantly increase the probability that Assad's regime would ultimately fall. Facing the loss of its bases, its ally in Assad, and potentially a weakening of its biggest natural gas export market, Putin initiated a preventive war in September 2015. The Russians opened air operations against the rebels in the north to relieve the Assad regime. Given falling oil prices, Putin had to act immediately, or he would face a loss of capability to stave off the impending permanent loss in the European market.

The Russian intervention enabled the Syrian Arab Army to retake parts of Aleppo previously lost to the rebels. However, a month into the intervention, on November 24, 2015, two Turkish F-16s shot down a Russian attack aircraft. The Russian Sukhoi fighter was immediately attacked after briefly entering Turkish airspace, which raised the strong possibility that the act was premeditated and deliberate. Russia immediately denounced the attack and claimed that Turkey was supporting terrorists in Syria. For the first time since the Cold War, a NATO country and the Russians stood on the brink of war.

Yet, early in 2016, Erdogan abruptly reversed course. In a meeting with Putin in March, Erdogan announced that Turkey would begin cooperating with Russia in an effort to bring an end to the war. This shift seemed to be motivated by the advance of the American-supported Kurdish Peshmerga in northern Syria and Iraq. From The advance of the Peshmerga against ISIS was now opening the possibility that the two Kurdish enclaves in the west and the east would unify. This unification created a substantial threat for Turkey, in that it could potentially encourage a new separatist challenge from the Kurdish population within Turkey itself. Worse, the Kurds maintained the backing of the

Pentagon, which saw them as the only force capable of fighting ISIS in Iraq. In the summer of 2016, Turkey invaded northern Syria under the guise of fighting ISIS. However, its mission was aimed at preventing the advance of the Peshmerga west of the Euphrates River. It appeared that Erdogan's desire for the Qatari-Turkish pipeline was trumped by his fear of increased Kurdish separatism, prompting him to switch sides. Additionally, Erdogan received guarantees of Russian cooperation and assurances not to bypass Turkey. These commitments seemed to secure Erdogan's energy desires, while simultaneously allowing him to prevent the unification of Kurdish territory.

Erdogan's shift to cooperate with the Russians spelled doom for the Army of Conquest. The Syrian Arab Army retook Palmyra from ISIS in 2016, and it followed by taking Aleppo with heavy Russian support in December. By January 2017, a ceasefire was declared between Assad and the rebels, with groups only controlling the city of Idlib. In September 2018, Russia and Turkey agreed to begin the process of demilitarizing Idlib if the Syrian Arab Army halted its bombing offensive. For the first time since the start of the war, Assad was close to unifying Syrian territory in the west under his control.

However, Syria's ability to reassert control over its eastern territory was stopped due to the advance of the American-backed Syrian Democratic Forces (SDF). The SDF is a coalition consisting mostly of Kurds but also includes numerous Turkmen, Arabs, and other ethnic minorities. Backed by approximately 2,000 American special operations forces and airpower, this group defeated ISIS for control of its capital of Raqqa in October 2017. The SDF continued to search for pockets of ISIS resistance fighters in the eastern part of the country. To support this counterinsurgency, the U.S. established multiple bases throughout northern Syria. Even as Assad moved toward victory in the west, the U.S. declared that it would keep these bases operational to continue hunting ISIS. With American forces entrenching themselves in Syria, it was clear that Assad could not reconsolidate his territory.

The construction of these bases within Syrian territory, and the continued American alliance with the SDF, were clear examples of the light footprint strategy in action—and the risks and damage associated with it. By keeping American forces in the eastern part of the country in support of the SDF, the U.S. secured control over most of Syria's oil and gas. More importantly, however, the presence of American forces all but ensured that the pipeline from Iran's Pars gas field to the west could never be constructed. This would prevent Iran from improving its access to the European market. This move was essential, given that Iran had long attempted to decouple energy sales from dollars. Further, by securing Syria's oil and gas, the U.S. ensured that the Russians would gain very little in terms of resources from their intervention into Syria, other than preventing the Qataris from encroaching on their European market. Finally, the bases would prevent Assad from ever developing his own internal power base and would ensure that the Russians would continue to have to spend resources to keep him in power and fend off an internal rebellion. This precarious position seemingly would undermine any effort Assad could make to rebuild his country, and perhaps establish himself as an energy transit hub.

Taken together, we see that the developments of the Syrian war can be explained as a series of predatory and preventive conflicts, driven by the loss of the stability provided by the U.S. security guarantee. The Russian intervention into Syria was motivated by the fear that the Qatari-Turkish pipeline would cause them to lose their status as supplier to Europe. This fear pushed the Russians to dissuade Assad from striking the agreement using security guarantees. When Assad fell under strain in 2011, the U.S. allies believed that the Americans would intervene against Assad. However, in this new state of the world, the U.S. simply could not. The Americans were still suffering from the financial crisis, and the politics of the U.S. gave no freedom to risk the possibility of a large-scale intervention. Once the American protector indicated that it would not assist significantly, Turkey, Qatar, and Saudi Arabia took it upon themselves to initiate a series of predatory wars. These predatory wars were met by preventive wars initiated by both the Iranians and the Russians. Eventually, the war died down once Turkey shifted from its predatory status and moved to initiate a preventive war to stop the unification of Kurdish territories on its border with Syria. While this decreased violence in the west, it raised the specter of conflict in the east, particularly with the U.S. cementing its bases in the region. In this environment, the jockeying for position and power politics between local actors was still ongoing in 2019. The Turkish military directly intervened in northern Syria in 2016 and 2018 to prevent the SDF from linking with the Kurdish Peoples' Protection Units (YPG) in the west. Additionally, in an effort to gain control of the resource-rich Deir ez-Zor Province, Syrian Arab Army units and a Russian mercenary group attacked American and SDF forces in May 2018. The Syrian effort failed and led to the deaths of hundreds of Russian fighters. Yet, this encounter was not expected to be a final one. The light footprint strategy allowed the U.S. to fight ISIS and prevent the Iranian pipeline, but did nothing to stop the enormous death toll in Syria, and it raised the specter of a military confrontation with the Russians.

## CONCLUSION: TERRORISM IN A TIME OF HEGEMONIC DECLINE

By 2010, with the cost of the war rising and the euro fading as a challenge to the dollar, the U.S. no longer seemed willing to guarantee security for all of the host states under its security umbrella. This created substantial security risks for the host states, who had long allowed terrorist challengers to survive within their territories and, in some cases, directly cultivated them. Now, with the U.S. unwilling to defend them, the hosts would be forced to fight these terrorists on their own. Unfortunately for the hosts, the terrorists at this stage were now far more powerful than they previously were, having seized territory and gained foreign support. The host states, on the other hand, were ill equipped to fight their terrorist challengers due to their exclusive dependence on the U.S. Sensing the rapid weakening of these hosts, rival states began supporting terrorists to further destabilize hosts, and perhaps seize portions of their territories. The threat of these predatory conflicts forced the host states to initiate their own wars to fight off their rival predators, before they lost all American military support. The loss of the credibility of the U.S. security guarantee therefore contributed to an escalation of terrorist violence and the initiation of several interstate conflicts.

As violence grew, the American foreign policy establishment became increasingly concerned with the limited level of U.S. engagement. By decoupling the U.S. from the ongoing conflicts, the U.S. was increasing the risk that its host states would seek protection elsewhere. The increased Russian involvement in the Middle East, and the willingness of traditional U.S. allies to cooperate with Putin, suggested that the days of American dominance were rapidly ending. In addition to increasing cooperation with Syria and Iran, Putin deepened Russia's ties with Egypt and Turkey, both of which were long-standing American allies. These moves to challenge American preeminence in the Middle East seemed unthinkable only a decade earlier. Yet, even as the Obama administration came to an end, and the new administration of Donald J. Trump assumed office in 2017, there seemed to be little appetite for reasserting American power on a large scale. Trump's new mantra for fighting the war on terror was to shift the burden to the hosts themselves. The danger, however, was that another state would assume the traditional role of the U.S. as protector of the host states that serve as the key suppliers and transit routes for global energy. Such a shift would forever alter the dynamics of the petrodollar system, and perhaps mark the beginning of the end of American hegemony.

# 6

# CONCLUSION

## THE WAR FOR EXORBITANT PRIVILEGE

If we had kept the oil, you wouldn't have ISIS because that's where they got their money from in the first place, but, OK, maybe we'll have another chance.[1]

—President Donald J. Trump
Speech to CIA, January 21, 2017

For almost three decades, the U.S. agreement to permanently defend the countries in OPEC supported the dominance of the American dollar in the global financial system. In exchange for American military protection, the OPEC states agreed to permanently sell their oil and energy products in American dollars, which created a permanent high global demand for U.S. currency. The OPEC states recycled their surplus dollars back to American treasuries, commercial banks, and eventually, investment houses. This system allowed the U.S. government to acquire capital at low interest rates despite its enormous debt. This

*Monsters to Destroy: Understanding the War on Terror*. Navin A. Bapat, Oxford University Press (2019).
© Oxford University Press.
DOI: 10.1093/oso/9780190061456.001.0001

system provided Americans with easy access to credit, low interest rates, and low taxes, all without cuts in government spending.

This system allowed Americans to enjoy a high quality of life in comparison to much of the rest of the world. However, the U.S. faced two threats to this system at the start of the new millennium. Osama bin Laden's challenge to the Saudi monarchy raised concerns of a populist revolt against the kingdom for its continued cooperation with the U.S. Second, Iraq's decision to exchange its oil for euros challenged the dollar's hold of the international market. The 9/11 terrorist attacks presented an opportunity to eliminate these threats to American hegemony. By deposing the Taliban in Afghanistan and Saddam Hussein in Iraq, the U.S. would place close to half of the world's proven energy reserves under its security umbrella. These moves permanently link global energy trades to American dollars and served as a deterrent to any state that would dare challenge U.S. hegemony. Although this position of domination appeared within America's grasp when Baghdad fell on April 14, 2003, this was as close as the Bush administration would come to fulfilling this vision.

The escalation of violence soon drove the war into its second phase. To ensure that energy continued to be sold in dollars, and profits from energy sales recycled back to American markets, the U.S. guaranteed permanent protection to the host states that both supplied energy and served as key transit routes. This guarantee encouraged these host states to both become increasingly corrupt and fostered the growth of terrorists within their territory. Since the U.S. would guarantee their safety, these hosts could ignore the needs of their populations, steal their countries' wealth, and repress all dissenters with impunity. This behavior gave rise to political opponents, who conveniently could be labeled as "terrorists" that needed to be repressed. The U.S. increased its military support to the hosts of these "terrorists," which cemented host leaders in power.

Perversely, this lucrative American support made it impossible for the host states to negotiate with their terrorists, while simultaneously making it impossible for the hosts to credibly disarm them. As a result, these terrorists transitioned into insurgencies by seizing control of territory. Gaining territory gave the groups control over a segment of the population, thereby providing them with tax revenue, infrastructure, and a base of support. These newfound resources for insurgencies forced the U.S. to increase its economic and military support to the host states. Over the course of the decade, the price to the U.S. for responding to these more powerful insurgencies in the energy market states quickly exceeded a trillion dollars. The rapid deterioration of the security situation suggested that the U.S. would need to continue spending at this level for the foreseeable future.

However, this situation soon became unsustainable. By 2006, military strains and congressional backlash signaled that the U.S. could no longer give host states a blank check in money, aid, and American blood. The threat to reduce support to the hosts was intended to follow the logic from Sun Tzu's 1521 treatise, *The Art of War*, "Confront them with annihilation, and they will then survive; plunge them into a deadly situation, and they will then live." The U.S. indicated that it would help states fight their terrorists, but it would no longer guarantee the security of hosts that made no effort to subdue their terrorists. The light footprint strategy bore fruit for a short time, as the governments in Iraq and Afghanistan initiated offensives to disarm their militants. However, the scars of Afghanistan and Iraq, the financial crisis of 2008, and the Arab Spring forced the U.S. to cease support for some of the key hosts in the system, most visibly in the case of Egypt's Mubarak.

This weakening of the American security guarantee ushered in a third phase of the war on terror. Without the certainty of American protection, the host states became increasingly vulnerable, and power appeared to shift in favor of these states' rivals. These rival states began initiating predatory wars to seize their opponents' resources. These challenges posed a critical strategic dilemma for the hosts under the U.S. security umbrella. They could initiate wars against their rivals while they still maintained significant American support, or they could wait and weaken if the U.S. chose to reduce its commitment. Facing an economically weakened Washington full of antiwar sentiment, the host states began initiating their own wars, using both conventional forces and non-state proxies. The unwillingness of the U.S. to maintain a large security commitment for the hosts further opened the door for American competitors. Russia began offering security guarantees to rivals in the region and struck deals with some U.S. allies. China continued to dangle the possibility of trading energy for RMB, and host states began holding Chinese currency and discussing accepting a basket of currencies.

While the euro lost stature due to the European sovereign debt crisis, China's RMB emerged as another viable challenger to the U.S. dollar following the financial crisis of 2008. With its enormous manufacturing base and population, China came to be a potential challenger to American hegemony. The Chinese economy exhibited substantial growth during the first decade of the twenty-first century. President Xi Jinping announced that he would push to make the Chinese RMB a world reserve currency and sought to increase worldwide demand for Chinese capital. While China maintained impressive economic growth, this growth seemed to be on shaky foundations by 2010. The Chinese government maintained strict capital controls, kept fewer banking regulations preventing the state from seizing assets, and had an opaque financial sector. Further, the Chinese invested considerably in infrastructure projects and underutilized housing. These deficiencies suggested real problems in the Chinese economy. In 2015, the Chinese stock market suffered a precipitous collapse. The government swiftly moved to prop up the banks, indicating that the poor lending practices would continue. Simultaneously, Chinese manufacturing started to cool, as some of the tasks became automated or outsourced to even cheaper labor markets. These deficiencies, coupled with dubious government practices, currently undermine China as a possible alternative haven.

There were few other attractive currencies after the euro and the RMB. Vladimir Putin perhaps wanted to translate Russian military successes into a greater global profile of the Russian ruble. However, the ruble was unattractive because of the limitations in its convertibility. Russia's economy remained almost completely dependent on energy. It therefore made no sense for energy producers to exchange their energy for rubles, which could only be used to purchase more energy. Alternatively, the yen remained unattractive due to Japan's economic stagnation, and the Swiss franc lacked the depth in capital markets to serve as a viable alternative. Given these constraints, the capital obtained by energy market states seemingly had only one place to go, even if the U.S. would no longer provide an indefinite and ironclad security guarantee.

These situations, coupled with the rising security threats in the Middle East, encouraged those with capital to flock to safe assets, which by default were American bonds and financial institutions. Additionally, the U.S. was consuming less energy and was increasingly less dependent on the energy market for its supply. The growth of fracking technology was generating a significant boost in American oil reserves. During the 2000s, the U.S. transitioned from importing the bulk of its oil from the Middle East to its own domestic supply and to imports from Canada and Venezuela. Additionally, as part of the American Recovery and Reinvestment Act of 2009 passed by Congress in response to the financial crisis, the U.S. made major moves to diversify its energy sources away from fossil fuels. By the mid-2010s, the solar and wind industries had made significant gains, and U.S. energy consumption rapidly dropped while productivity remained high.

We can therefore see that the U.S. seemed to stumble into a "win" in the global war on terror. Despite its setbacks in Egypt, Yemen, and Syria, the U.S. ended 2018 with ISIS all but defeated, and with key territories in Syria needed to contain Iran and check Russian influence under control. The U.S. remained a pivotal player in the Middle East and Central Asia, and with the fading of the euro, no other currency could challenge American control over global energy markets. If the war started to maintain the peg between dollars and oil, it appeared that at the end of 2018, the mission was accomplished.

## THE LONG-TERM STRATEGIC FAILURE

Unfortunately for the U.S, this "success" wasn't what the Bush administration initially hoped for, and it certainly did not accomplish the goal of permanently securing American financial hegemony. The war has taken the lives of over 5,000 Americans and has left tens of thousands with significant wounds. The war cost the U.S. $5 trillion during the period 2001–2016, and promises to cost much more in veterans' health care and benefits well into the future. The U.S. further failed to secure total domination of the global energy market's producers and transit routes. Russia and China continued to build links with the hosts of the energy market. China began construction of a naval base in Djibouti adjacent to the U.S. naval base, Camp Lemmonier, indicating that the People's Liberation Army Navy was interested in projecting power close to Bab el-Mandeb and into the Red Sea. On the other hand, Putin opened negotiations with Saleh's Houthi rebels about the possibility of a naval facility in Yemen, moving the Russian navy into a position to challenge the U.S. for dominance of Bab el-Mandeb. For its part, Iran continues to challenge the U.S. in the Strait of Hormuz and continues its support for both antiregime militants and militia groups throughout the Middle East. These three states, along with Venezuela, are all abandoning the dollar in energy trades. Iran initially began exchanging oil and energy for a basket of currencies with the opening in 2008 of an international oil bourse (commodity exchange) on the Iranian resort island of Kish. This plan to denominate oil sales in non-dollar currencies continued in response to President Trump's Muslim ban following his inauguration in 2017. However, in addition to the Iranians, Russia and China agreed to begin swapping energy in their own currencies in 2016. Collectively, these moves may be laying the groundwork for a future transition away from the peg between energy trades and the dollar. While the U.S. may have "won" in the sense that the dollar is now supreme, the war on terror has set the groundwork for the hosts under the U.S. security umbrella to consider transitioning away from their support of American financial dominance.

The waning of U.S. influence is opening the door for its rivals to assert themselves globally, particularly China. One of President's Xi's initiations was to increase the global use of the Chinese RMB as a reserve currency. The Chinese rapidly increased investment in Europe and Latin America, both traditionally dominated by the U.S. In 2009, China's footprint in Africa grew larger than that of the U.S. as the Chinese surpassed the U.S. in investment. The Chinese were further willing to cooperate with states under U.S. sanctions, such as Sudan and Zimbabwe. These actions radically increased the circulation of the RMB globally.

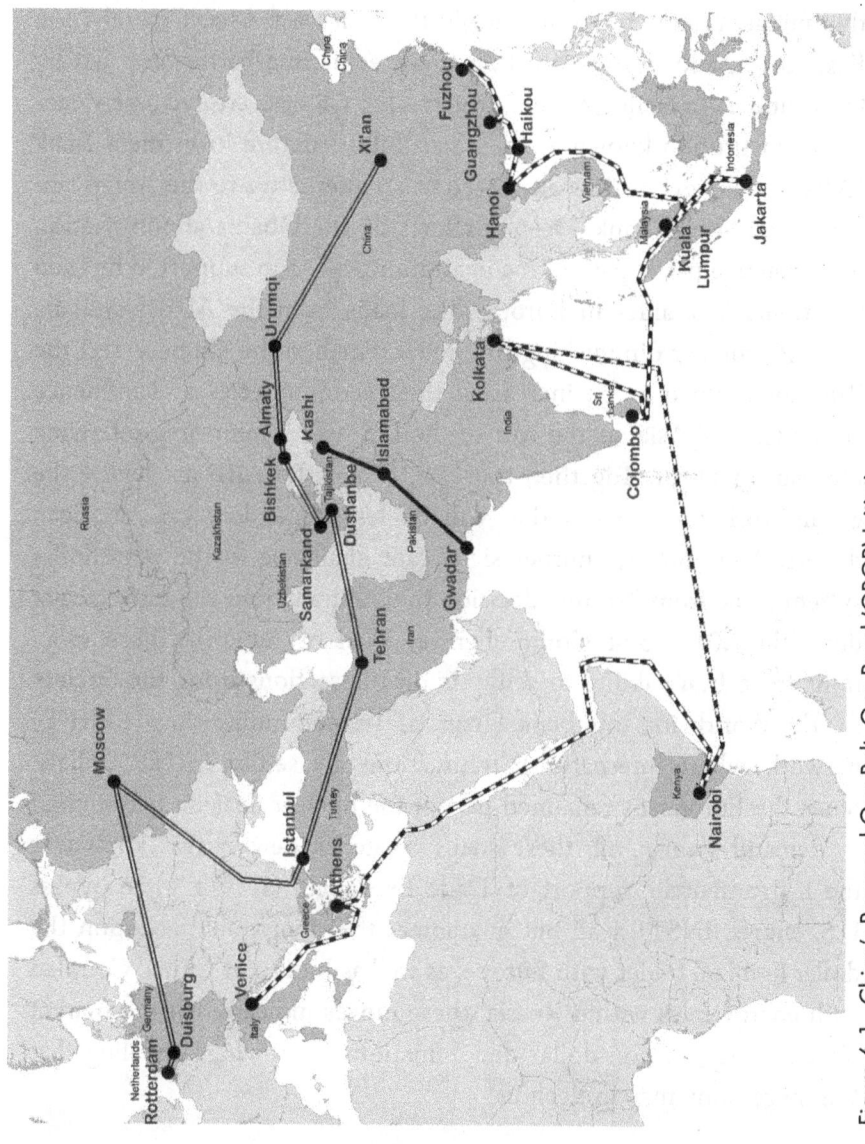

Figure 6.1. China's Proposed One Belt, One Road (OBOR) Initiative.
Note. Data from McBride (2016).

This growing clout allowed the Chinese to pursue an initiative known as One Belt, One Road (OBOR). Figure 6.1 demonstrates that this initiative aims to economically tie Southeast Asia, Central Asia, East Africa, and Europe together in an economic partnership led by the Chinese. To facilitate these projects, the Chinese created a new economic institution known as the Asian Infrastructure Investment Bank (AIIB). This new institution served as an alternative to the American-supported World Bank. Despite efforts by the Obama administration to discourage participation, the institution was soon supported by even traditional U.S. allies in Europe. The loans from the AIIB would be in RMB, further diminishing the dollar. Further, the Chinese and the Russians seemed to be increasing their economic ties and influence across Central Asia, as the role of the U.S. was diminishing following the war on terror. Together, the OBOR and the AIIB are laying the groundwork for a world that will be less dependent on American dollars. Additionally, another significant challenge to the petrodollar system came from Trump's decision to withdraw from the Iran nuclear deal (the 2015 Joint Comprehensive Plan of Action). These sanctions froze Iran's ability to settle its oil transactions using the Society for the Worldwide Interbank Financial Telecommunication (SWIFT) network, where international transactions are settled in U.S. dollars. Since the Europeans remained part of the nuclear deal, and continued to demand Iranian oil, these states created a new system known as the Instrument In Support of Trade Exchanges (INSTEX) to bypass U.S. efforts. INSTEX all but guarantees that Iran would abandon the dollar in its oil trades with Europe, as well as India and China. Coupled with energy sales within Russia, these moves indicate that the market to sell energy in non-dollar denominations is growing, signaling that U.S. hegemony may in decline.[2]

### DOMESTIC UNREST AND FADING MEMORY

Yet, the U.S. will still enjoy several advantages over its competitors in terms of maintaining the dollar as the world's reserve currency. First, the U.S. has the advantage of the status quo, meaning that any shift toward a different order would entail some transaction cost. Second, the U.S. liberal order led to an increase in real income for most of the world.[3] These changes have led to remarkable reductions in global poverty and malnourishment, while increasing access to clean water and improving life expectancy.[4] These positive outcomes may give states little incentive to shift away from the American-led order. Third, the potential challengers to the U.S.-led order face significant demographic challenges. While Russia's population is in decline, China's population is aging quickly as a consequence of its one-child policy. These changes may make it difficult for both states to remain economically competitive and project military power in the future. By contrast, large immigrant demographics are allowing the U.S. to buck this trend and are likely to support U.S. population growth for the foreseeable future.

Interestingly enough, despite these positive trends, the domestic politics of the U.S. threaten to undermine its own hegemony. For example, in the summer of 2011, the U.S. nearly refused to raise its debt ceiling, or the amount of money the government could borrow. If the U.S. failed to do so, there was a chance that at some point the U.S. would need to default on repaying its debt to its creditors. If the states of OPEC were to conclude that U.S. treasuries were not safe assets, there would be no reason to buy these assets. The U.S. government would therefore be forced to borrow at higher rates, or raise taxes and cut spending to continue functioning. The U.S. seemed to be risking its own privilege as a result of partisan political debates. The larger issue was whether the political system of the U.S. was still equipped to serve as a stabilizing force in global economics.

The election of 2016 only worsened these concerns. Trump openly stated that the U.S. could ask its creditors to take a "haircut," meaning that the U.S would refuse to pay back the money it borrowed.[5] Trump further claimed that global forces were harming American workers, and he denounced trade and international engagement in conflict. Trump's argument was that U.S. workers' wages stagnated as a result of global engagement and that only elites were gaining from the system. On the other side of the political aisle, the Democratic candidates also denounced increasing globalization. Although former Secretary of State Hillary Clinton at one point claimed that the proposed Trans-Pacific Partnership was the gold standard in trade agreements, she quickly shifted her position on the TPP during the Democratic primary against Senator Bernie Sanders, an avid protectionist. These actions raised concerns that the U.S. was simply unreliable as a hegemon and that the U.S. public would demand actions that would undermine the entire dollar-based financial system. Recent American behavior in the Trump administration has done little to quell these fears. From the time of his inauguration in 2017, Trump's foreign policy increasingly alienated key European allies, undermined trade agreements that encourage financial flows into the U.S., pulled the U.S. back from extensive engagement in Asia, and haphazardly threatened to withdraw American forces from Afghanistan and Syria.

Even as these actions seem to pull the U.S. away from hegemony, it seems that the U.S. will continue to fight the war on terror and could potentially escalate it. Unlike Obama, Trump frequently portrayed ISIS, along with other Islamic groups, as existential threats. While this claim is empirically false, this threat does motivate Americans to support U.S. actions in the war on terror. For example, after images of violence perpetuated by ISIS emerged, 65% of Americans believed that the group was a "major threat" to the U.S., and 57% supported sending Americans ground troops into the fight in Iraq and Syria.[6] Americans became willing to support a ground war against the terrorist group despite the public's long aversion to remaining in Iraq. Given these fears, the threat of terrorism seems to be the best way to maintain the U.S. position as protector of the international energy markets. Therefore, to continue projecting American power, we might expect the foreign policy establishment to continue emphasizing the danger of terrorist threats to the international system.

There is, however, a qualitative difference between terrorist threats following 9/11 and threats today. In the past, the U.S. used the threat of terrorism to justify the expansion of its presence in the host states of the energy market. Terrorism was a cover to provide security to these states to cement American hegemony. Today, the threat of terrorism reflects more of a desperate effort by the U.S. to maintain its remaining forward presence in the hosts under its umbrella. For example, following the campaign against ISIS, the U.S. may attempt to make some of its military bases in Iraqi territory permanent. The motivation for this action is to maintain American influence over parts of Iraq's oil reserves and defend these areas against Russian or Iranian influence. We therefore see the qualitative change in how the threat of terrorism is used. In the past, the motivation for U.S. intervention against terrorism was to cement its dominance over the world's global energy market. Today, the motivation for intervening against terrorists is to maintain control over key territories, contain the growing power of its rivals, and prevent the further decline of American influence in the global energy market.

## TERRORISM AND INTERNATIONAL WAR

This study began with the puzzle: why would a state like the U.S. fight a global war against terrorism? Terrorism kills fewer people annually than motor vehicle accidents, lightning strikes, or even toddlers that mishandle firearms. Society views these unfortunate events as acceptable risks. Yet, when it comes to terrorism, the U.S. was willing to sacrifice thousands of its citizens, tens of thousands of foreign citizens, and over $3 trillion to wage war against those that would engage in this activity. This behavior seems even more puzzling when we consider that most terrorist groups typically fail to accomplish their strategic goals, suffer from incredible internal dysfunction, and often collapse in less than a decade. Why then would the U.S. feel so threatened by small groups of individuals willing to use this tactic called terrorism, and why was the U.S., with all its economic and military power, unable to emerge victorious from the war on terror?

This book has argued that the war on terror began because of the Bush administration's determination to maintain the place of the dollar as the world's reserve currency. The possibility that energy could be sold in euros as opposed to dollars created risk to the status of the U.S. dollar as the world's foremost reserve currency. The loss of this status could potentially force the U.S. to pay higher borrowing costs or to increase taxes and reduce government spending. Even today, after so much violence and war, it is unlikely that a president will retain power if any of these outcomes are realized. This leads us to our first key lesson from this research: if currencies are tied to their convertibility into critical goods (i.e., water, food, or energy), the potential loss of these resources may create a shift in power that can push states into war. By linking conflict studies to studies in political economy, we can see that shifts in power may be caused by currency depreciation. Depreciation of a state's currency means that it will be less able to maintain a balance of power with its rivals and finance the public or private goods that a leader needs to stay in power. If, however, a leader who faces a risk of currency depreciation has a powerful military at her disposal, she can prevent her currency from losing convertibility by seizing control of the critical good through war.

The answer to the second question of why the U.S. was unable to emerge victorious is that American protection gave host states no incentive to disarm their terrorists. If State A is willing to provide State B with military resources to fight terrorists, State B will have an incentive to continue fighting terror so long as it knows that State A will not abandon it. In the case of the U.S., no host state believed that the Americans would abandon them, given the lucrative nature of remaining the world's hegemon and protector of the global energy trade. As a result, none of the states that comprised the suppliers and the transit routes had any incentive to disarm their terrorists. More generally, this study demonstrates that providing a government with protection against an internal adversary perversely gives the government the incentive to allow the internal adversary to exist.

This yields a third lesson about how terrorism may contribute to larger conflicts. While terrorists typically fail to accomplish their strategic objectives, these groups may thrive in smaller geographic areas within states, particularly if they are facing corrupt or bureaucratically weak adversaries. In these areas, terrorists may use the threat of violence to compel civilians to cease their cooperation with the state. These activities may endogenously weaken the state, particularly if terrorists destabilize an area that is critical to sustaining the state's economy. If this occurs, terrorist activity may shift the balance of power between states. In a more global picture, terrorist activities may disrupt the ability to extract energy from key supply sites, or disrupt the ability to move the energy to the market. In both of these cases, terrorist activity at a local level may contribute to larger economic disruptions and may significantly harm both hegemons that protect these routes and the states that depend on these trades. This harm may weaken both the hegemon and the hosts it depends on, and it may open the door for challenges from hostile rivals. Facing these declines, hegemons such as the U.S. as well as their proxies may initiate preventive wars out of desperation to fend off their rivals and maintain their control of their markets and trade routes, both of which are critical to sustaining their power. We see that although the damage from terrorist activity is minimal, the ability of terrorists to destabilize a state's control of its territory is a key reason for why non-state actors are a cause of interstate conflict.

Taken together, these findings indicate that as the war on terror progresses, and as the U.S. faces increasing competition for the goodwill of its allies and control over the energy market, the U.S. is likely to become more aggressive. The advantage for the U.S. is that unlike Russia or China, it can still project power anywhere in a short period of time and it is able to sustain its presence. The U.S. is also the foremost exporter of weaponry in the world, and it maintains an advantage in that the U.S. dollar is the status quo way of settling international trades. These tools give the U.S. the ability to defend host states anywhere from their "terrorists." Given the lucrative nature of hegemony, and the political repercussion of allowing it to slip away, it is unlikely that the U.S. will quietly cede its position. As a result, we may expect new wars on terror to emerge in the future, and expect that the U.S. will continue seeking monsters to destroy.

# Appendix

# GAME THEORETICAL SOLUTIONS AND STATISTICAL MODELS

### 3.1 FORMAL MODEL DESCRIPTION FOR CHAPTER 3

Figure A.1 presents a stylized model of a terrorist campaign occurring in a foreign host state that is a key player in the American-supported petrodollar system. The conflict is simplified to three players: the U.S. government (US), the host state (H), and a terrorist group (T) that operates within H's territory. H begins the game in complete control of his territory, which allows him to distribute the territory's benefits to his supporters.[1] Additionally, by supporting the petrodollar system, H's control of the territory provides a foreign policy benefit to US, which is normalized to 1. On the other hand, T seeks to destabilize H's government and assume sovereignty over the territory for itself. We can therefore normalize H's utility function such that he receives a payoff of 1 for each round in which he survives and a payoff of 0 if he is destabilized by T. Similarly, assume that T's utility function is normalized such that it receives a payoff of 0 for each round in which

156 • APPENDIX

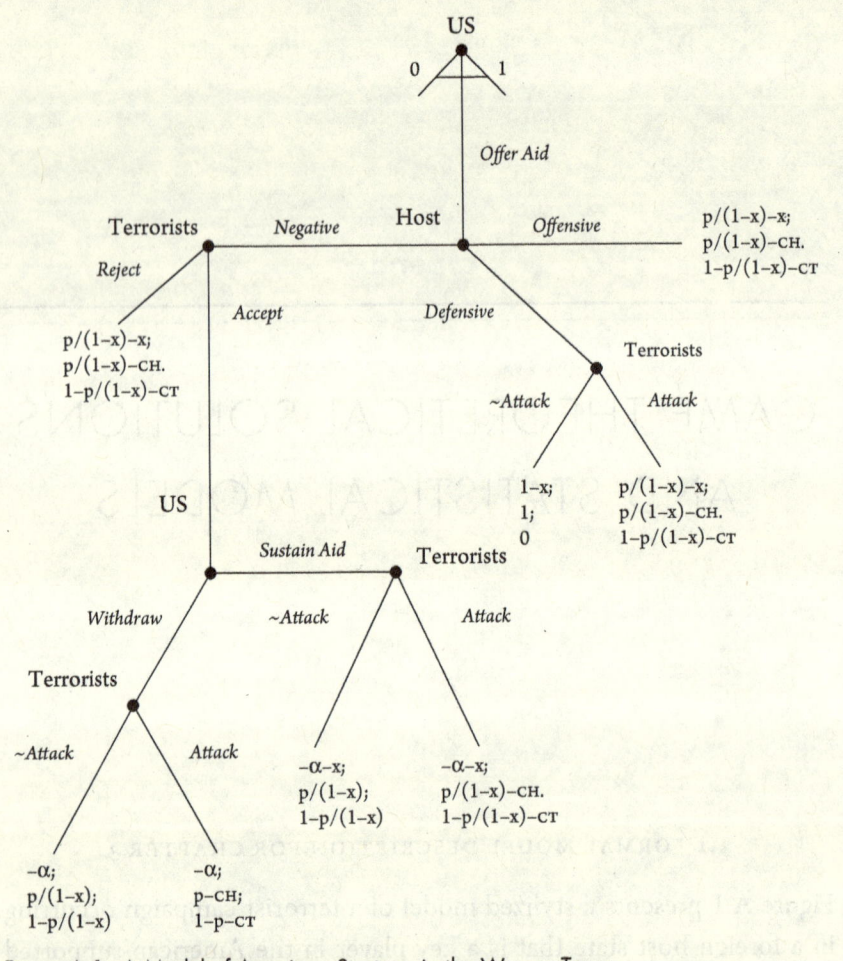

Figure A.1. A Model of American Strategy in the War on Terror.
Note. Each p in the model is superscripted with a $\lambda t$ to capture the state of the game t. Figure A.1, however, represents $p^{\lambda t}$ as p for ease of presentation.

H survives and receives a payoff of 1 if H destabilizes. In addition to facing opposition from H, T also faces opposition from US, which seeks to keep T out of power.[2]

The game presented in Figure A.1 represents a single round of an infinitely repeated game, which continues until one of three outcomes occurs. First, the game ends if both H and T engage in a direct military encounter. This may occur if H engages in an offensive against T or if T makes an attempt to seize power at H's center. A third possibility is for H and T to reach a negotiated settlement, which breaks H's cooperation with US. The game terminates with any of these three outcomes (H engages in an offensive, T attacks H at the center, or H and T reach a negotiated settlement).

In the event of an offensive or attack by T at the center, assume that H defeats T with probability $p^{\lambda t} \in [0,1]$ and fails do so with the corresponding probability $(1-p^{\lambda t})$, where t represents the state of the game and $\lambda \in [0,L]$ represents a normalizing parameter. Assume that the state of the game represents the number of rounds previously played and that the game transitions from state t to state $(t+1)$ with probability $\omega = 1$. Substantively, the setup of the model therefore assumes that H's probability of defeating T with military force declines over time, though the rate of decline slows as $\lambda \to 0$ and accelerates as $\lambda \to L$. The assumption that H's ability to survive a direct military encounter with T declines with time is based on several studies of both terrorism and insurgency that conclude that terrorists typically strengthen as the organization persists over time.[3]

## 3.1.1 Moves

Each round begins with US's decision of whether or not to provide some level of military aid to H to improve his chances of surviving an attempt by T to destabilize him. US assistance is formally represented by $x \in [0,1]$, which is assumed to be a continuous and increasing level of assistance to H's regime. US provides increasing military aid as $x \to 1$, and relatively less as $x \to 0$. This aid directly increases H's probability of survival to $p^{\lambda} = \dfrac{p^{\lambda t}}{1-x}$, where $p^{\lambda} > p$ so long as $x > 0$.[4] This indicates that US effectively guarantees H's survival if $x=(1-p^{\lambda t})$. On the other hand, if US sets $x = 0$, H's probabilty of survival is equal to $\dfrac{p^{\lambda t}}{1-0}=p^{\lambda t}$. We therefore see that US's aid increases the probability that H survives a destabilization attempt by T, but it is possible for H to survive without US's support.

Once US allocates military aid, H has three possible options. First, H may use the military aid provided by US to mount an offensive against

T in an effort to disarm it. In this case, H actively makes an effort to end the game by destroying T's organization. Second, H can choose to stay on the defensive and simply wait for T to attack. If H adopts the defensive posture, the game next moves to T, which decides whether or not to attack H. If T attacks, H disarms T with probability $\frac{p^{\lambda t}}{1-x}$ and T destabilizes H with probability $1-\frac{p^{\lambda t}}{1-x}$. On the other hand, if T does not attack, the game moves to the next round, given that neither H nor T are disarmed.

The final option for H is to negotiate with T in an effort to induce the group to cease its violence. Numerous studies in the bargaining and conflict literature indicate that negotiated settlements which reflect the balance of military power should be preferable to conflict.[5] Therefore, T might prefer some negotiated settlement if H makes some offer that reflects the balance of military power between the two sides. With US's military assistance, H makes an offer of $1-\frac{p^{\lambda t}}{1-x}$, which reflects T's probability of surviving a military encounter when H receives US support x. We can see that H's offer to T declines as $x \rightarrow 1-p^{\lambda t}$, indicating greater support from US. This indicates that H does not make an offer that reflects the actual balance of power between himself and T, but rather the balance of power created by US military assistance. The only case in which H makes an offer that does reflect the actual balance of power is if x=0, in which case, H offers $1-\frac{p^{\lambda t}}{1-0}=1-p^{\lambda t}$. A key component, however, is that H's cooperation with US's supported petrodollar system becomes compromised as a result of the settlement.

Once H makes the offer, T either accepts or rejects it. If T accepts, T agrees to cease its political violence in exchange for the concessions offered by H. Given that the deal compromises petrodollar cooperation in some way, the US next decides whether to continue providing H with economic and military support or whether to withdraw this support. Following this decision, T chooses either to fulfill its commitment to

H and disarm or to renege on the deal and attempt to destabilize H at the center. Should T resume fighting, H survives with probability $p^{\lambda t}$ if US withdraws and survives with probability $\frac{p^{\lambda t}}{1-x}$ if US does not.

## 3.1.2 Payoffs

H receives a payoff of 1 for each round in which he survives as the sole sovereign over the territory. If H negotiates with T, and T fulfills its obligations and terminates its violence, H's payoff reflects the negotiated distribution of benefits. Should H make an offer of $1-\frac{p^{\lambda t}}{1-x}$ to T, and should T accept, H's payoff would be $\frac{p^{\lambda t}}{1-x}$. If H refuses to negotiate, and chooses to mount an offensive against T, H's payoff is equal to his probability of disarming T minus the cost $c_H \in [0,1]$ he must pay to engage in military conflict. H's payoff for the offensive is therefore equal to $\frac{p^{\lambda t}}{1-x}(1) + (1-\frac{p^{\lambda t}}{1-x})(0) - c_H = \frac{p^{\lambda t}}{1-x} - c_H$. If H adopts defensive tactics, and T responds by attacking, H receives the same payoff of $\frac{p^{\lambda t}}{1-x} - c_H$ since this outcome also involves a military conflict against T. However, if H adopts a defensive posture and T chooses not to attack, H receives a payoff of 1 and pays no cost, since there is no conflict with T.

Although both H and US are aligned, the utility functions of these players are slightly different. While H's primary objective is to maintain power over the territory, US does not derive utility from keeping H in power but rather from keeping T out of power. Let us therefore specify that US receives a payoff of 1 if and only if T is kept out of power, and US receives a payoff of 0 if T gains *any* political power. This means that US receives a payoff of 0 if T either defeats H militarily or if H grants T any power as part of a negotiated settlement. Assume that if T gains any power in the territory, the US-supported petrodollar system becomes compromised, producing a cost to US of $\alpha \in [0, A]$. If conflict occurs between H and T, US's utility for supporting H can therefore be represented by the following expression: $\frac{p^{\lambda t}}{1-x}(1) + (1 - \frac{p^{\lambda t}}{1-x})(0) - x$. On the other hand, if US support H, but there is no conflict, the US payoff is equal to 1−x. Finally, if US does not provide aid to H in his first move, and T assumes some control over the territory either through force or negotiation, the US payoff is equal to—α.

Let us now consider T's payoffs. T receives a payoff of 0 in each round if H survives, and receives a payoff of 1 if H destabilizes. If a negotiated settlement is reached, T's payoff corresponds to the offer that H makes. Like H, T is also assumed to pay a cost $c_T \in [0,1]$ if it fights, which represents the utility of the cost of conflict to T. However, since terrorist groups are typically non-transparent, and have incentives to misrepresent their true resolve, let us assume that both US and H have incomplete information as to the value of $c_T$, whereas T has complete and perfect information (Fearon 1995; Powell 2000; Reiter 2003; Schelling 1960). This ability to misrepresent is often characteristic of terrorist groups, which frequently engage in behaviors intended to signal intense resolve, such as suicide bombings (Arce and Sandler 2007; Bloom 2005; Kydd and Walter 2006; Lapan and Sandler 1993; Pape 2003). Let us therefore assume that US and H are both uncertain as to the value of $c_T$ but are both aware that $c_T \sim U[0,1]$, or distributed according to a standard uniform distribution ranging between 0 and 1.

### 3.1.3 Solution

Since the game is repeated infinitely and involves incomplete information, I solve the game using the Markov perfect Bayesian equilibrium concept (MPBE). Stationary MPBE assume that in any subgame, the behavior of each of the players is dependent on only the current value of a particular state variable (Carter 2015; Mailath and Samuelson 2006; Maskin and Tirole 2001; Slantchev 2002). In this case, let us characterize t as the state variable, which determines the value of p, or the current likelihood that H will survive a direct military encounter with T. This makes intuitive sense, as we would expect US, H, and T to base

### 3.1.3.1 Case 1. Host Negotiates $x = 1 - p^*$

Let us first identify the set of conditions under which H chooses to negotiate. In this case, T's decision to defect on the agreement or to maintain it is contingent on whether or not US supports H after negotiation. If US maintains the support, T defects if $1 - \frac{p^{\lambda t}}{1-x} - c_T > 1 - \frac{p^{\lambda t}}{1-x}$. We see that because of the costly nature of conflict, this expression can never be true, even if $x = 0$. We can therefore see that if US maintains support for H following negotiation, T will never defect from the agreement. However, since US's utility is solely based on keeping T out of power, US receives a payoff of $-\alpha$ if H negotiates. Therefore, the payoff to US for maintaining support for H following negotiation is equal to $-\alpha - x$. On the other hand, if US withdraws and conflict between H and T erupts, the US payoff is equal to $p^{\lambda t}(1) + (1-p^{\lambda t})(-\alpha)$. If US knew with certainty that conflict would occur, she would prefer to maintain support for H after negotiation if $-\alpha - x > p^{\lambda t}(1) + (1-p^{\lambda t})(-\alpha)$, which reduces to

$$p^{\lambda t} \in \hat{I}[0,1], (1-p^{\lambda t}) > 0 - x > p^{lt}(1+\alpha) \qquad (1)$$

This condition cannot be fulfilled if $x > 0$. We therefore see that if US provides support to H, she cannot credibly sustain this support if H negotiates with T. Both H and T therefore know that US will withdraw if a negotiated settlement is reached. If this is true, T will *Attack* following the US withdrawal if $1 - p^{\lambda t} - c_T > 1 - \frac{p^{\lambda t}}{1-x}$. Rearranging terms, this indicates that T is indifferent between abiding by the deal and attacking if $c_T = \frac{p^{\lambda t}}{1-x} - p^{\lambda t}$, which simplifies to $\frac{p^{\lambda t} x}{1-x}$. We can therefore state that T plays *Attack* if $c_T < \frac{p^{\lambda t} x}{1-x}$ and plays *~Attack* if $c_T \geq \frac{p^{\lambda t} x}{1-x}$. Define H's belief that T plays *Attack* as $c_T' = \frac{p^{\lambda t} x}{1-x}$. We can see that $c_T' \to 1$ as $x \to 1 - p^{\lambda t}$, which demonstrates that T is more likely to *Attack* as the level of aid that US provides increases. Substantively, this indicates that the greater the level of military aid provided by US, the more likely it is that T will defect from a negotiated settlement. However, notice that if x = 0, the offer made by H is equal to $1 - p^{\lambda t}$. If this is true, the probability that T defects is equal to $\frac{p^{\lambda t} 0}{1-0} = 0$. In other words, if H makes an offer that reflects the balance of power between H and T without US's support, T can be considered perfectly credible. This reflects something interesting: *the more aid US provides, the less credible any deal is with T, whereas T is credible if US provides no military support to H.*

Given that both players are aware of this, how do they behave in negotiation? Interestingly enough, the model demonstrates that both T for which $c_T < \frac{p^{\lambda t} x}{1-x}$ and T for which $c_T \geq \frac{p^{\lambda t} x}{1-x}$ will always accept H's initial offer to negotiate. In the latter case, T will not *Attack* at the end of the game, even if US withdraws. The latter T therefore accepts any deal if $1 - \frac{p^{\lambda t}}{1-x} \geq 1 - \frac{p^{\lambda t}}{1-x} - c_T$, which must always be true. In the former case, where T will renege on the settlement once US withdraws, T accepts if $1 - p^{\lambda t} - c_T \geq 1 - \frac{p^{\lambda t}}{1-x} - c_T$. Again, this condition is always fulfilled, which indicates that these T will accept and subsequently *Attack* so long as x > 0. If x = 0, these T accept and abide by the negotiated settlement. Therefore, H knows that if he plays *Negotiate*, T will always *Accept* and US will always *Withdraw*. Since H is unaware of what type of T he is facing, H's payoff for negotiation can be defined as

$$\frac{p^{\lambda t} x}{1-x}(p^{\lambda t} - c_H) + (1 - \frac{p^{\lambda t} x}{1-x})(\frac{p^{\lambda t}}{1-x}) \qquad (2)$$

Negotiation is therefore a risky strategy for H. H is aware that T will accept negotiation, but making this offer will cost H his US support, since US is only interested in preventing T from entering into H's government. Negotiation therefore requires H to gamble that T is of the type for which $c_T \geq \frac{p^{\lambda t}x}{1-x}$. However, if the probability that Nature draws this type is equal to $(1-\frac{p^{\lambda t}x}{1-x})$, we see that it is increasingly unlikely as $x \to 1$. In other words, *if H is heavily reliant on US military aid, it is unlikely that negotiation will succeed, and highly likely that T will respond to US's withdrawal by reigniting terrorist violence.*

### 3.1.3.2 Case 2. Host Adopts Defensive Tactics

Let us consider H's second possible strategy, in which H plays *Defensive*. In this case, H does not mount an offensive against T, but instead gambles that T will be deterred by US's provision of military aid and its subsequent increase in military power. If H adopts this strategy, T plays *Attack* if $1-\frac{p^{\lambda t}}{1-x}-c_T>0$. Rearranging terms, T plays *Attack* if $c_T<1-\frac{p^{\lambda t}}{1-x}$. Let us therefore define the probability that T *Attack* | H *Defensive* as $c_T''=1-\frac{p^{\lambda t}}{1-x}$. H's expected utility for this strategy is equal to

$$(c_T'')(\frac{p^{\lambda t}}{1-x}-c_H)+(1-c_T'')(1) \qquad (3)$$

If we compare H's payoff for *Defensive* with his payoff for *Negotiate*, we quickly see that if $x > 0$, H's strategy to play *Defensive* dominates *Negotiate*.

**Lemma 3.1.** H strictly prefers *Defensive* to *Negotiate* if $x > 0$.

*Proof.* H's expected utility for *Negotiate* is equal to $c_T'(p-c_H)+(1-c_T')(\frac{p^{\lambda t}}{1-x})$. On the other hand, H's expected utility for *Defensive* is equal to $(c_T'')(\frac{p^{\lambda t}}{1-x}-c_H)+(1-c_T'')(1)$. If $x > 0$, it must be true that it must be true that $\frac{p^{\lambda t}}{1-x}-c_H>p-c_H$. It must also be true that Pr since [2] Therefore, for H, EU(*Defensive*) >> EU(*Negotiate*) if $x > 0$. □

**Corollary 3.1.** If x=0, H prefers *Defensive* if $p^{\lambda t} > c_H$ and prefers *Negotiate* otherwise.

*Proof.* If US sets x=0, the payoff to H for *Negotiate* is equal to $p^{\lambda t}$. H's payoff for *Defensive* is equal to $(1-p^{\lambda t})(p^{\lambda t} - c_H) + p^{\lambda t}$. H therefore prefers *Negotiate* to *Defensive* if $p^{\lambda t} \geq (1-p^{\lambda t})(p^{\lambda t} - c_H) + p^{\lambda t} \equiv 0 \geq (1-p^{\lambda t})(p^{\lambda t} - c_H)$. Since $(1-p^{\lambda t}) > 0$, the expression is true if $(p^{\lambda t} - c_H) < 0$ and is false otherwise. Therefore, we see that if x=0, H plays *Negotiate* if $0 \geq (p^{\lambda t} - c_H)$ and *Defensive* if $(p^{\lambda t} - c_H) > 0$. □

This yields an interesting insight as to the effect of US support on H's behavior. If $p^{\lambda t}$ is relatively low, H responds to a lack of US support by reaching some negotiated settlement with T in order to avoid continued violence. Since the US does not interfere, H's offer would reflect the balance of power between himself and T, thereby rendering the agreement between the two parties credible. However, if US provides military aid while $p^{\lambda t} < c_H$, H has a disincentive to negotiate because US support decreases the cost of keeping T out of power. Since H knows that he is likely to survive conflict with T with US support, H is given an disincentive to negotiate versus adopt defensive postures.

### 3.1.3.3 Case 3. Host Attempts Offensive

We see that US support gives H a disincentive to negotiate. Ideally, US support should allow H to engage in an offensive to eliminate T rather than adopting defensive postures. H's payoff for engaging in an offensive is equal to $\frac{p^{\lambda t}}{1-x}(1) + (1 - \frac{p^{\lambda t}}{1-x})(0) - c_H = \frac{p^{\lambda t}}{1-x} - c_H$. This payoff is also dominated by H's strategy of adopting a defensive posture unless x=0.

**Lemma 3.2.** If $x > 0$, H weakly prefers playing *Defensive* over *Offensive*.

*Proof.* If $x > 0$, H's payoff for playing *Defensive* is equal to $(c_T'')(\frac{p^{\lambda t}}{1-x} - c_H) + (1-c_T'')(1)$. On the other hand, H's payoff for playing *Offensive* is $\frac{p^{\lambda t}}{1-x} - c_H$. Since $(c_T'')(\frac{p^{\lambda t}}{1-x} - c_H) + (1-c_T'')(1) \geq \frac{p^{\lambda t}}{1-x} - c_H$, H weakly prefers *Defensive* to *Offensive* if $x > 0$. □

## APPENDIX • 165

**Corollary 3.2.** If x=0, H strictly prefers to *Defensive* to *Offensive*.

*Proof.* If x=0, H prefers *Offensive* over *Defensive* if: $(1-p^{\lambda t})(p^{\lambda t}-c_H)+(p^{\lambda t})(1)<p^{\lambda t}-c_H$. This expression cannot be true since $p^{\lambda t}>0$. Therefore, H weakly prefers *Defensive* to *Offensive* if x=0. □

### 3.1.3.4. U.S. Behavior

Given H's behavior, US is faced with one of two choices. First, US can provide some economic and military support to H, which will prevent H from negotiating and may deter T from attacking. Second, US can refuse to support H. If US chooses the latter, she risks that H will negotiate with T or that T will successfully destabilize H by attacking at his center. However, if US supports H, she will not accomplish her objective of disarming T, unless T is so resolute that it will play *Attack* despite US assistance. We can identify the level of support US provides H by maximizing her utility for this strategy, represented by the following expression:

$$(1-\frac{p^{\lambda t}}{1-x})(\frac{p^{\lambda t}}{1-x}(1)+(1-\frac{p^{\lambda t}}{1-x})(0))+(\frac{p^{\lambda t}}{1-x})(1)-x \quad (4)$$

The US payoff is dependent on the probability (T *Attack* | x*), where x* is defined as the level of support that maximizes US utility if H plays *Defensive*.

**Definition 3.1.** The US optimal level of military support for H is x=x*.

*Proof.* We can identify the US optimal level of economic and military by maximizing her utility should H play *Defensive* with respect to x:

$$\frac{\partial((1-\frac{p^{\lambda t}}{1-x})(\frac{p^{\lambda t}}{1-x}(1)+(1-\frac{p^{\lambda t}}{1-x})(0))+(\frac{p^{\lambda t}}{1-x})(1)-x)}{\partial x} \quad (5)$$

After setting this derivative equal to zero, we establish that

$$x^*=\frac{1}{3}(3-\frac{2*3^{\frac{2}{3}}p^{\lambda t}}{(-9p^{2\lambda t}+\sqrt{3}\sqrt{p^{3\lambda t}(-8+27p^{\lambda t})})^{\frac{1}{3}}}$$

$$-(-27p^{2\lambda t}+3\sqrt{3}\sqrt{p^{3\lambda t}(-8+27p^{\lambda t})})^{\frac{1}{3}}).$$

This level of support x* maximizes the expected utility to US if H plays *Defensive*, which he will do if x* > 0. □

**Definition 3.2.** The lower bound of US economic and military support to H is equal to x=x'.

*Proof.* The expected utility to US of providing military support x=x* to H declines as t → ∞. At some point t* it may be true that $EU_{US}(x=x^*)<-\alpha$. In these cases, if $p^{\lambda t}>c_H$, H plays *Defensive* instead of *Negotiate* even without US support. However, if $p^{\lambda t}<c_H$, US guarantees herself a payoff of —α if x=0. Alternatively, US may allocate x=x', which is defined as a level of military support that produces an expected utility equal to —α. Define x' as the value of x for which

$$(1-\frac{p^{\lambda t}}{1-x})(\frac{p^{\lambda t}}{1-x}(1)+(1-\frac{p^{\lambda t}}{1-x})(0))+(\frac{p^{\lambda t}}{1-x})(1)-x=-\alpha.^6$$

**Lemma 3.3.** US sets x=x* if $EU_{US}(x=x^*) \geq --$

*Proof.* Lemma 3.1 establishes that if x > 0, H prefers *Defensive* to *Negotiate*, while Lemma 3.2 shows that H prefers *Defensive* to *Offensive*. If US sets x > 0, H plays *Defensive*. From the above definition, we establish that US maximizes her expected utility for supporting H by allocating x=x*. US prefers this strategy unless the $EU_{US}(x=x^*)<EU_{US}(x=0) \equiv EU_{US}(x=x^*)<-\alpha$. Therefore, US sets x=x* in all cases where $EU_{US}(x=x^*)>-\alpha$. □

**Corollary 3.3.** If $EU_{US}(x=x^*)<-\alpha$, but x' > 0, US sets x=x' to x=0.

*Proof.* Formally, $EU_{US}(x=x')=-\alpha$. However, x' > 0, H plays *Defensive* if US sets x=x' since x > 0. Therefore, H refuses to negotiate, and there is some positive probability that T will either be deterred or that T will fail to destabilize H if it attacks the center. Therefore, if $EU_{US}(x=x^*)<-\alpha$, but x' > 0, US sets x=x' instead of x=0 unless x' < 0. □

### 3.1.4 Equilibria

**Proposition 3.1.** If $EU_{US}(x=x^*)>-\alpha$, the following constitutes a Markov perfect Bayesian equilibrium:

1. US: {x=x*, *Withdraw*}
2. H: *Defensive*

3. T: $\{(Accept; Attack); Attack\}$ if $c_T < \min\{\frac{p^{\lambda t}x}{1-x}; 1-\frac{p^{\lambda t}}{1-x}\}$, $\{\sim Attack;$ $Attack\}$ if $\frac{p^{\lambda t}x}{1-x} < c_T < 1-\frac{p^{\lambda t}}{1-x}$; $\{Attack; \sim Attack\}$ if $1-\frac{p^{\lambda t}}{1-x} < c_T < \frac{p^{\lambda t}x}{1-x}$; $\{\sim Attack; \sim Attack\}$ if $c_T > \max\{\frac{p^{\lambda t}x}{1-x}; 1-\frac{p^{\lambda t}}{1-x}\}$

4. Beliefs: $\{\Pr. Attack \mid Negotiate\} = c_T'$; $\{\Pr. Attack \mid Defensive\} = c_T''$.

*Proof.* Lemma 3.3 establishes that US sets $x=x^*$ if $EU_{US}(x=x^*) > -\alpha$. Lemma 3.2 and Corollary 3.2 establish that if $x > 0$, H strictly prefers to play *Defensive* to both *Negotiate* and *Offensive*. T's strategies and the beliefs are established by the above discussion. □

**Proposition 3.2.** If $EU_{US}(x=x^*) < -\alpha$ & $x' > 0$, the following constitutes a Markov perfect Bayesian equilibrium:

1. US: $\{x=x'; Withdraw\}$
2. H: *Defensive*
3. T: $\{(Accept; Attack); Attack\}$ if $c_T < \min\{\frac{p^{\lambda t}x}{1-x}; 1-\frac{p^{\lambda t}}{1-x}\}$, $\{\sim Attack;$ $Attack\}$ if $\frac{p^{\lambda t}x}{1-x} < c_T < 1-\frac{p^{\lambda t}}{1-x}$; $\{Attack; \sim Attack\}$ if $1-\frac{p^{\lambda t}}{1-x} < c_T < \frac{p^{\lambda t}x}{1-x}$; $\{\sim Attack; \sim Attack\}$ if $c_T > \max\{\frac{p^{\lambda t}x}{1-x}; 1-\frac{p^{\lambda t}}{1-x}\}$
4. Beliefs: $\{\Pr. Attack \mid Negotiation = 0\} = \frac{p^{\lambda t}x'}{1-x}$; $\{\Pr. Attack \mid Defensive\} = 1-\frac{p^{\lambda t}}{1-x}$.

*Proof.* Corollary 3.3 demonstrates that if $EU_{US}(x=x^*) < -\alpha$, US set $x = x'$. If $x' > 0$, Lemma 3.2 and Corollary 3.2 establish that H strictly prefers to play *Defensive* to both *Negotiate* and *Offensive*. To establish the belief that T will *Attack* following negotiation, which is off the equilibrium path, consider what occurs if US plays *Withdraw* in her second move. In this case, the $\{\Pr. Attack \mid Negotiate\}$ can be identified by examining

T's expected utilities. T *Attack* if $1-p^{\lambda t}-c_t>1-\frac{p^{\lambda t}}{1-x}$. Solving for $c_T$, we see that this is true if $c_T<\frac{p^{\lambda t}x'}{1-x}$. Define {Pr. *Attack* | *Negotiate*} = $\frac{p^{\lambda t}x'}{1-x}$. If H plays *Defensive*, T *Attack* if $1-\frac{p^{\lambda t}}{1-x}-c_T>0$. Solving for $c_T$, this is true if $c_T<1-\frac{p^{\lambda t}}{1-x}$. Define {Pr. *Attack* | *Defensive*} = $1-\frac{p^{\lambda t}}{1-x}$. □

**Proposition 3.3.** If $EU_{US}(x=x^*)<-\alpha$, $x'\leq 0$, & $p^{\lambda t}>c_H$, the following constitutes a Markov perfect Bayesian equilibrium:

1. US: {$x=0$, *Withdraw*}
2. H: *Defensive*
3. T: {*Accept*; ~*Attack*); *Attack*} if $c_T<1-p$ and {~*Attack*; ~*Attack*} otherwise.
4. Beliefs: {Pr. *Attack* | *Negotiate* =0; {Pr. *Attack*| *Defensive*} =$1-p^{\lambda t}$.

*Proof.* Corollary 3.3 demonstrates that if $EU_{US}(x=x^*)<-\alpha$, US sets $x=x'$, where $x'=0$ if $x'<0$. We again define {Pr. *Attack* | *Negotiate* } by examining T's expected utilities. Since US plays *Withdraw* if H plays *Negotiate*, T *Attack* if $1-p^{\lambda t}-c_T>1-\frac{p^{\lambda t}}{1-x}$, which reduces to $1-p^{\lambda t}-c_T>1-p^{\lambda t}$ if $x=0$. Since this cannot be true, the {Pr. *Attack* | *Negotiate*} = 0. On the other hand, if H plays *Defensive*, T *Attack* if $1-\frac{p^{\lambda t}}{1-x}-c_T>0 \equiv 1-p^{\lambda t}-c_T>0$. This expression is true if $c_T<1-p^{*t}$. Define {Pr. *Attack* | *Defensive*} = $1-p^{\lambda t}$. Since Corollary 2 establishes that $EU_H(\text{Defensive})>>EU_H(\text{Offensive})$, H plays either *Negotiate* or *Defensive*. H prefers *Negotiate* if $p^{\lambda t}>(1-p^{\lambda t})(p^{\lambda t}-c_H)+p^{\lambda t} \equiv 0>(1-p^{\lambda t})(p^{\lambda t}-c_H)$. Since $p^{\lambda t} \in [0,1]$, $(1-p^{\lambda t})>0$. This condition is therefore only true if $p^{\lambda t}<c_H$. However, in this case, $p^{\lambda t}>c_H$, meaning that H prefers *Defensive* to *Negotiate*. Therefore, if $EU_{US}(x=x^*)<-\alpha$, $x'\leq 0$, & $p^{\lambda t}>c_H$, H plays *Defensive* with belief {Pr. *Attack* | *Defensive*} = $1-p^{\lambda t}$. □

**Proposition 3.4.** If $EU_{US}(x=x^*)<-\alpha$, $x'\leq 0$, $\& p^{\lambda t}<c_H$, the following constitutes a Markov perfect Bayesian equilibrium:

1. US: {x=0; *Withdraw*}
2. H: *Negotiate*
3. T: ({*Accept*; *~Attack*); *Attack*} if $c_T<1-p^{\lambda t}$ and {*~Attack*; *~Attack*} otherwise.
4. Beliefs: {Pr. *Attack* | *Negotiate*} =0; {Pr. *Attack*| *Defensive*} =$1-p^{\lambda t}$.

*Proof.* Corollary 3.3 demonstrates that if $EU_{US}(x=x^*)<-\alpha$, US sets x=x', where x'=0 if x' < 0. From Proposition 3.3, we know know that if H *Negotiate*, {Pr. *Attack* | *Negotiate*} = 0 and that {Pr. *Attack* | *Defensive*} = $1-p^{\lambda t}$. We further know that H plays *Negotiate* if $p^{\lambda t}>(1-p^{\lambda t})(p^{\lambda t}-c_H)+p^{\lambda t}\equiv 0>(1-p^{\lambda t})(p^{\lambda t}-c_H)$. If $p^{\lambda t}<c_H$, it must be true that $0>(1-p^{\lambda t})(p^{\lambda t}-c_H)$. This means that H prefers *Negotiate* to *Defensive*. US responds by playing *Withdraw*, and the {Pr. *Attack* | *Negotiate*} = 0. □

### 3.2 TESTING THE MODEL DESCRIPTION FOR CHAPTER 3

The model predicts that the provision of American military aid should prolong the survival of terrorist groups for two reasons. First, military aid gives weaker host states no incentive to negotiate and instead encourages them to play defensive strategies. This allows terrorist organizations to persist in the host state's peripheral areas and perhaps transition into insurgencies. Second, military aid may deter some terrorist groups from attacking the center of stronger host states, which could bring about their demise earlier. The empirically testable implication from the model is therefore:

**Hypothesis 3.1. The provision of U.S. military aid decreases the hazard of terrorist group collapse.**

I test this hypothesis using data from the U.S. Overseas Loans and Grants, Obligations and Loan Authorizations Greenbook (2008).[7]

Although this publication details numerous aspects of American foreign aid, I restrict the analysis to only aid that falls under the category titled Nonproliferation, Anti-terrorism, Demining, and Related Programs (NADR), which began in 1997. The NADR supports programs that use the Terrorism Interdiction Program (TIP) to "meet the evolving terrorist threat" and improve "TIP countries' efforts to interdict terrorists."[8] This program appears to best match the type of aid detailed in the model. The Greenbook provides a list of U.S. military aid disbursements aimed at fighting terrorists in each year during the period 1997–2006 in constant 2008 American dollars.

To examine if these aid programs prolong terrorist campaigns, I combine the data from the Greenbook with Jones and Libicki's (2008) dataset on the duration of terrorist campaigns. This dataset contains information on 648 groups in the period 1968–2006. Since we are only interested in how the NADR affects the duration of terrorist campaigns, we restrict the analysis to campaigns that were ongoing in 1997–2006. Additionally, since the model assumes that the U.S. is supporting a host that can substantially benefit from aid, I exclude the terrorist campaigns that were operating against major powers. The new dataset therefore consists of 184 terrorist campaigns directed against 48 host states during 1997–2006. The data from Jones and Libicki are time-invariant, meaning that the dataset examines each campaign as a single observation, rather than looking at campaign years. The analysis therefore examines each campaign as individual units of analysis.

### 3.2.1 Dependent Variable

The dependent variable is the duration until a terrorist group is defeated. Jones and Libicki identify that terrorist campaigns terminate if the group splinters or is defeated by police work.[9] I consider both of these cases to be instances in which the host disarms its group. I create a dichotomous variable labeled "Terrorist Group Collapse," which is coded as 1 if the campaign terminates from policing or with the group splintering and as 0 otherwise. In the dataset, 58 of the 184 cases (31.52%) terminated with the group's collapse.

## 3.2.2. Independent Variables

The key independent variable is the military aid provided by the U.S. to the host. I measure this in three ways. First, I use a simple dichotomous variable titled US Aid. This variable is coded as 1 if the U.S. provided any military aid to the particular host and as 0 otherwise. My expectation is that the provision of aid should decrease the hazard of terrorist group collapse.

Figure A.2 compares the ability of terrorist groups to survive against hosts that receive U.S. military aid to terrorists fighting hosts without American support using Kaplan-Meier survival curves. These curves indicate the fraction of terrorist campaigns that survive, given that the host receives or does not receive U.S. military support. We see clearly that the probability that terrorists survive is *greater* in cases where the host receives U.S. military support (dashed line) than in cases where the host receives none (solid line). While this provides support for the hypothesis that military aid prolongs terrorist campaigns, a key concern is whether this finding is robust and has the potential for endogeneity. For example, it is entirely conceivable that the reason terrorist campaigns

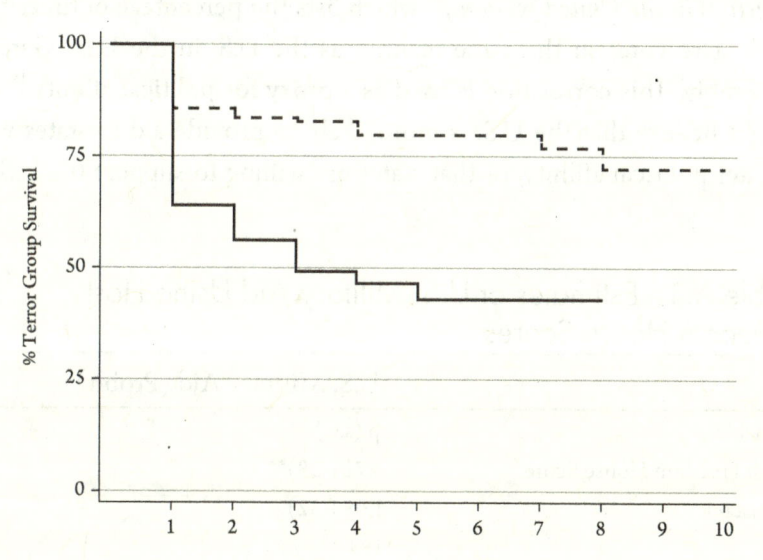

Figure A.2. Kaplan-Meier Curves Comparing Probability of Terrorist Survival in Cases Where Hosts Receive and Do Not Receive U.S. Military Aid.
Note. Solid line represents cases where US military aid =0; dashed line represents cases where US military aid =1.

go on longer in states that receive military aid is because the U.S. only chooses to fight the most difficult terrorist groups. To address the possibility for endogeneity, I create an instrumental variable using the host's Freedom House score.[10] Freedom House divides states into three groups: 0) Not Free; 1) Partially Free; and 3) Free. Using the Freedom House score as an instrument effectively handles the problem of endogeneity, in that the Freedom House measure should be correlated with military aid but uncorrelated with the length of the terrorist campaign.[11] I use a probit model to estimate the "U.S. aid" variable with the Freedom House and logged population variables. I then save the predicted probabilities as the variable "instrument U.S. aid."[12] The estimate of U.S. aid using the Freedom House scores are presented in Table A.1. The model clusters the standard errors on each host state's respective country code, given that within-host observations are probably not independent. The analysis indicates that the instrument is correlated with U.S. aid.

I use four additional control variables in the model. First, I develop a measure of affinity between the U.S. and a particular host using information from the U.S. State Department's annual report titled *Voting Practices in the United Nations*,[13] which lists the percentage of times that each state votes in the same manner as the U.S. in the U.N. General Assembly. This correlation is used as a proxy for political affinity.[14] We might believe that the U.S. is more likely to provide aid to states with greater political affinity, or that states are willing to support the U.S. in

Table A.1. Estimates of U.S. Military Aid Using Host Freedom House Scores

| Variable | U.S. Military Aid (Probit) $\beta$ (s.e.) |
|---|---|
| Host Freedom House Score | -.71 (.28)** |
| Constant | 1.08 (.32) |
| N | 184 |
| Log Likelihood | -105.15 |
| Pr. > chi$^2$ | .01 |

*p < .1; **p < .05

the U.N. in order to gain support against hostile terrorists. Second, I include the host's logged per capita GDP score for the first year of the terrorist campaign. Several studies associate higher per capita GDP scores with a more powerful and developed central government, which decreases the ability of militants to operate.[15] This variable therefore controls for the host's ability to suppress its terrorists without help from the U.S. Third, I include the logged population score for the host in the first year of the terrorist campaign as a second control variable. This variable is also included as an ancillary parameter in the tests that do not use the instrumental variable. Finally, I include the host's logged number of military personnel in the first year of the campaign to control for the militarization of the host. Each of these variables is intended to hold the baseline conditions that favor terrorism constant in order to focus on the effect of military aid on the duration of the campaign.

### 3.2.3. Results

I test the hypotheses using duration analysis (Box-Steffensmeier and Zorn 2002). The hypotheses are tested using two parametric Gompertz models (Table A.2) and two semi-parametric Cox models (Table A.3). The hazard rates are reported for ease of interpretation.

The first column in Table A.2 presents the results using the dichotomous military aid variable; the second column presents the instrumental variable results. We see that in both cases, hazard rates associated with military aid is less than 1, indicating that the provision of U.S. military aid *decreases* the hazard that terrorist groups collapse. In the first model, using the military aid dummy, the hazard of terrorist group collapse decreases by 78%, whereas the hazard decreases by 49% in the model using the instrumental variable. This demonstrates support for Hypothesis 3.1 that U.S. military support does increase the time until terrorist groups collapse.

Figure A.3 plots the predicted hazard rates from the Gompertz models both with no U.S. military aid and with military aid using the dichotomous military aid variable and the instrumental variable. In both cases, we see that with U.S. military aid, the hazard that terrorists collapse both proportionately drops and decreases throughout the

## Table A.2. Effect of U.S. Military Aid on the Duration of Terrorist Campaigns (Gompertz)

| Gompertz (Hazard Ratio) | U.S. Military Aid (0,1) | Instrument |
|---|---|---|
| Military Aid | .22 (.08)*** | .51 (.19)* |
| LN US Affinity | .58 (.15)** | .65 (.19) |
| LN per Capita GDP | .96 (.18) | 1.02 (.19) |
| LN Population | .72 (.12)* | .58 (.09)*** |
| LN Armed Force | 1.77 (.41)** | 2.04 (.42)*** |
| Constant | .06 (.16) | .32 (1.1) |
| Gamma | -.23 (.09)** | -.26 (.1)*** |
| N | 174 | 174 |
| Log Likelihood | -150.27 | -160.43 |
| Chi$^2$ | .00 | .00 |

## Table A.3. Effect of U.S. Military Aid on the Duration of Terrorist Campaigns (Cox)

| Cox (Hazard Ratio) | US Military Aid (0,1) | Instrument |
|---|---|---|
| Military Aid | .22 (.08)*** | .21 (.18)* |
| LN US Affinity | .58 (.15)** | .58 (.19)* |
| LN per Capita GDP | .97 (.18) | 1.08 (.2) |
| LN Population | .7 (.12)** | .58 (.09)*** |
| LN Armed Force | 1.95 (.45)*** | 2.3 (.48)*** |
| N | 174 | 174 |
| Log Likelihood | -260.07 | -270 |
| Chi$^2$ | .00 | .00 |

course of the campaign. These results are consistent with the prediction of Hypothesis 3.1: if the U.S. provides military aid, the U.S. decreases the probability that the terrorist campaign will terminate. This supports the model's contention that providing military aid to host states can effectively make the business of fighting terrorists quite profitable, thereby giving host states no incentive to actually terminate these conflicts. Additionally, we see that the Cox results from Table A.3 are also consistent with Hypothesis 3.1. These models estimate that the provision of U.S. military aid decreases the hazard of terrorist group collapse by 78% in the case of the dummy variable and by 79% using

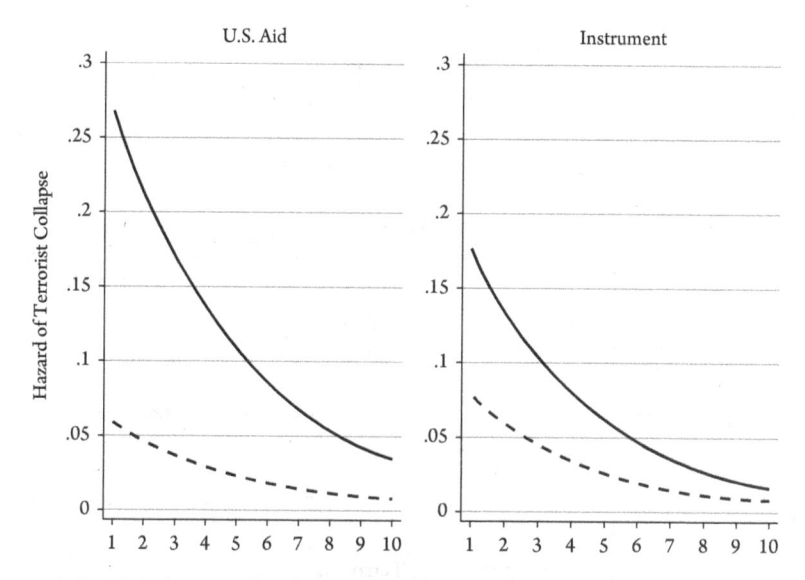

[Figure: two plots labeled "U.S. Aid" and "Instrument", y-axis "Hazard of Terrorist Collapse", x-axis 1–10]

Figure A.3. US Military Aid and Terrorist Group Survival
Note. Estimated using a survival model with a Gompertz distribution. Solid line represents hazard using dichotomous without U.S. aid variable; dashed line represents estimate with U.S. aid.

the instrument. We can therefore conclude that the results are consistent with both Hypothesis 1 and the theoretical model's empirical implications.

## 4.1 FORMAL MODEL DESCRIPTION FOR CHAPTER 4

Figure A.4 again presents the model of the strategic interaction between the U.S. (US), a host state (H) in the petrodollar system, and a hostile terrorist group (T). The key features of the model remain the same as they were in chapter 3, except here we have a war on terror with increasing cost. The game is infinitely repeated until H engages in an offensive against T, T attacks H at his center, or H and T reach a negotiated settlement. Let us again assume that H survives a direct military encounter with T with probability $p^{\lambda t} \in [0,1]$ and destabilizes in such an encounter with probability $(1-p^{\lambda t})$, and that H's probability of survival declines with time. We also know that the game transitions from state t to state t+1 with probability $\omega = 1$. This indicates that H will decline in power if the game continues and that the amount of support x US will need to provide increases as $t \to \infty$. The key difference in this version

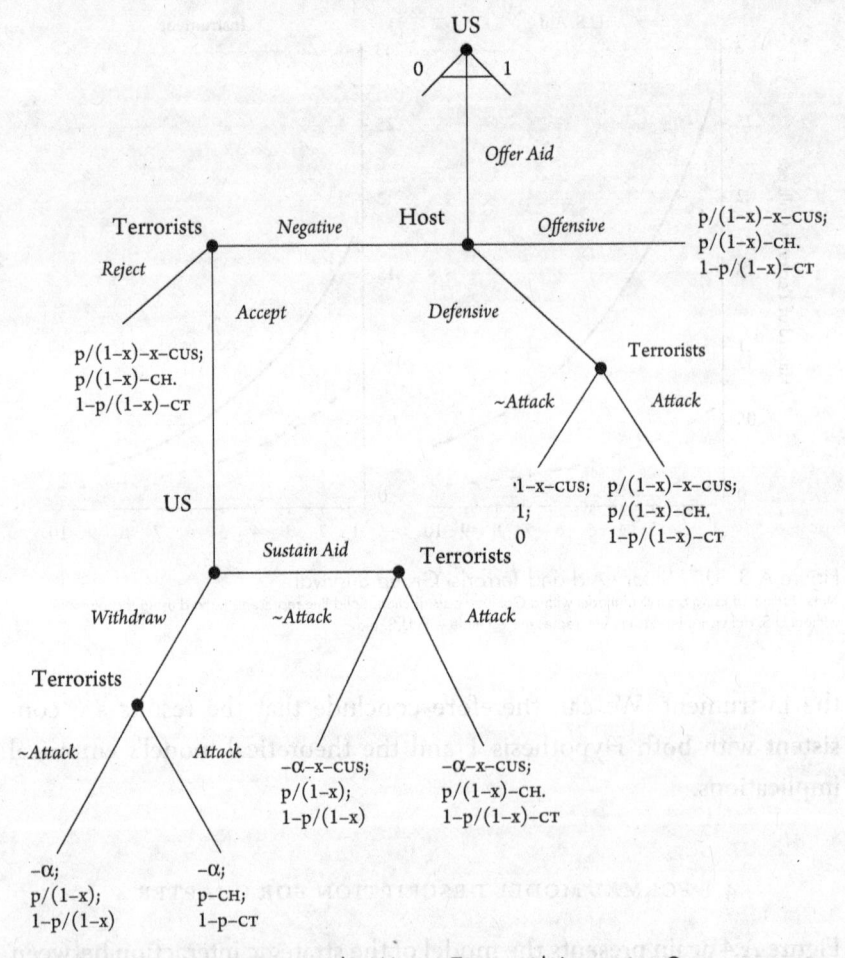

**Figure A.4. American Strategy in the War on Terror with Increasing Cost.**
Note. Each p in the model is superscripted with a λt to capture the state of the game t. Figure A.1, however, represents $p^{\lambda t}$ as p for ease of presentation.

of the game is that in addition to paying the cost of economic and military support x, US also suffers some cost if the conflict continues $c_{US} \in [0,1]$. Substantively, this cost represents the political backlash suffered by the U.S. in addition to the military strain of continuing the conflict. This mechanism of public backlash and military cost is only likely to alter U.S. behavior when the U.S. is fighting on behalf of weaker host states. It is unlikely that the U.S. public, for example, would object to American support for stable host states that would likely fight terrorists even in the absence of American support. The hosts that are likely to generate public backlash are those that face high levels of violence and appear prone to destabilization. Formally, let us therefore restrict this analysis to the cases where $p^{\lambda t} < c_H$.

**Lemma 4.1.** There are no conditions where US sets x=0 if $c_{US} = 0$.

*Proof.* US prefers setting x=0 if $(1-p^{\lambda t})(p^{\lambda t})+p^{\lambda t}-c_{US} \geq -\alpha$. Rearranging terms, we see that this expression is true if $(1-p^{\lambda t})(p^{\lambda t})+p^{\lambda t}+\alpha \geq c_{US}$. Since $\{p^{\lambda t},\alpha\} \in [0,1]$, this expression is always true if $c_{US} = 0$. □

Lemma 4.1 demonstrates that in the absence of a political cost for fighting the war on terror, the U.S. would continue to support even the weakest hosts indefinitely to protect the petrodollar system.

**Lemma 4.2.** If $c_{US} > 0$ and x' > 0, US sets x=x' if t > t*.

*Proof.* US prefers setting x=x* if $(1-p^{\lambda t})(p^{\lambda t})+p^{\lambda t}+\alpha \geq c_{US}$, but sets x = {x', 0} otherwise. The value of the left-hand side of the equation decreases as t → ∞. This demonstrates that there is a horizon at time t*. If t < t*, US setx x=x*. However, if t ≥ t*, US will set x = x' if x' > 0 and sets x=0 otherwise. We can define t* by solving $(1-p^{\lambda t})(p^{\lambda t})+p^{\lambda t}+\alpha \geq c_{US}$ for t:

$$t^* = \frac{\ln[1-\sqrt{1-c_{US}+\alpha}]}{\lambda * \ln[p]}$$

We therefore see that if t ≥ t*, $EU_{US}(x=x^*) < --$. US therefore sets x=x' since x' > 0. □

**Corollary 4.2.** If $c_{US} > 0$ and x' < 0, US sets x=0 if t > t*.

*Proof.* If t ≥ t*, $EU_{US}(x=x^*) < -\alpha$. US therefore sets x=0 since x' < 0. □

Lemma and Corollary 4.2 demonstrate that if there is a cost to continuing the war, a state t* exists where US will cease providing the optimal level of economic and military support x* to H. Instead, US reduces her military support to a lower level x'. Substantively, this is taken to mean that the U.S. adopts the light footprint if and only if x' > 0. If x' < 0, this indicates that the U.S. abandons the host completely. If x' > 0, the U.S. reduces its support for the host government and turns to local actors to protect the energy market. Examples might include the Obama administration's shift from the COIN counterinsurgency strategy in Afghanistan to a strategy with more limited aims, such as former Vice President Biden's preferred counterterrorism plus. Interestingly, the shift away from sustained and continued support for the hosts of the petrodollar system does not occur unless there is an increased political and military cost $c_{US} > 0$. This demonstrates that some public aversion to continuing the war on terror is necessary for US to reduce her support to H. If the costs of the war are minimal, the U.S. will continue providing economic and military assistance to the host states critical to supporting the petrodollar.

Let us now examine how the possibility of losing US support affects the strategic behavior of H. From previous models, we know that sudden collapses in power may motivate preemptive war (Powell 2004, 2006; Fearon 2004). In this case, the prospect of losing American support in the future may motivate host states to play *Offensive* before the U.S. reduces her support. This reduction in support would subject H to a greater risk of destabilization, which in turn may force H to negotiate with T on unappealing terms. The key question then is whether a reduction in military support from $x^*$ to $x'$ can induce H to play *Offensive* in the period prior to $t^*$ when the US will reduce her support. To address this question, let us assume that the game is played over two rounds. Assume the game begins in state $t^*-1$ and will transition to $t^*$ in the second round. This means that the first round under examination is the last period where US provides $x=x^*$. In the next round, the US will reduce her allocation of economic and military support to $x=x'$. Since we are examining how the prospect of losing support in the future affects present behavior, let us assume that each player shares a common discount factor $\cdot \in [0,1]$ for future payoffs. To further simplify the notation, define the level of support H receives in the first period as

$$p = \frac{p}{1-x^*}.$$

**Lemma 4.3.** If US will reduce her aid from $x^*$ at time $t-1$ to $x'$ at time $t$, H plays Offensive at time $t-1$ iff $\lambda > \max\{\lambda^*, \lambda^{**}\}$.

*Proof.* Suppose that H's probability of disarming T falls from $p$ at time $t-1$ to $\varphi p$ at time $t$, which implies that $p^{2\lambda} = \varphi p$. Solving for $\varphi$, we see that $\varphi = p^{2\lambda-1}$. Let us now compare H's payoff for playing *Offensive* with his payoff for playing *Defensive*. Over the two periods, $EU_H(Offensive) = p*(1+\delta(1)) - c_H$. Should H disarm T, he receives a payoff 1 in the first round, followed by a discounted payoff of 1 for the second, minus the conflict cost. On the other hand, over two periods, the $EU_H(Defensive) = (1-p)*(p-c_H) + p + \delta((1-\varphi p)*(\phi p - c_H) + \varphi p)$. H therefore prefers *Offensive* to *Defensive* if

$$p*(1+\delta(1)) - c_H > (1-p)*(p-c_H) + p + \delta((1-\varphi p)*(\phi p - c_H) + \varphi p).$$

Solving in terms of $\varphi$, we see that H is indifferent between *Offensive* and *Defensive* if $\varphi = \dfrac{\delta(2+c_H) + \sqrt{-\delta}\sqrt{4p^2 - 4p(1+c_H-\delta) - (4+c_H^2)\delta}}{2\delta p}$.

This implies that H is indifferent between *Offensive* and *Defensive* if $p^{2\lambda-1} = \dfrac{\delta(2+c_H) + \sqrt{-\delta}\sqrt{4p^2 - 4p(1+c_H-\delta) - (4+c_H^2)\delta}}{2\delta p}$.

Solving for $\lambda$, this is true if

$$\lambda = \dfrac{\ln(p) + \ln\left(\dfrac{\delta(2+c_H) + \sqrt{-\delta}\sqrt{4p^2 - 4p(1+c_H-\delta) - (4+c_H^2)\delta}}{2\delta p}\right)}{2\ln(p)}.$$

Define

$$\lambda^* = \dfrac{\ln(p) + \ln\left(\dfrac{\delta(2+c_H) + \sqrt{-\delta}\sqrt{4p^2 - 4p(1+c_H-\delta) - (4+c_H^2)\delta}}{2\delta p}\right)}{2\ln(p)}.$$

If $\lambda > \lambda^*$, H prefers playing *Offensive* to *Defensive* but prefers *Defensive* to *Offensive* otherwise. However, we must next establish that H also prefers *Offensive* to *Negotiate*. H's payoff for *Negotiate* over two rounds is equal to $(1-\varphi p)(\phi p - c_H) + \varphi p(p + \delta p)$. The different belief that T will *Attack* reflects the decision by US to *Withdraw* following H's decision to *Negotiate*. US cannot credibly commit to continuing her support for H once he compromises with T. Therefore, if T plays *Attack*, it is more likely to succeed against H without US support than in the case where H plays *Defensive*. However, if T plays ~*Attack*, H receives the payoff for the settlement he offered, which reflects his power relative to T prior to the US withdrawal. If T plays ~*Attack*, H receives a payoff of p > φp for negotiation in the first round and a discounted value of p for the second. H prefers *Offensive* to *Negotiate* over the final two rounds if $p*(1+\delta(1))-c_H > (1-\varphi p)(\varphi p - c_H)+\varphi p(p+\delta p)$.

Solving in terms of φ, H is indifferent between *Offensive* and *Negotiate* if

$$\varphi = \frac{1+c_H+p+\delta p-\sqrt{-4p(1+\delta)+(1+c_H+p+\delta p)^2}}{2p}.$$

H is therefore indifferent between *Offensive* and *Negotiate* if

$$p^{2\lambda-1} = \frac{1+c_H+p+\delta p-\sqrt{-4p(1+\delta)+(1+c_H+p+\delta p)^2}}{2p}.$$

Solving for λ, this is true if

$$\lambda = \frac{\ln(p)+\ln(\frac{1+c_H+p+\delta p-\sqrt{-4p(1+\delta)+(1+c_H+p+\delta p)^2}}{2p})}{2\ln(p)} \quad \text{D.}$$

Define

$$\lambda^{**} = \frac{\ln(p)+\ln(\frac{1+c_H+p+\delta p-\sqrt{-4p(1+\delta)+(1+c_H+p+\delta p)^2}}{2p})}{2\ln(p)}.$$

If $\lambda > \lambda^{**}$, H prefers playing *Offensive* to *Negotiate* but prefers *Negotiate* to *Offensive* otherwise. We therefore see that if $\lambda > \max\{\lambda^*, \lambda^{**}\}$, H prefers *Offensive* to both *Defensive* and *Negotiate*. This demonstrates that a weaker H is more likely to attack T in response to a weakening of US commitment, given that a decrease in US economic and military support will trigger a substantial loss in power.

# NOTES

## CHAPTER 1

1. Costs of War Project, "Costs of War," Watson Institute for International and Public Affairs, Brown University, November 2018, https://watson.brown.edu/costsofwar/figures/2018/budgetary-costs-post-911-wars-through-fy2019-59-trillion. U.S. population figure from U.S. Census Bureau estimated 2018 population for the United States.
2. John Mueller, *Overblown: How Politicians and the Terrorism Industry Inflate National Security Threats, and Why We Believe Them* (New York: Free Press, 2000).
3. Bruce Bueno de Mesquita, *The Predictioneer's Game* (New York: Random House, 2009); James D. Morrow, *Game Theory for Political Scientists* (Princeton, NJ: Princeton University Press, 1994).
4. Title 22 of the U.S. Code, section 2656f(d).

## CHAPTER 2

1. Dave Mosher and Skye Gould, "How Likely Are Foreign Terrorists to Kill Americans? The Odds May Surprise You," *Business Insider*, January 31, 2017, http://www.businessinsider.com/death-risk-statistics-terrorism-disease-accidents-2017-1.
2. See Alex P. Schmid and Albert J. Jongman, *Political Terrorism: A New Guide to Actors, Authors, Concepts, Databases, Theories, and Literature*, 2nd ed. (Abingdon: Routledge, 1988); Navin A. Bapat, "Insurgency and the Opening of Peace Processes," *Journal of Peace Research* 42, no. 6 (2005): 699–717; Audrey K. Cronin, *How Terrorism Ends: Understanding the Decline and Demise of Terrorist Campaigns* (Princeton, NJ: Princeton University Press, 2009); Khusarav Gaibulloev and Todd Sandler, "Determinants of the Demise of Terrorist Organizations," *Southern Economic Journal* 79, no. 4 (2013): 774–792; Seth Jones and Martin Libicki, *How Terrorist Groups End: Lessons for Countering al Qa'ida* (Santa Monica, CA: RAND Corporation, 2008); Brian J. Phillips, "Terrorist Group Cooperation

and Longevity," *International Studies Quarterly* 58, no. 2 (2014): 336–347; James J. F. Forest, Jarret Brachman, and Joseph Felter. *Harmony and Disharmony : Exploiting al Qa'ida's Organizational Vulnerabilities*. West Point, NY: Combating Terrorism Center, 2006. A later study examining similar themes is Jacob N. Shapiro, *The Terrorists' Dilemma: Managing Violent Covert Organizations* (Princeton, NJ: Princeton University Press, 2013).
3. Robert Gilpin, *The Political Economy of International Relations* (Princeton, NJ: Princeton University Press, 1987). Robert Keohane, *After Hegemony: Cooperation and Discord in the World Economy* (Princeton, NJ: Princeton University Press, 1984); Charles P. Kindleberger, *The World in Depression, 1929–1939* (Berkeley and Los Angeles: University of California Press, 1973); David A. Lake, "Leadership, Hegemony, and the International Economy: Naked Emperor or Tattered Monarch with Potential," *International Studies Quarterly* 37 (1993): 459–489; A. F. K. Organski and Jacek Kugler, *The War Ledger* (Chicago: University of Chicago Press, 1980).
4. Kenneth J. Arrow, *Social Choice and Individual Values* (New Haven, CT: Yale University Press, 1951); Richard D. McKelvey, "Intransitivities in Multidimensional Voting Models and Some Implications for Agenda Control," *Journal of Economic Theory* 12, no. 3 (1976): 472–482; Kenneth A. Shepsle, "Institutional Arrangements and Equilibrium in Multidimensional Voting Models," *American Journal of Political Science* 23, no. 1 (1979): 27–49.
5. G. John Ikenberry and Charles A. Kupchan, "Socialization and Hegemonic Power," *International Organization* 44, no. 3 (1990): 283–315. Bruce Russett, "The Mysterious Case of Vanishing Hegemony; or, Is Mark Twain Really Dead?" *International Organization* 39, no. 2 (1985): 207–231.
6. Andrew C. Sobel, *Birth of Hegemony: Crisis, Financial Revolution, and Emerging Global Networks* (Chicago: University of Chicago Press, 2012), 175.
7. I. C. B. Dear and M. R. D. Foot, eds., *The Oxford Companion to World War II*, (Oxford: Oxford University Press, 2002); Meredith R. Sarkees and Frank Wayman, *Resort to War 1816–2007*, (Washington DC: CQ Press, 2010). Please see Correlates of War Project (COW) v. 4, 1816–2007., n.d., http://www.correlatesofwar.org/data-sets/COW-war.
8. Robert Z. Aliber, *The New International Money Game*, 7th ed. (New York: Palgrave MacMillan, 2011); Thomas Oatley, *International Political Economy*, 5th ed. (Milton Park: Routledge, 2016).
9. An account of the Bretton Woods negotiation is presented in Benn Steil, *The Battle of Bretton Woods: John Maynard Keynes, Harry Dexter White, and the Making of a New World Order* (Princeton, NJ: Princeton University Press).
10. Michael J. Hiscox, "The Magic Bullet? The RTAA, Institutional Reform, and Trade Liberalization," *International Organization* 53, no. 4 (1999): 669–698.
11. Secretary of State George Marshall, June 5, 1947, commencement address at Harvard University. https://www.marshallfoundation.org/marshall/the-marshall-plan/marshall-plan-speech/

12. Timothy Green, "Central Bank Gold Reserves: A Historical Perspective since 1945," World Gold Council, Research Study no. 23.
13. After World War I and the successful Bolshevik Revolution in Russia, Communist parties emerged throughout Western Europe and insurgencies began in Germany, Hungary, Ireland, and Italy. Fascist movements also emerged in Germany, Austria, Spain, Poland, Romania, Croatia, and Portugal.
14. The 7.4% reduction is calculated by Arthur F. Jones and Daniel H. Weinberg. "The Changing Shape of the Nation's Income Distribution," *Current Population Reports* P60-204. U.S. Census Bureau (2000), https://www.census.gov/prod/2000pubs/p60-204.pdf. See also Claudia Goldin and Robert Margo, "The Great Compression: The Wage Structure in the United States at Mid-Century," *Quarterly Journal of Economics* 107, no. 1 (1992): 1–34.
15. Gilpin 1987; Joanne S. Gowa, *Closing the Gold Window: Domestic Politics and the End of Bretton Woods* (Ithaca, NY: Cornell University Press, 1983); Keohane 1984.
16. M. King Hubbert, "Nuclear Energy and the Fossil Fuel." *American Petroleum Institute Drilling and the Production Practice.* 1956, pp. 7–25. In this paper, the Shell geophysicist famously predicted that U.S. oil production would peak in the early 1970s and subsequently decline. Interestingly, Hubbert's prediction about "peak oil" appeared to be realized.
17. White House, Gerald R. Ford Presidential Library and Museum, "National Security Adviser, Memoranda of Conversations, 1973–1977," memorandum of conversation between President Richard Nixon, Secretary of the Treasury William Simon, and Major General Brent Scowcroft, July 9, 1974, https://www.fordlibrarymuseum.gov/library/document/0314/1552732.pdf.
18. Alan S. Blinder, "The Anatomy of Double Digit Inflation in the 1970s," in Robert E. Hall, ed., *Inflation: Causes and Effects*, 261–282 (Chicago: University of Chicago Press, 1983).
19. This follows much of the current research in international relations, in which studies using the bargaining model suggest that power is endogenous. For example, see, Robert Powell, "War as a Commitment Problem," *International Organization* 60, no. 1 (2006): 169–203; David Carter, "The Strategy of Territorial Conflict," *American Journal of Political Science* 54, no. 4 (2010): 969–987.
20. See Robert Powell, "The Inefficient Use of Power: Costly Conflict with Complete Information," *American Political Science Review* 98, no. 2 (2004): 231–241; Powell 2006; and James D. Fearon, "Rationalist Explanations for War," *International Organization* 49, no. 3 (1995): 379–414.
21. This remained true until the mid-1980s when production peaked, and the Saudis rapidly decreased the price of oil by increasing production. See Thane Gustafson, "The Origins of the Soviet Oil Crisis, 1970–1985," *Soviet Economy* 1, no. 2 (1985): 103–135.
22. White House, July 9, 1974.

23. White House, Gerald R. Ford Presidential Library and Museum, "National Security Adviser, Memoranda of Conversations, 1973–1977," memorandum of conversation between President Nixon, Secretary of the Treasury William Simon, Assistant to the President Kenneth Rush, and Deputy Assistant to the President for National Security Affairs Brent Scowcroft, July 30, 1974, https://www.fordlibrarymuseum.gov/library/document/0314/1552737.pdf.
24. Andrea Wong, "The Untold Story behind Saudi Arabia's 41-Year U.S. Debt Secret," Bloomberg News, May 30, 2016, https://www.bloomberg.com/news/features/2016-05-30/the-untold-story-behind-saudi-arabia-s-41-year-u-s-debt-secret.
25. Andrew Scott Cooper, *The Oil Kings: How the U.S., Iran, and Saudi Arabia Changed the Balance of Power in the Middle East* (New York: Simon and Schuster, 2011), 230–237.
26. Cooper 2011, 230–237.
27. Not only did the Shah oversee a more liberal government but he also did not join the original boycott, which appeared to increase his credibility with the three. Nixon and Kissinger also believed that the Shah was a stronger ally against the Soviets and radical forces throughout the Middle East.
28. White House, July 30, 1974.
29. White House, Gerald R. Ford Presidential Library and Museum, "National Security Adviser, Memoranda of Conversations, 1973–1977," memorandum of conversation between President Gerald Ford, Secretary of State Henry Kissinger, and Shah of Iran Mohammad Reza Pahlavi, May 15, 1975, https://www.fordlibrarymuseum.gov/library/document/0314/1553077.pdf. The plan involved a joint operation involving Iran and Egypt.
30. U.S. Department of Agriculture Economic Research Service, Data from the International Macroeconomic Data Set, http://www.ers.usda.gov/data-products/international-macroeconomic-data-set.aspx#.UfZngiPlX34.
31. B. Zahlungsausgleich, "Triennial-Central Bank Survey-Report on Global Foreign exchange market activity in 2010." *The Bank for International Settlements* (2010). Available at: www.bis.org/publ/rpfxf10t.pdf.
32. Although the bursting of the real estate bubble in 2008 and the following crash of the stock market in 2009 certainly appeared to harm the U.S. economy, the subsequent financial crises in Europe and other areas of the world appear to have caused investors to double down on U.S. investments. Indeed, the U.S. share of world banking markets appears to have *increased* since the financial crisis rather than decreasing, which again signals that the attractiveness of the U.S. market is high. Additionally, despite several years of quantitative easing by the Federal Reserve, demand for U.S. bonds remains stable, further supporting the idea that the U.S. market remains an attractive place for investment. The financial crisis will be discussed in greater detail in later chapters.
33. William K. Winecoff, "Financial Power and the Global Crisis," PhD diss., University of North Carolina–Chapel Hill.

34. Jonathan Kirshner, "Dollar Primacy and American Power: What's at Stake?" *Review of International Political Economy* 15, no. 3 (2008): 418–438.
35. David A. Lake, *Entangling Relations: American Foreign Policy in Its Century* (Princeton, NJ: Princeton University Press, 1999).
36. Figure from Marc Auboin, "Use of Currencies in International Trade: Any Changes in the Picture?" *Working Paper*, (World Trade Organization Economic Research and Statistics Division, 2012). Available at: https://www.wto.org/english/res_e/reser_e/ersd201210_e.pdf.
37. President Bill Clinton, State of the Union Address, January 27, 2000, http://www.presidency.ucsb.edu/ws/?pid=58708.
38. The rise of China posed another potential security challenge. This threat did not appear acute at the turn of the millennium, though it would certainly become more relevant as the war on terror progressed. The later part of the argument in this book explores how competition for markets with China is currently working to continue the war on terror.
39. Bob Dudley, British Petroleum Statistical Review of World Energy, 68th edition, 2019, http://www.bp.com/en/global/corporate/energy-economics/statistical-review-of-world-energy.html.
40. Information according to the Correlates of War Dataset. See Meredith R. Sarkees and Frank Wayman, *Resort to War 1816–2007*, (Washington DC: CQ Press, 2010). Data available from Correlates of War Project (COW) v. 4, 1816–2007., n.d., http://www.correlatesofwar.org.
41. Steve Coll, *Ghost Wars: The Secret History of the CIA, Afghanistan, and bin Laden, from the Soviet Invasion to September 10, 2001* (New York: Penguin, 2004).
42. See Mahmoud A. El-Gamal and Amy Myers Jaffe, *Oil, Dollars, Debt, and Crises* (Cambridge: Cambridge University Press, 2010), 66
43. El-Gamal and Jaffe 2010.
44. El-Gamal and Jaffe 2010.
45. Source: U.S. Energy Information Administration (February 2017).
46. Bin Laden interview with *Frontline* correspondent Josh Miller, May 1998, https://www.pbs.org/wgbh/pages/frontline/shows/binladen/who/interview.html.
47. Stathis Kalyvas, *The Logic of Violence in Civil War* (Cambridge: Cambridge University Press, 2006); Stathis Kalyvas and Matthew Kocher, "How 'Free' Is Free-Riding in Civil Wars? Violence, Insurgency, and the Collective Action Problem." *World Politics* 59, no. 2 (2007): 177–216; Laia Balcells, *Rivalry and Revenge: The Politics of Violence during Civil Wars* (Cambridge: Cambridge University Press, 2017).
48. For example, on September 8, 2002, U.S. National Security Advisor Condoleeza Rice famously stated, "We don't want the smoking gun to be a mushroom cloud." Four days later, in his speech to the U.N. General Assembly on September 12, 2002, President George W. Bush stated, "The first time we may be completely certain he has nuclear weapons is when, God forbids, he uses one."

49. Information on attacks and fatalities from National Consortium for the Study of Terrorism and Responses to Terrorism (START). 2018. Global Terrorism Database [Data file]. Retrieved from https://www.start.umd.edu/gtd.
50. See United States Department of State, *Patterns of Global Terrorism 2002*, https://www.state.gov/j/ct/rls/crt/2002/pdf/index.htm.

# CHAPTER 3

1. James Fearon and David Laitin, "Ethnicity, Insurgency, and Civil War," *American Political Science Review* 97, no. 1 (2003): 75–90; Håvard Hegre and Nicholas Sambanis, "Sensitivity Analysis of Empirical Results on Civil War Onset," *Journal of Conflict Resolution* 50, no. 4 (2006): 508–535.
2. President George W. Bush, Remarks to the George C. Marshall ROTC Award Seminar on National Security, Virginia Military Institute, Lexington, Virginia, April 17, 2002, https://georgewbush-whitehouse.archives.gov/news/releases/2002/04/20020417-1.html.
3. Brian L. Steed, ed. *Voices of the Iraq War* (Santa Barbara:, CA: Greenwood Press, 2016), pp. 58–61.
4. U.S. State Department, "National Strategy for Combating Terrorism," February 2003, 15–22, https://2001-2009.state.gov/s/ct/rls/wh/71803.htm.
5. Amy Belasco, "The Cost of Iraq, Afghanistan, and Other Global War on Terror Operations since 9/11," *Congressional Research Service*, Document no. 7-5700 RL33110, March 29, 2011, http://www.fas.org/sgp/crs/natsec/RL33110.pdf.
6. James D. Fearon and David Laitin, "Neotrusteeship and the Problem of Weak States." *International Security* 28, no. 4 (2004): 5–43.
7. For example, see James A. Piazza, "Incubators of Terror: Do Failed and Failing States Promote Transnational Terrorism?" *International Studies Quarterly* 52, no. 3 (2008): 469–488. See also Navin A. Bapat, "The Internationalization of Terrorist Campaigns," *Conflict Management and Peace Science* 24, no. 4 (2007): 265–280.
8. The Greenbook provides data on U.S. military aid disbursements through various programs during the period FY1946–FY2008. Data from https://explorer.usaid.gov/reports
9. Data from Seth G. Jones and Martin C. Libicki. *How Terrorist Groups End: Lessons for Countering Al Qa'ida*. Santa Monica: RAND Corporation, 2008. The dataset contains information on 648 groups from 1968–2006. Since I am focusing on the effect of counterterrorism assistance, I examine only the aid that is part of the Nonproliferation, Anti-terrorism, Demining and Related Programs (NADR) account. This program began in 1997, so the analysis is restricted to campaigns that were ongoing between 1997–2006. Additionally, since the model assumes that U.S. military support substantially improves the capacity of host states to fight their terrorists, the analysis excludes campaigns against major powers, such as the Provisional Irish Republican Army's campaign in Northern Ireland.

10. The duration analysis is performed with two Gompertz models and two Cox models, each using instrumental variables.
11. Bruce Bueno de Mesquita and Alastair Smith, "Foreign Aid and Policy Concessions," *Journal of Conflict Resolution* 51, no. 2 (2007): 251–284; David L. Cingranelli and Thomas E. Pasquarello, "Human Rights Practices and the Distribution of US Foreign Aid to Latin American Countries," *American Journal of Political Science* 29, no. 3 (1985): 539–563; James M. McCormick and Neil Mitchell, "Is US Aid Really Linked to Human Rights in Latin America?" *American Journal of Political Science* 32, no. 1 (1988): 231–239;, James Meernik, Eric L. Krueger, and Steven C. Poe, "Testing Models of US Foreign Policy: Foreign Aid during and after the Cold War," *Journal of Politics* 60, no. 1 (1998): 63–85; Steven C. Poe, "Human Rights and US Foreign Aid: A Review of Quantitative Studies and Suggestions for Future Research," *Human Rights Quarterly* 12 (1990): 499–512.
12. Navin A. Bapat, "Transnational Terrorism, U.S. Military Aid, and the Incentive to Misrepresent," *Journal of Peace Research* 48, no. 3 (2011): 303–318; Andrew Boutton and David Carter, "Fair Weather Allies? Terrorism and the Allocation of U.S. Foreign Aid," *Journal of Conflict Resolution* 58, no. 7 (2014): 1144–1173; Tiberiu Dragu, "The Moral Hazard of Terrorism Prevention," *Journal of Politics* 79, no. 1 (2017): 223–236.
13. See Freedom House, *Freedom in the world 2010: The Annual Survey of Political Rights and Civil Liberties.* Rowman & Littlefield and Amnesty International. *Amnesty International Report: The State of the World's Human Rights.* London: Amnesty International Publications, 2010.
14. Jean-Paul Azam and Alexandra Delacroix, "Aid and the Delegated Fight against Terrorism," *Review of Development Economics* 10, no. 2 (2006): 330–344; Subhayu Bandyopadhyay, Todd Sandler, and Javed Younas, "Foreign Direct Investment, Aid, and Terrorism." *Oxford Economic Papers* 66, no. 1 (2013): 25–50; Walter Enders and Todd Sandler, *The Political Economy of Terrorism* (Cambridge: Cambridge University Press, 2006).
15. Ethan Bueno de Mesquita, "Conciliation, Counterterrorism, and Patterns of Terrorist Violence." *International Organization* 59, no. 1 (2005): 145–176; Kalyvas 2006; Reed M. Wood, Jacob D. Kathman, and Stephen E. Gent, "Armed Intervention and Civilian Victimization in Intrastate Conflicts," *Journal of Peace Research* 49, no. 5 (2012): 647–660.
16. Max Abrahams, "What Terrorists Really Want: Terrorist Motives and Counterterrorism Strategy," *International Security* 32, no. 4 (2008): 78–105; Bryan Caplan, "Terrorism: The Relevance of the Rational Choice Model," *Public Choice* 128, no. (2006): 91–107.
17. Ethan Bueno de Mesquita, "A Political Economy of Terrorism: A Selected View of Recent Work," unpublished manuscript, University of Chicago, 2008; Enders and Sandler 2006; Shapiro 2013.
18. The term 'Shi'ite' refers to individuals practicing the faith of Shi'a Islam, whereas the term 'Shi'a' refers to a collective practicing the faith, or a group of Shi'ites.
19. Navin A. Bapat, "State Bargaining with Transnational Terrorist Groups," *International Studies Quarterly* 50, no. 1 (2006): 213–229; Bueno de

Mesquita 2005; Barbara F. Walter, *Committing to Peace: The Successful Settlement of Civil Wars* (Princeton, NJ: Princeton University Press, 2002).
20. Ngozi Okonjo-Iweala and Philip Osafo-Kwaako, "Nigeria's Economic Reforms: Progress and Challenges," Brookings Global Economy and Development. Working Paper no. 6, 2007. Available at: https://papers.ssrn.com/sol3/papers.cfm?abstract_id=1080251.
21. The death toll for this incident, known as the Odi massacre, was forty-three according to the Nigerian military, but Human Rights Watch places the figure at 2,500 civilians. See http://pantheon.hrw.org/legacy/press/1999/dec/nibg1299.htm.

## CHAPTER 4

1. Civil wars are defined as armed conflicts between a government and a non-state actor that produces at least one thousand fatalities. See Fearon and Laitin 2003;Nils Petter Gleditsch, Peter Wallensteen, Mikael Eriksson, Margareta Sollenberg, and Håvard Strand, "Armed Conflict 1946–2001: A New Dataset," *Journal of Peace Research* 39, no. 5 (2002): 615–637; Nicholas Sambanis, "What Is a Civil War?" *Journal of Conflict Resolution* 48, no. 6 (2004): 814–858; Melvin Small and J. David Singer, *Resort to Arms: International and Civil War, 1816–1980* (Beverly Hills, CA: Sage, 1982).
2. Congressional Budget Office, "Recruiting, Retention, and Future Levels of U.S. Military Personnel," 2006, https://www.cbo.gov/sites/default/files/109th-congress-2005-2006/reports/10-05-recruiting.pdf.
3. In addition to the key issue of maintaining the petrodollar, an alternative, complementary argument centers on leader accountability. Since Bush started the war, he was ultimately culpable for its outcome, giving him a disincentive to terminate it on unfavorable terms. For a full presentation of this argument, see Sarah E. Croco, *Peace at What Price? Leaders and the Domestic Politics of War Termination* (Cambridge: Cambridge University Press, 2015).
4. Michael Spence and Richard Zeckhauser, "Insurance, Information, and Individual Action," *American Economic Review* 61, no. 2 (1971): 380–381; Steven Shavell, "Risk Sharing and Incentives in the Principal and Agent Relationship," *Bell Journal of Economics* 10, no. 1 (1979): 55–73; George W. Downs and David M. Rocke, "Conflict, Agency, and Gambling for Resurrection: The Principal-Agent Problem Goes to War," *American Journal of Political Science* 38, no. 2 (1994): 362–380; Gary J. Miller, "The Political Evolution of Principal-Agent Models," *Annual Review of Political Science* 8 (2005): 203–225.
5. Bengt Holmstrom, "Moral Hazard and Observability," *Bell Journal of Economics* 10, no. 1 (1979): 74–91.
6. Barry R. Weingast and Mark J. Moran, "Bureaucratic Discretion or Congressional Control? Regulatory Policymaking by the F.E.C.," *Journal of Political Economy* 91, no. 5 (1983): 765–800; Andrew B. Whitford, "Decentralization and Political Control of the Bureaucracy," *Journal of Theoretical Politics* 14, no. 2 (2002): 167–194; Dan B. Wood, "Principal,

Bureaucrats, and Responsiveness in Clean Air Enforcement," *American Political Science Review* 82, no. 1 (1988): 213–234.
7. Navin A. Bapat, Luis de la Calle, Kaisa Hinkkainen, and Elena McClean, "Economic Sanctions, Transnational Terrorism, and the Incentive to Misrepresent," *Journal of Politics* 78, no. 1 (2016); Nikolay Marinov, "Do Economic Sanctions Destabilize Country Leaders?" *American Journal of Political Science* 49, no. 3 (2005): 564–576; Fiona McGillivray and Allan Stam, "Political Institutions, Coercive Diplomacy, and the Duration of Sanctions," *Journal of Conflict Resolution* 48, no. 2 (2004): 154–172.
8. Ramon P. DeGennaro, "Market Imperfections," *Journal of Financial Transformation* 14 (2005): 107–117; Bruce C. Greenwald and Joseph E. Stiglitz, "Financial Market Imperfections and Business Cycles," *Quarterly Journal of Economics* 108, no. 1 (1993): 77–114.
9. Elena V. McLean, Kaisa Hinkkainen, Luis de la Calle, and Navin A. Bapat, "Economic Sanctions and the Dynamics of Terrorist Campaigns," *Conflict Management and Peace Science* 35, no, 4 (2018): 378–401; Piazza 2008.
10. Fearon 1995; Powell 2006; Dan Reiter, "Exploring the Bargaining Model of War," *Perspectives on Politics* 1, no. 1 (2003): 27–43; R. Harrison Wagner, "Bargaining and War," *American Journal of Political Science* 44, no. 3 (2000): 469–484.
11. Croco 2015.
12. Morris P. Fiorina, *Retrospective Voting in American National Elections* (New Haven, CT: Yale University Press, 1981); Bruce Bueno de Mesquita, Alastair Smith, Randolph Siverson, and James Morrow, *The Logic of Political Surivval* (Cambridge, MA: MIT Press, 2005); Scott S. Gartner and Gary Segura, "War, Casualties, and Public Opinion," *Journal of Conflict Resolution* 42, no. 3 (1998): 278–300; Chris F. Gelpi, Peter D. Feaver, and Jason Reifler, "Iraq the Vote: Retrospective and Prospective Foreign Policy Judgments on Candidate Choice and Casualty Tolerance," *Political Behavior* 29, no. 2 (2007): 151–174; Chris F. Gelpi, Peter D. Feaver, and Jason Reifler, *Paying the Human Costs of War* (Princeton, NJ: Princeton University Press, 2009); Kenneth A. Schultz, *Democracy and Coercive Diplomacy* (Cambridge: Cambridge University Press, 2001).
13. Gelpi et al. 2009; Scott S. Gartner, "The Multiple Effects of Casualties on Public Support for War: An Experimental Approach," *American Political Science Review* 102, no. 1 (2008): 95–106.
14. Samuel Popkin, *The Reasoning Voter* (Chicago: University of Chicago Press, 1991); Adam J. Berinsky, "Assuming the Costs of War: Events, Elites, and American Public Support for Military Conflict," *Journal of Politics* 69, no. 4 (2007): 975–997; Elizabeth N. Saunders, "War and the Inner Circle: Democratic Elites and the Politics of Using Force," *Security Studies* 24, no. 3 (2015): 466–501.
15. Lake 1999; Brett Ashley Leeds, "Do Alliances Deter Aggression? The Influence of Military Alliances on the Initiation of Militarized Interstate Disputes," *American Journal of Political Science* 47, no. 3 (2003): 427–439;

James D. Morrow, "Alliances: Why Write Them Down?" *Annual Review of Political Science* 3 (2000): 63–83.
16. William G. Howell and Jon C. Pevehouse, *While Dangers Gather: Congressional Checks on Presidential War Powers* (Princeton, NJ: Princeton University Press, 2007).
17. Thomas Schelling, *The Strategy of Conflict* (Cambridge, MA: Harvard University Press, 1960).
18. Schelling 1960.
19. Bob Woodward, *The War Within: A Secret White House History, 2006–2008* (New York: Simon and Schuster), 163.
20. David Cloud and Greg Jaffe, *The Fourth Star: Four Generals and the Epic Struggle for the Future of the United States Army* (New York: Crown, 2009); Stephen B. Dyson, "George W. Bush, the Surge, and Presidential Leadership," *Political Science Quarterly* 125, no. 4 (2010): 557–585.
21. Michael R. Gordon and Bernard E. Trainor, *The Endgame: The Inside Story of the Struggle for Iraq* (New York: Pantheon, 2012); Michael R. Gordon, "The Secret Surge Debate," *Foreign Policy*, March 18, 2013, https://foreignpolicy.com/2013/03/18/the-secret-surge-debate/; C. Christine Fair, "False Choices in Afghanistan," *Foreign Policy*, January 11, 2011, https://foreignpolicy.com/2011/01/11/false-choices-in-afghanistan/; Seth G. Jones, "Going Local: The Key to Afghanistan," August 8, 2009, https://www.rand.org/blog/2009/08/going-local-the-key-to-afghanistan.html.
22. Navin A. Bapat, "Terrorism, Democratization, and U.S. Foreign Policy," *Public Choice* 149, nos. 3–4 (2011): 315–335; Navin A. Bapat, "The Escalation of Terrorism: Microlevel Violence and Interstate Conflict," *International Interactions* 40, no. 4 (2014): 568–578; Navin A. Bapat and Sean Zeigler, "Terrorism, Dynamic Commitment Problems, and Military Conflict," *American Journal of Political Science* 60, no. 2 (2016): 337–351.
23. Gordon and Trainor 2012, 31.
24. Michael R. Gordon, "The Secret Surge Debate," *Foreign Policy*, March 18, 2013, https://foreignpolicy.com/2013/03/18/the-secret-surge-debate/.
25. Formally, the host's ability to resist destabilization p has declined to $p^t$. This indicates that the host will receive less in a power-sharing agreement in the second round than if it had negotiated a power sharing agreement in the first $(p > p^t)$.
26. See November 29, 2006, memo by National Security Advisor Stephen Hadley to National Security Council, http://www.nytimes.com/2006/11/29/world/middleeast/29mtext.html?pagewanted=alhttp://www.nytimes.com/2006/world/middleeast/29mtext.html?pagewanted=all.
27. Woodward 2008, 175.
28. According to National Security Advisor Stephen Hadley, Secretary of State Condoleezza Rice told Maliki in a meeting, "You are failing." Maliki responded, "I feel it too. What should I do?" Hadley interpreted this to mean that Maliki recognized the severity of his situation and his

willingness to comply with American demands. For information about the political trouble this caused for Maliki's ruling coalition, see http://www.washingtonpost.com/wp-dyn/content/article/2006/11/29/AR2006112901624.html.

29. All Iraq fatality data from Iraq Body Count (IBC), https://www.iraqbodycount.org/database/.
30. Cordesman 2008.
31. See Gordon and Trainor 2012.
32. Stephen Biddle, Jeffrey A. Friedman, and Jacob N. Shapiro, "Testing the Surge: Why Did Violence Decline in Iraq in 2007?" *International Security* 37, no. 1 (2012): 7–40.
33. Shailagh Murray, "Symbolic Measure to End War Voted Down 67 to 29 in Senate," *Washington* Post, A03, 17 May 2007. Available at: http://www.washingtonpost.com/wp-dyn/content/article/2007/05/16/AR2007051600708.html.
34. Joshua Thiel and Joyce Hogan, "The Statistical Irrelevance of American SIGACT data: Iraq Surge Analysis Reveals Reality," Monterray, CA: Naval Postgraduate School, 2011.
35. BBC News, "Sadr 'Freezes' Militia Activities," 29 August 2007, Available at: http://news.bbc.co.uk/2/hi/middle_east/6968720.stm. See also Aymen Jawad, "Assessing the Surge in Iraq," *Middle East Review of International Affairs* 15, no. 4 (2011): 26–38.
36. Data on Awakening Councils from Biddle, Friedman, and Shapiro 2012.
37. Consistent with the model, the Sunnis who cooperated against al Qaeda received marginal, if any, political concessions from Maliki's government. According to Patrick Cockburn's (2008) analysis, the Shi'a government was "prepared to accommodate the Sunni, but not at the cost of diluting Shia dominance." See Patrick Cockburn, "Violence is down—but not because of America's 'Surge,'" *The Independent on Sunday*, 14 September 2008. Retrieved from http://libproxy.lib.unc.edu/login?url=https://search-proquest-com.libproxy.lib.unc.edu/docview/337049336?accountid=14244.
38. Ali Khedery, "Why We Stuck with Maliki—and Lost Iraq," *Washington Post*, July 3, 2014, https://www.washingtonpost.com/opinions/why-we-stuck-with-maliki--and-lost-iraq/2014/07/03/0dd6a8a4-f7ec-11e3-a606-946fd632f9f1_story.html?utm_term=.107c987e0d42.
39. Stephen Farrell and Ammar Karim, "Drive in Basra by Iraqi Army Makes Gains: Control called Fragile Despite Optimism." *The New York Times*, A1, 12 May 2008. Retrieved from http://libproxy.lib.unc.edu/login?url=https://search-proquest-com.libproxy.lib.unc.edu/docview/897147443?accountid=14244.
40. Khedery 2014.
41. Jon Boone, "Wikileaks Cables Portray Hamid Karzai as Corrupt and Erratic," *The Guardian*, 2 December 2010. Cable available at: https://www.theguardian.com/world/us-embassy-cables-documents/181930.

42. It is therefore possible to interpret the shift in behavior to a change in the presidency from Bush to Obama. However, if we examine the data systematically, we see that Obama's policies appear consistent with Bush's, indicating that U.S. strategic behavior is driven by shifts external to the presidency.
43. Ahmed Rashid, "How Obama Lost Karzai" *Foreign Policy,* Issue 185, March 2011. Available at: http://foreignpolicy.com/2011/02/21/how-obama-lost-karzai-2/.
44. Bob Woodward, *Obama's Wars* (New York: Simon and Schuster, 2010), 279.
45. Amir Shah and Christopher Bodeen, "Karzai Warns He Might Join the Taliban?" Associated Press, *Daily Herald,* p. 9, 6 April 2010.
46. Margaret Warner, "Karzai on Firing Corrupt Officials: 'We Have and We Will.'" *Public Broadcasting Service,* 9 November 2009. Available at: https://www.pbs.org/newshour/show/karzai-on-firing-corrupt-officials-we-have-and-we-will
47. Robert Gates, *Duty: Memoirs of a Secretary at War* (New York: Vintage, 2015).
48. Barack H. Obama, "Remarks by the President on a New Strategy for Afghanistan and Pakistan." 27 March 2009. Available at: https://obamawhitehouse.archives.gov/the-press-office/remarks-president-a-new-strategy-afghanistan-and-pakistan
49. Steve Coll, "The Unblinking Stare," *The New Yorker* 90(37), p. 98.
50. See UN Report of the Secretary General, "The Situation in Afghanistan and Its Implications for International Peace and Security," https://unama.unmissions.org/sites/default/files/SG_Report_to_Security_Council_March_2011_0.pdf.
51. Barack H. Obama, "Osama Bin Laden Dead," 2 May 2011. Speech available at: https://obamawhitehouse.archives.gov/blog/2011/05/02/osama-bin-laden-dead
52. Mark Landler, "The Afghan War and the Evolution of Obama," *New York Times,* 1 January 2017.
53. Tim Craig and Sayed Salahuddin, "Karzai Rejects Call for Quick Decision on U.S. Troop Agreement," *Washington Post,* 22 November 2013.
54. Landler, 2017.
55. Peter D. Feaver, "Right to Be Right: Civil-Military Relations and the Iraq Surge Decision," *International Security* 35, no. 4 (2011): 87–125.
56. Thomas Oatley, William Kindred Winecoff, Andrew Pennock, and Sarah Baurle Danzman, "The Political Economy of Global Finance," *Perspectives on Politics* 11, no. 1 (2013): 133–153.
57. For a discussion of the Greek financial crisis, see Stathis Kalyvas, *Modern Greece: What Everyone Needs to Know* (Oxford: Oxford University Press, 2015).
58. http://ec.Europa.eu/Eurostat/statistics-explained/index.php/Unemployment_statistics.
59. "A New Beginning," June 4, 2009, Cairo University; full text at http://www.nytimes.com/2009/06/04/us/politics/04obama.text.html.

## CHAPTER 5

1. Lally Weymouth, "In Rare Interview, Egyptian General has Harsh Words for U.S", *The Washington Post*, 2013. Available at: https://www.washingtonpost.com/world/middle_east/rare-interview-with-egyptian-gen-abdel-fatah-al-sissi/2013/08/03/a77eb37c-fbc4-11e2-a369-d1954abcb7e3_story.html?utm_term=.8550a7a4aa9c.
2. Ben Hubbard and Nicholas Kulish, "Obama to Visit a Saudi Arabia Deep in Turmoil", *The New York Times*, 2016, pp. A1.
3. This motivation was discussed in a leaked memo between Secretary of State Hillary Clinton and her political aide Sidney Blumenthal; see: U.S. Department of State Case No. F-2014-20439 Doc No. C05779612 Date: 12/31/2015, Available at: https://www.foreignpolicyjournal.com/wp-content/uploads/2016/01/110402-France-client-gold-State-Dept.pdf.
4. Michael Hastings, "Inside Obama's War Room," *Rolling Stone*, no. 1142, 2011, pp. 47–52.
5. Once the U.S. and its allies intervened, the rebels created a new central bank and oil company that would conduct oil sales in U.S. dollars; see Bloomberg News, "Libyan Rebels Form Own Oil Company: Nation Pumping Less than a Third as Much as before Unrest," *Lincoln Journal Star*, 2011. Also see: http://www.cnbc.com/id/42308613; http://www.reuters.com/article/us-libya-oil-rebels-idUSTRE72R6X620110328.
6. Ralph Sundberg, Kristine Eck, and Joakim Kreutz, "Introducing the UCDP Non-State Conflict Dataset," *Journal of Peace Research* 49, no. 2 (2012): 351–362; Erik Melander, Therése Pettersson, and Lotta Themenér, "Organized Violence, 1989–2015," *Journal of Peace Research* 53, no. 5 (2016): 727–742..
7. Remarks by President Obama to the White House Press Corps, August 20, 2012; see https://obamawhitehouse.archives.gov/the-press-office/2012/08/20/remarks-president-white-house-press-corps.
8. Amena Bakr and Warren Strobel, "Saudi Arabia/Syria/Iran/United States: Saudi Arabia Warns of Shift Away from US Over Syria, Iran," *Asia News Monitor*, 2013.
9. Jeffrey Goldberg, "The Obama Doctrine," *The Atlantic* 317(3): 70–90, 2016.
10. Goldberg 2016.
11. Melander et. al. 2016; Gleditsch et al. 2002.
12. Max Weber, *Politics as a Vocation*. Munich: Duncker and Humblodt, 1919.
13. David B. Carter and Hein Goemans, "The Making of Territorial Order: New Borders and the Emergence of Interstate Conflict," *International Organization* 65, no. 2 (2011): 275–309; R. Harrison Wagner, *War and the State: The Theory of International Politics* (Ann Arbor: Michigan, 2007).
14. Daron Acemoglu, Simon Johnson, and James Robinson, "The Colonial Origins of Comparative Development," *American Economic Review* 91, no. 5 (2001): 1369–1401; Michael Bernhard, Christopher Reenock, and Timothy Nordstrom, "The Legacy of Western Overseas Colonialism on Democratic Survival," *International Studies Quarterly* 48, no. 1

(2004): 225–250; Pierre Englebert, *State Legitimacy and Development in Africa* (Boulder: Lynne Reinner, 2000); Douglas Lemke and Jeff Carter. "Birth Legacies, State Making, and War," *Journal of Politics* 78, no. 2 (2016): 497–511.
15. Jeffrey Herbst, *States and Power in Africa: Comparative Lessons in Authority and Control* (Princeton, NJ: Princeton University Press, 2014).
16. Jørgen Anderson and Silje Alsaksen, "Oil and Political Survival," *Journal of Developmental Economics* 100, no. 1 (2013): 89–106; Bruce Bueno de Mesquita and Alastair Smith, "Leader Survival, Revolutions, and the Nature of Government Finance," *American Journal of Political Science* 54, no. 4 (2010): 936–950; Jesus Crespo Cuaresma, Harald Oberofer, and Paul Raschky, "Oil and the Duration of Dictatorships," *Public Choice* 148, no. 3 (2010): 505–530; Luc Désiré Omgba, "On the Duration of Political Power in Africa: The Role of Oil Rents," *Comparative Political Studies* 42, no. 3 (2009): 416–436; Kristopher W. Ramsay, "Revisiting the Resource Curse: Natural Disasters, the Price of Oil, and Democracy," *International Organization* 65, no. 3 (2011): 507–529; Michael Ross, *The Oil Curse: How Petroleum Wealth Shapes the Development of Nations* (Princeton, NJ: Princeton University Press, 2013).
17. Cullen Hendrix and Marcus Noland, *Confronting the Curse: The Economics and Politics of Natural Resource Governance* (New York: Columbia University Press, 2014).
18. Kalyvas 2006; Jeremy Weinstein, *Inside Rebellion: The Politics of Insurgent Violence* (Cambridge: Cambridge University Press, 2007).
19. Luis De la Calle, and Ignacio Sánchez-Cuenca, "Rebels without a Territory: An Analysis of Nonterritorial Conflicts in the World, 1970–1997," *Journal of Conflict Resolution* 56, no. 4 (2012): 580–603; Zachariah Cherian Mampilly, *Rebel Rulers: Insurgent Governance and Civilian Life during War* (Ithaca, NY: Cornell University Press, 2011).
20. Bapat and Zeigler 2016.
21. Fearon and Laitin 2003; Cullen S. Hendrix, "Head for the Hills? Rough Terrain, State Capacity, and Civil War Onset," *Civil Wars* 13, no. 4 (2011): 345–370.
22. The slow seizure of territory by terrorists is referred to as a salami tactic because of the analogy to slicing sausage. When sausage is sliced, small pieces are cut off, but the bulk of the sausage appears to remain. However, as small pieces are gradually sliced off, eventually, the entire sausage disappears. In this case, terrorists slowly destabilize villages or towns, which gradually leads to a loss of the entire territory. James D. Fearon, "Bargaining over Objects that Influence Future Power," unpublished manuscript, University of Chicago, 1996; Robert Powell, "Uncertainty, Shifting Power, and Appeasement," *American Political Science Review* 90, no. 4 (1996): 749–764; Powell 2006; Thomas Schelling, *Arms and Influence* (New Haven, CT: Yale University Press, 1966).
23. Bapat 2014; Bapat and Zeigler 2016.

24. Daniel Byman, Peter Chalk, Bruce Hoffman, William Rosenau, and David Brannan, *Trends in Outside Support for Insurgent Movements* (Santa Monica, CA: RAND Corporation, 2001); Daniel Byman, *Deadly Connections: States That Sponsor Terrorism* (Cambridge: Cambridge University Press, 2005).
25. Byman 2005; Idean Salehyan, *Rebels without Borders: Transnational Insurgencies in World Politics* (Ithaca, NY: Cornell University Press, 2009); I. William Zartman, *Elusive Peace: Negotiating an End to Civil Wars* (Washington DC: Brookings, 1995).
26. Alan J. Kuperman, "The Moral Hazard of Humanitarian Intervention: Lessons from the Balkans," *International Studies Quarterly* 52, no. 1 (2008): 49–80; Lake 1999; Miller 2005.
27. Bryan Brophy-Baermann and John A. C. Conybeare, "Retaliating against Terrorism: Rational Expectations and the Optimality of Rules versus Discretion," *American Journal of Political Science* 38, no. 1 (1994): 196–210; Byman 2005; David B. Carter, "The Compellence Dilemma: International Disputes with Violent Groups," *International Studies Quarterly* 59, no. 3 (2015): 461–476; Kristian Skrede Gleditsch, Idean Salehyan, and Kenneth Schultz, "Fighting at Home, Fighting Abroad: How Civil Wars Lead to International Disputes," *Journal of Conflict Resolution* 52, no. 4 (2008): 479–506; David Lake and Donald Rothchild, eds., *The International Spread of Ethnic Conflict* (Princeton, NJ: Princeton University Press, 1998), 3–33; Salehyan 2009.
28. Bapat and Zeigler 2016; Bapat 2014.
29. In these cases, natural resource revenues may be needed to support a government's economy, pay off elites to keep the government in power, or both. Natural resources are therefore not only strategically necessary but may also be necessary for governments to be sustained politically. See also Jeff D. Colgan, *Petro-Aggression: When Oil Causes War* (Cambridge, Cambridge University Press, 2013).
30. This behavior would be true regardless of whether the neighbor is an active sponsor or passive host (Byman 2005). In the former case, the neighbor actively supports the group, thereby giving the government an incentive to disrupt the shipment of resources from the neighbor's territory. In the latter case, the government may attack because of its concerns that the neighbor either lacks the capacity or the will to disarm the terrorists in its territory.
31. Idean Salehyan, "The Externalities of Civil Strife: Refugees as a Source of International Conflict," *American Journal of Political Science* 52, no. 4 (2008): 787–801, demonstrates that not a single one of the nineteen attempts by governments to destroy the transnational bases of rebel groups during the 1990s achieved success.
32. John O. Brennan, Speech to the Council on Foreign Relations. 8 August 2012. Transcript available at: https://www.cfr.org/event/conversation-john-o-brennan-0.
33. See Wikileaks, "The Yemen Files," https://wikileaks.org/yemen-files/document/.

34. For a formal discussion of majority-minority ethnic relations and potential commitment problems, see James Fearon, "Commitment Problems and the Spread of Ethnic Conflict," chapter 5 in David A. Lake and Donald Rothchild, eds., *The International Spread of Ethnic Conflict* (Princeton, NJ: Princeton University Press 1998), 107–126.
35. Chris Zamelis, "Syria's Sunnis and the Regime's Resistance," *Combatting Terrorism Center Sentinel* 8, no. 5 (2015): 5–9, https://www.ctc.usma.edu/v2/wp-content/uploads/2015/05/CTCSentinel-Vol8Issue52.pdf.
36. See Mert Bilgin, "Geopolitics of European Natural Gas Demand: Supplies from Russia, Caspian, and the Middle East," *Energy Policy* 37, no. 11 (2009): 4482–4492.
37. Sydney Thomas and Richard A. Dawe, "Review of Ways to Transport Natural Gas Energy from Countries Which Do Not Need the Gas for Domestic Use," *Energy* 28: 1461–1477.
38. Juan Montes, "IEA Economist: Russia is no longer Reliable Gas Supplier" *Dow Jones Institutional News* 15 January 2009.
39. Axel M. Wietfeld, "Understanding Middle East Gas Exporting Behavior," *The Energy Journal*, 32, no. 2 (2011): 203–228.
40. Although no source directly attributes the quote to Assad, the motivation typically attributed to the Syrian leader is that Syria rejected the Qatari pipeline "to protect the interests of its Russian ally"; see Agence France-Presse, "Moscow Rejects Saudi Offer to Drop Assad for Arms Deal," *Hürriyet Daily News*, August 8, 2013, http://www.hurriyetdailynews.com/moscow-rejects-saudi-offer-to-drop-assad-for-arms-deal-52245.
41. In private correspondence between former Secretary of State Hillary Clinton and her eventual presidential campaign chair John Podesta, Secretary Clinton wrote on August 17, 2014 that the governments of Qatar and Saudi Arabia "are providing clandestine financial and logistic support to ISIL and other radical Sunni groups in the region." See Wikileaks, "The Podesta Emails," https://wikileaks.org/podesta-emails/emailid/55380#efmA_RBEL.
42. An additional motivation was to undercut the growing American shale-drilling industry.
43. Agence France-Presse 2013.

## CHAPTER 6

1. Danny McDonald, "Trump on Iraq: 'We Should Have Kept the Oil.'" *Boston Globe*, 21 January 2017.
2. For an argument that the decision by states to diversify their currency holdings away from dollars to RMB is driven by the waning support for the U.S. liberal order, see Stephen Liao and Daniel McDowell "No Reservations: International Order and Demand for the Renminbi as a Reserve Currency," *International Studies Quarterly* 60, no. 2 (2016): 272–293.
3. Branko Milanovic and Christoph Lakner, "Global Income Distribution: From the Fall of the Berlin Wall to the Great Recession," *Revista de Economía*

*Institucional* 17, no. 32 (2015): 71–128. For a counterargument suggesting that lower and middle classes are benefiting from globalization, see Adam Corlett, "Examining an Elephant: Globalization and the Lower Middle Class of the Rich World," Resolution Foundation, September 2016, http://www.resolutionfoundation.org/app/uploads/2016/09/Examining-an-elephant.pdf.

4. See Johan Norberg, *Progress: Ten Reasons to Look Forward to the Future* (London: Oneworld Publishers, 2016).
5. Andrew Stuttaford, "Giving our Lenders a Haircut?" *Weekly Standard* 21, no. 35: 14–16.
6. Sarah Dutton, Jennifer De Pinto, Anthony Salvanto, and Fred Backus, "Do Americans want to Send Groud Troops to Fight ISIS?" *CBS News*, 19 February 2015. See: http://www.cbsnews.com/news/do-americans-want-to-send-ground-troops-to-fight-isis/.

## APPENDIX

1. In the text, I refer to US as "she," H as "he," and T as "it."
2. A case example of this situation might be the U.S.-Saudi relationship. The host (the Saudi monarchy) is in control of its territory and distributes the benefits of ruling largely to members of the monarchy. In response, al Qaeda and other militant groups organized to destabilize the regime. Since keeping the monarchy in power benefits the U.S., American foreign policy seems oriented to keeping al Qaeda and its supporters out of power in this territory.
3. See Bapat 2005; Cronin 2009; Jones and Libicki 2008; Zartman 1995.
4. Since $p^*$ is a probability, and must be bounded between 0 and 1, the maximum level of x US can provide at time t is $(1-p^{\lambda t})$.
5. Fearon 1995; Matthew Hoddie and Caroline Hartzell, "Civil War Settlements and the Implementation of Military Power-Sharing Arrangements," *Journal of Peace Research* 40, no. 3 (2003): 303–320; Wagner 2000.
6. While this value of x does exist, its solution is very cumbersome. The value of x' is available by request.
7. The Greenbook provides data on U.S. military aid disbursements through various programs from FY1946—FY2008. http://gbk.eads.usaidallnet.gov/.
8. U.S. State Department document, http://www.state.gov/documents/organization/28971.pdf.
9. "Splintering" in the Jones and Libicki data refers to the collapse of the group. It does not refer to cases where a terrorist organization splits into multiple terrorist groups, which would in effect make the problem of terrorism worse.
10. *Freedom in the World*, 1997–2006, http://www.freedomhouse.org/template.cfm?page=15.
11. Numerous studies indicate that the presence of terrorist groups is correlated with regime type; see Quan Li, "Does Democracy Promote or Reduce Transnational Terrorist Incidents?" *Journal of Conflict Resolution*

49, no. 2 (2005): 278–297; Todd Sandler, "On the Relationship between Democracy and Terrorism," *Terrorism and Political Violence* 7, no. 4 (1995): 1–9. However, few suggest that the duration of a terrorist campaign is a function of regime type. Therefore, while regime type has been shown to be correlated with the presence of terrorists, it has not been theoretically demonstrated to be correlated with duration.

12. In addition to testing with the dichotomous instrument, I also created an instrument for the logged maximum level of U.S. aid. However, while this instrument yielded results that were consistent with the theoretical hypotheses, this instrument was not effective in removing the possibility of endogeneity. I therefore only present the results using the first instrument.

13. U.S. State Department, *Voting Practices in the United Nations*, http://www.state.gov/p/io/rls/rpt/.

14. See Erik Gartzke, "Preferences and the Democratic Peace," *International Studies Quarterly* 44, no. 2 (2000): 191–212.

15. See James D. Fearon and David Laitin, "Ethinicity, Insurgency, and Civil War," *American Political Science Review* 97, no. 1 (2003): 75–90.

# BIBLIOGRAPHY

Abrahams, Max. 2008. "What Terrorists Really Want: Terrorist Motives and Counterterrorism Strategy." *International Security* 32(4): 78–105.

Acemoglu, Daron, Simon Johnson, and James Robinson. 2001. "The Colonial Origins of Comparative Development." *American Economic Review* 91(5): 1369–1401.

Agence France-Presse. 2013. "Moscow Rejects Saudi Offer to Drop Assad for Arms Deal." *Hürriyet Daily News*, August 8, 2013. http://www.hurriyetdailynews.com/moscow-rejects-saudi-offer-to-drop-assad-for-arms-deal-52245.

Aliber, Robert Z. 2011. *The New International Money Game*. 7th ed. New York, NY: Palgrave MacMillan.

Amnesty International. 2010. *Amnesty International Report: The State of the World's Human Rights*. London: Amnesty International Publications.

Anderson, Jørgen, and Silje Alsaksen. 2013. "Oil and Political Survival." *Journal of Developmental Economics* 100(1): 89–106.

Arrow, Kenneth J. 1951. *Social Choice and Individual Values*. New Haven, CT: Yale University Press.

Auboin, Marc. 2012. "Use of Currencies in International Trade: Any Changes in the Picture?" Working Paper, World Trade Organization Economic Research and Statistics Division. Available at: https://www.wto.org/english/res_e/reser_e/ersd201210_e.pdf.

Austin, Steve. 2015. "Oil Prices and the Syrian Civil War." Oil-Price.net, October 14, 2015. http://www.oil-price.net/en/articles/oil-prices-and-syrian-civil-war.php.

Azam, Jean-Paul, and Alexandra Delacroix. 2006. "Aid and the Delegated Fight against Terrorism." *Review of Development Economics* 10(2): 330–344.

Balcells, Laia. 2017. *Rivalry and Revenge: The Politics of Violence during Civil Wars*. Cambridge: Cambridge University Press.

Bandyopadhyay, Subhayu, Todd Sandler, and Javed Younas. 2013. "Foreign Direct Investment, Aid, and Terrorism." *Oxford Economic Papers* 66(1): 25–50.

Bapat, Navin A. 2005. "Insurgency and the Opening of Peace Processes." *Journal of Peace Research* 42(6): 699–717.

Bapat, Navin A. 2006. "State Bargaining with Transnational Terrorist Groups." *International Studies Quarterly* 50(1): 213–229.

Bapat, Navin A. 2007. "The Internationalization of Terrorist Campaigns." *Conflict Management and Peace Science* 24(4): 265–280.

Bapat, Navin A. 2011. "Transnational Terrorism, U.S. Military Aid, and the Incentive to Misrepresent." *Journal of Peace Research* 48(3): 303–318.

Bapat, Navin A. 2011. "Terrorism, Democratization, and U.S. Foreign Policy." *Public Choice* 149(3/4): 315–335.

Bapat, Navin A. 2014. "The Escalation of Terrorism: Microlevel Violence and Interstate Conflict." *International Interactions* 40(4): 568–578.

Bapat, Navin A., and Kanisha D. Bond. 2012. Alliances Between Militant Groups. *British Journal of Political Science* 42(4): 793–824.

Bapat, Navin A., Luis de la Calle, Kaisa Hinkkainen, and Elena McClean. 2016. "Economic Sanctions, Transnational Terrorism, and the Incentive to Misrepresent." *Journal of Politics* 78(1): 249–264.

Bapat, Navin A., and Sean Zeigler. 2016. "Terrorism, Dynamic Commitment Problems, and Military Conflict." *American Journal of Political Science* 60(2): 337–351.

Bartels, Larry M. 1996. "Uninformed Votes: Information Effects in Presidential Elections." *American Journal of Political Science* 40(1): 194–230.

Belasco, Amy. 2011. "The Cost of Iraq, Afghanistan, and Other Global War on Terror Operations since 9/11." *Congressional Research Service*. Document # 7-5700 RL33110. March 29, 2011. http://www.fas.org/sgp/crs/natsec/RL33110.pdf.

Berinsky, Adam J. 2007. "Assuming the Costs of War: Events, Elites, and American Public Support for Military Conflict." *Journal of Politics* 69(4): 975–997.

Bernhard, Michael, Christopher Reenock, and Timothy Nordstrom. 2004. "The Legacy of Western Overseas Colonialism on Democratic Survival." *International Studies Quarterly* 48(1): 225–250.

Biddle, Stephen, Jeffrey A. Friedman, and Jacob N. Shapiro. 2012. "Testing the Surge: Why Did Violence Decline in Iraq in 2007?" *International Security* 37(1): 7–40.

Bilgin, Mert. 2009. "Geopolitics of European Natural Gas Demand: Supplies from Russia, Caspian, and the Middle East." *Energy Policy* 37(11): 4482–4492.

Blinder, Alan S. 1982. "The Anatomy of Double Digit Inflation in the 1970s." In Robert E. Hall, ed., *Inflation: Causes and Effects*, 261–282. Chicago: University of Chicago Press.

Boutton, Andrew, and David Carter. 2014. "Fair Weather Allies? Terrorism and the Allocation of U.S. Foreign Aid." *Journal of Conflict Resolution* 58(7): 1144–1173.

Brennan, John O. 2012. Speech to the Council on Foreign Relations. 8 August 2012. See: https://www.cfr.org/event/conversation-john-o-brennan-0

Brophy-Baermann, Bryan, and John A. C. Conybeare. 1994. "Retaliating against Terrorism: Rational Expectations and the Optimality of Rules versus Discretion." *American Journal of Political Science* 38(1): 196–210.

Bueno de Mesquita, Ethan. 2005. "Conciliation, Counterterrorism, and Patterns of Terrorist Violence." *International Organization* 59(1): 145–176.

Bueno de Mesquita, Ethan. 2008. "A Political Economy of Terrorism: A Selected View of Recent Work." Unpublished manuscript, University of Chicago.

Bueno de Mesquita, Bruce. 2009. *The Predictioneer's Game*. New York: Random House.

Bueno de Mesquita, Bruce, and Alastair Smith. 2007. "Foreign Aid and Policy Concessions." *Journal of Conflict Resolution* 51(2): 251–284.

Bueno de Mesquita, Bruce, and Alastair Smith. 2010. "Leader Survival, Revolutions, and the Nature of Government Finance." *American Journal of Political Science* 54(4): 936–950.

Bueno de Mesquita, Bruce, Alastair Smith, Randolph Siverson, and James Morrow. 2005. *The Logic of Political Surivval*. Cambridge, MA: MIT Press.

Byman, Daniel. 2005. *Deadly Connections: States That Sponsor Terrorism*. Cambridge: Cambridge University Press.

Byman, Daniel, Peter Chalk, Bruce Hoffman, William Rosenau, and David Brannan. 2001. *Trends in Outside Support for Insurgent Movements*. Santa Monica, CA: Rand Corporation.

Caplan, Bryan. 2006. "Terrorism: The Relevance of the Rational Choice Model." *Public Choice* 128(1): 91–107.

Carter, David B. 2010. "The Strategy of Territorial Conflict." *American Journal of Political Science* 54(4): 969–987.

Carter, David B. 2015. "The Compellence Dilemma: International Disputes with Violent Groups." *International Studies Quarterly* 59(3): 461–476.

Carter, David B., and Hein Goemans. 2011. "The Making of Territorial Order: New Borders and the Emergence of Interstate Conflict." *International Organization* 65(2): 275–309.

Cingranelli, David L., and Thomas E. Pasquarello. 1985. "Human Rights Practices and the Distribution of US Foreign Aid to Latin American Countries." *American Journal of Political Science* 29(3): 539–563.

Clapham, Christopher. 1996. *Africa and the International System: The Politics of State Survival*. Cambridge: Cambridge University Press.

Clark, William R. 2005. *Petrodollar Warfare: Oil, Iraq, and the Future of the Dollar*. Gabriola Island: New Society Publishers.

Cloud, David, and Greg Jaffe. 2009. *The Fourth Star: Four Generals and the Epic Struggle for the Future of the United States Army*. New York: Crown.

Cockburn, Patrick. 2008. "Violence is down—but not because of America's 'Surge'," *The Independent on Sunday*. Retrieved from http://libproxy.lib.unc.edu/login?url=https://search-proquest-com.libproxy.lib.unc.edu/docview/337049336?accountid=14244.

Colgan, Jeff D. 2013. *Petro-Aggression: When Oil Causes War*. Cambridge: Cambridge University Press.

Coll, Steve. 2004. *Ghost Wars: The Secret History of the CIA, Afghanistan, and bin Laden, from the Soviet Invasion to September 10, 2001*. New York, NY: Penguin.

Coll, Steve, "The Unblinking Stare," *The New Yorker* 90(37): 98.

Collier, Paul, and Anke Hoeffler. 2004. "Greed and Grievance in Civil War." *Oxford Economic Papers* 56(4): 563–595.

Congressional Budget Office. 2006. "Recruiting, Retention, and Future Levels of U.S. Military Personnel." https://www.cbo.gov/sites/default/files/109th-congress-2005-2006/reports/10-05-recruiting.pdf.

Cooper, Andrew S. 2008. "Showdown at Doha: The Secret Oil Deal that Helped Sink the Shah of Iran." *Middle East Journal* 62(4): 567–591.

Cooper, Andrew S. 2011. *The Oil Kings: How the U.S., Iran, and Saudi Arabia Changed the Balance of Power in the Middle East*. New York: Simon and Schuster.

Cordesman, Anthony H. 2008. *The Iraq War: Key Trends and Developments.* Washington, DC: Center for Strategic and International Studies.

Corlett, Adam. 2016. "Examining an Elephant: Globalization and the Lower Middle Class of the Rich World." Resolution Foundation, September 2016. http://www.resolutionfoundation.org/app/uploads/2016/09/Examining-an-elephant.pdf.

Costs of War Project. 2018. "Costs of War." Watson Institute for International and Public Affairs, Brown University. November 2018. https://watson.brown.edu/costsofwar/figures/2018/budgetary-costs-post-911-wars-through-fy2019-59-trillion.

Croco, Sarah E. 2015. *Peace at What Price? Leaders and the Domestic Politics of War Termination.* Cambridge: Cambridge University Press.

Cronin, Audrey K. 2009. *How Terrorism Ends: Understanding the Decline and Demise of Terrorist Campaigns.* Princeton, NJ: Princeton University Press.

Cuaresma, Jesus Crespo, Harald Oberofer, and Paul Raschky. 2010. "Oil and the Duration of Dictatorships." *Public Choice* 148(3): 505–530.

Cunningham, Kathleen G. 2014. *Inside the Politics of Self Determination.* Oxford: Oxford University Press.

De la Calle, Luis, and Ignacio Sánchez-Cuenca. 2012. "Rebels without a Territory: An Analysis of Nonterritorial Conflicts in the World, 1970–1997." *Journal of Conflict Resolution* 56(4): 580–603.

Dear, I. C. B., and M. R. D. Foot, eds. 2002. *The Oxford Companion to World War II.* Oxford: Oxford University Press.

DeGennaro, Ramon P. 2005. "Market Imperfections." *Journal of Financial Transformation* 14:107–117.

Downs, George W., and David M. Rocke. 1994. "Conflict, Agency, and Gambling for Resurrection: The Principal-Agent Problem Goes to War." *American Journal of Political Science* 38(2): 362–380.

Downes, Alexander B. 2004. "The Problem with Negotiated Settlements to Ethnic Civil Wars." *Security Studies* 13(4): 230–279.

Dragu, Tiberiu. 2017. "The Moral Hazard of Terrorism Prevention." *Journal of Politics* 79(1): 223–236.

Dyson, Stephen B. 2010. "George W. Bush, the Surge, and Presidential Leadership." *Political Science Quarterly* 125(4): 557–585.

El-Gamal, Mahmoud A., and Amy Myers Jaffe. 2010. *Oil, Dollars, Debt, and Crises.* Cambridge: Cambridge University Press.

Enders, Walter, and Todd Sandler. 2006. *The Political Economy of Terrorism.* Cambridge: Cambridge University Press.

Englebert, Pierre. 2000. *State Legitimacy and Development in Africa.* Boulder: Lynne Reinner.

European Council of Foreign Relations. 2017. "Mapping the Yemen Conflict: Current Front Lines." http://www.ecfr.eu/mena/yemen.

Fair, C. Christine. 2011. "False Choices in Afghanistan." *Foreign Policy*, January 11, 2011. https://foreignpolicy.com/2011/01/11/false-choices-in-afghanistan/.

Fearon, James D. 1995. "Rationalist Explanations for War." *International Organization* 49(3): 379–414.

Fearon, James D. 1996. "Bargaining over Objects that Influence Future Power." Unpublished manuscript, University of Chicago.

Fearon, James D. 1998. "Commitment Problems and the Spread of Ethnic Conflict." Chapter 5 in David A. Lake and Donald Rothchild, eds. *The International Spread of Ethnic Conflict*, 107–126. Princeton, NJ: Princeton University Press.

Fearon, James D., and David D. Laitin. 2003. "Ethnicity, Insurgency, and Civil War." *American Political Science Review* 97(1): 75–90.

Fearon, James D., and David D. Laitin. 2004. "Neotrusteeship and the Problem of Weak States. *International Security* 28(4): 5–43.

Feaver, Peter D. 2011. "Right to Be Right: Civil-Military Relations and the Iraq Surge Decision." *International Security* 35(4): 87–125.

Fiorina, Morris P. 1981. *Retrospective Voting in American National Elections*. New Haven, CT: Yale University Press.

Fjelde, Hanne, and Indra De Soysa. 2009. "Coercion, Co-optation, or Cooperation? State Capacity and the Risk of Civil War, 1961–2004."*Conflict Management and Peace Science* 26(1): 5–25.

Fjelde, Hanne, and Desirée Nilsson. 2012. "Rebels against Rebels: Explaining Violence between Rebel Groups." *Journal of Conflict Resolution* 56(4): 604–628.

Forest, James J. F., Jarret Brachman, and Joseph Felter. 2006. *Harmony and Disharmony : Exploiting al Qa'ida's Organizational Vulnerabilities*. West Point, NY: Combating Terrorism Center.

Freedom House. 2010. *Freedom in the world 2010: The Annual Survey of Political Rights and Civil Liberties*. Lanham, MD: Rowman & Littlefield.

Gaibulloev, Khusrav, and Todd Sandler. 2013. "Determinants of the Demise of Terrorist Organizations." *Southern Economic Journal* 79(4): 774–792.

Gartner, Scott S. 2008. "The Multiple Effects of Casualties on Public Support for War: An Experimental Approach." *American Political Science Review* 102(1): 95–106.

Gartzke, Erik. 2000. "Preferences and the Democratic Peace." *International Studies Quarterly* 44(2): 191–212.

Gartner, Scott S., and Gary Segura. 1998. "War, Casualties, and Public Opinion." *Journal of Conflict Resolution* 42(3): 278–300.

Gates, Robert S. 2015. *Duty: Memoirs of a Secretary at War*. New York: Vintage.

Gelpi, Chris F., Peter D. Feaver, and Jason Reifler. 2007. "Iraq the Vote: Retrospective and Prospective Foreign Policy Judgments on Candidate Choice and Casualty Tolerance." *Political Behavior* 29(2): 151–174.

Gelpi, Chris F., Peter D. Feaver, and Jason Reifler. 2009. *Paying the Human Costs of War*. Princeton, NJ: Princeton University Press.

Ghoborah, Hazem A., Paul Huth, and Bruce Russett. 2003. "Civil Wars Kill and Maim People – Long after the Shooting Stops." *American Political Science Review* 97(2): 189–202.

Gilpin, Robert. 1987. *The Political Economy of International Relations*. Princeton, NJ: Princeton University Press.

Gleditsch, Kristian Skrede, Idean Salehyan, and Kenneth Schultz. 2008. "Fighting at Home, Fighting Abroad: How Civil Wars Lead to International Disputes." *Journal of Conflict Resolution* 52(4): 479–506.

Gleditsch, Nils Petter, Peter Wallensteen, Mikael Eriksson, Margareta Sollenberg, and Håvard Strand. 2002. "Armed Conflict, 1946–2001: A New Dataset." *Journal of Peace Research* 39(5): 615–637.

Global Terrorism Database: 2019. Codebook: Inclusion Criteria and Variables (https://www.start.umd.edu/gtd/downloads/Codebook.pdf)

Goldberg, Jeffrey. 2016. "The Obama Doctrine." *The Atlantic* 317(3): 70–90.

Goldin, Claudia, and Robert Margo. 1992. "The Great Compression: The Wage Structure in the United States at Mid-Century." *Quarterly Journal of Economics* 107(1): 1–34.

Gordon, Michael R. 2013. "The Secret Surge Debate." *Foreign Policy*, March 18, 2013. https://foreignpolicy.com/2013/03/18/the-secret-surge-debate/.

Gordon, Michael R., and Bernard E. Trainor. 2012. *The Endgame: The Inside Story of the Struggle for Iraq, from George W. Bush to Barack Obama*. New York: Pantheon.

Gowa, Joanne S. 1983. *Closing the Gold Window: Domestic Politics and the End of Bretton Woods*. Ithaca, NY: Cornell University Press.

Green, Timothy. 1999. "Central Bank Gold Reserves: A Historical Perspective since 1945." World Gold Council, Research Study #23.

Greenwald, Bruce C., and Joseph E. Stiglitz. 1993. "Financial Market Imperfections and Business Cycles." *Quarterly Journal of Economics* 108(1): 77–114.

Gustafson, Thane. 1985. "The Origins of the Soviet Oil Crisis, 1970–1985." *Soviet Economy* 1(2): 103–135.

Hegre, Håvard, and Nicholas Sambanis. 2006. "Sensitivity Analysis of Empirical Results on Civil War Onset." *Journal of Conflict Resolution* 50(4): 508–535.

Hendrix, Cullen S. 2011. "Head for the Hills? Rough Terrain, State Capacity, and Civil War Onset." *Civil Wars* 13(4): 345–370.

Hendrix, Cullen, and Marcus Noland. 2014. *Confronting the Curse: The Economics and Politics of Natural Resource Governance*. New York, NY: Peterson Institute for International Economics.

Herbst, Jeffrey. 2014. States and Power in Africa: Comparative Lessons in Authority and Control. Princeton, NJ: Princeton University Press.

Hiscox, Michael J. 1999. "The Magic Bullet? The RTAA, Institutional Reform, and Trade Liberalization." *International Organization* 53(4): 669–698.

Hoddie, Matthew, and Caroline Hartzell. 2003. "Civil War Settlements and the Implementation of Military Power-Sharing Arrangements." *Journal of Peace Research* 40(3): 303–320.

Holmstrom, Bengt. 1979. "Moral Hazard and Observability." *Bell Journal of Economics* 10(1): 74–91.

Howell, William G., and Jon C. Pevehouse. 2007. *While Dangers Gather: Congressional Checks on Presidential War Powers*. Princeton, NJ: Princeton University Press.

Hubbert, M. King. 1956. "Nuclear Energy and the Fossil Fuel." *American Petroleum Institute Drilling and the Production Practice*.

Ikenberry, G. John, and Charles A. Kupchan. 1990. "Socialization and Hegemonic Power." *International Organization* 44(3): 283–315.

Jawad, Aymen. 2011. "Assessing the Surge in Iraq." *Middle East Review of International Affairs* 15(4): 26–38.

Jones, Arthur F. and Daniel H. Weinberg. 2000. "The Changing Shape of the Nation's Income Distribution," *Current Population Reports* P60-204. U.S. Census Bureau, https://www.census.gov/prod/2000pubs/p60-204.pdf

Jones, Seth G. 2009. "Going Local: The Key to Afghanistan." The RAND Blog. August 8, 2009. https://www.rand.org/blog/2009/08/going-local-the-key-to-afghanistan.html.

Jones, Seth, and Martin Libicki. 2008. *How Terrorist Groups End: Lessons for Countering al Qa'ida*. Santa Monica, CA: RAND Corporation.

Kalyvas, Stathis N. 2006. *The Logic of Violence in Civil War*. Cambridge: Cambridge University Press.

Kalyvas, Stathis N. 2015. *Modern Greece: What Everyone Needs to Know*. Oxford: Oxford University Press.

Keohane, Robert. 1984. *After Hegemony: Cooperation and Discord in the World Political Economy*. Princeton, NJ: Princeton University Press.

Khedery, Ali. 2014. "Why We Stuck with Maliki—and Lost Iraq." *Washington Post*, July 3, 2014. https://www.washingtonpost.com/opinions/why-we-stuck-with-maliki--and-lost-iraq/2014/07/03/0dd6a8a4-f7ec-11e3-a606-946fd632f9f1_story.html?utm_term=.107c987e0d42.

Kindleberger, Charles P. 1973. *The World in Depression 1929–1939*. Berkeley, CA: University of California Press.

Kirshner, Jonathan. 2008. "Dollar Primacy and American Power: What's at Stake?" *Review of International Political Economy* 15(3): 418–438.

Kuperman, Alan J. 2008. "The Moral Hazard of Humanitarian Intervention: Lessons from the Balkans." *International Studies Quarterly* 52(1): 49–80.

Lake, David A. 1993. "Leadership, Hegemony, and the International Economy: Naked Emperor or Tattered Monarch with Potential." *International Studies Quarterly* 37:459–489.

Lake, David A. 1999. *Entangling Relations: American Foreign Policy in Its Century*. Princeton, NJ: Princeton University Press.

Lake, David A., and Donald Rothchild, eds. 1998. *The International Spread of Ethnic Conflict*. Princeton, NJ: Princeton University Press.

Leeds, Brett Ashley. 2003. "Do Alliances Deter Aggression? The Influence of Military Alliances on the Initiation of Militarized Interstate Disputes." *American Journal of Political Science* 47(3): 427–439.

Lemke, Douglas, and Jeff Carter. 2016. "Birth Legacies, State Making, and War." *Journal of Politics* 78(2): 497–511.

Li, Quan. 2005. "Does Democracy Promote or Reduce Transnational Terrorist Incidents?" *Journal of Conflict resolution* 49(2): 278–297.

Liao, Stephen, and Daniel McDowell. 2016. "No Reservations: International Order and Demand for the Renminbi as a Reserve Currency." *International Studies Quarterly* 60(2): 272–293.

Lister, Tim. 2016. "Terror Export Fears as ISIS 'Caliphate' Shrinks," CNN, July 11, 2016, https://www.cnn.com/2016/07/11/middleeast/isis-territory-analysis-lister/.

Lujala, Päivi, Nils Petter Gleditsch, and Elisabeth Gilmore. 2005. "A Diamond Curse? Civil War and Lootable Resource." *Journal of Conflict Resolution* 49(4): 538–562.

Mampilly, Zachariah Cherian. 2011. *Rebel Rulers: Insurgent Governance and Civilian Life during War.* Ithaca, NY: Cornell University Press.

Marinov, Nikolay. 2005. "Do Economic Sanctions Destabilize Country Leaders?" *American Journal of Political Science* 49(3): 564–576.

Martin-Vézian, Louis, Evan Centanni, and Djordje Djukic. 2016. Political Geography Now. "Yeman Control Map and Report: December 2016." http://www.polgeonow.com/2016/12/houthis-in-yemen-control-map-2016.html.

McLean, Elena V., Kaisa Hinkkainen, Luis de la Calle, and Navin A. Bapat. 2018. "Economic Sanctions and the Dynamics of Terrorist Campaigns." *Conflict Management and Peace Science* 35(4): 378–401.

McBride, James. "Building the New Silk Road." Council on Foreign Relations, May 22, 2015. https://www.cfr.org/backgrounder/building-new-silk-road.

McCormick, James M., and Neil Mitchell. 1988. "Is US Aid Really Linked to Human Rights in Latin America?" *American Journal of Political Science* 32(1): 231–239.

McGillivray, Fiona, and Allan Stam. 2004. "Political Institutions, Coercive Diplomacy, and the Duration of Sanctions." *Journal of Conflict Resolution* 48(2): 154–172.

McKelvey, Richard D. 1976. "Intransitivities in Multidimensional Voting Models and Some Implications for Agenda Control." *Journal of Economic Theory* 12(3): 472–482

Meernik, James, Eric L. Krueger, and Steven C. Poe. 1998. "Testing Models of US Foreign Policy: Foreign Aid during and after the Cold War." *Journal of Politics* 60(1): 63–85.

Melander, Erik, Therése Pettersson, and Lotta Themenér. 2016. "Organized Violence, 1989–2015." *Journal of Peace Research* 53(5): 727–742.

Mentan, Tatah. 2004. *Dilemmas of Weak States: Africa and Transnational Terrorism in the Twenty-First Century.* Burlington, VT: Ashgate.

Milanovic, Branko, and Christoph Lakner. 2015. "Global Income Distribution: From the Fall of the Berlin Wall to the Great Recession." *Revista de Economía Institucional* 17(32): 71–128.

Miller, Gary J. 2005. "The Political Evolution of Principal-Agent Models." *Annual Review of Political Science* 8:203–225.

Morrow, James D. 1994. *Game Theory for Political Scientists.* Princeton, NJ: Princeton University Press.

Morrow, James D. 2000. "Alliances: Why Write Them Down?" *Annual Review of Political Science* 3:63–83.

Mosher, Dave, and Skye Gould. 2017. "How Likely Are Foreign Terrorists to Kill Americans? The Odds May Surprise You." Business Insider, January 31, 2017. http://www.businessinsider.com/death-risk-statistics-terrorism-disease-accidents-2017-1.

Mueller, John. 2006. *Overblown: How Politicians and the Terrorism Industry Inflate National Security Threats, and Why We Believe Them.* New York, NY: Free Press.

National Consortium for the Study of Terrorism and Responses to Terrorism (START). 2018. Global Terrorism Database [Data file]. Retrieved from https://www.start.umd.edu/gtd

National Highway Traffic Safety Administration. 2019. NCSA Data Resource Website. *Fatality Analysis Reporting System Encyclopedia.* Available at: https://www-fars.nhtsa.dot.gov/Main/index.aspx

Norberg, Johan. 2016. *Progress: Ten Reasons to Look Forward to the Future.* London: Oneworld Publishers.

Oatley. Thomas. 2012. *International Political Economy.* 5th ed. Milton Park: Routledge.

Oatley. Thomas. 2015. *A Political Economy of American Hegemony: Buildups, Booms, and Busts.* Cambridge: Cambridge University Press.

Oatley, Thomas, William Kindred Winecoff, Andrew Pennock, and Sarah Baurle Danzman. 2013. "The Political Economy of Global Finance." *Perspectives on Politics* 11(1): 133–153.

Okonjo-Iweala, Ngozi. 2007. "Nigeria's Economic Reforms: Progress and Challenges." Brookings Global Economy and Development. Working Paper no. 6.

Omgba, Luc Désiré. 2009. "On the Duration of Political Power in Africa: The Role of Oil Rents." *Comparative Political Studies* 42(3): 416–436.

Oppenheim, Ben, Abbey Steele, Juan F. Vargas, and Michael Weintraub. 2015. "True Believers, Deserters, and Traitors: Who Leaves Insurgent Groups and Why." *Journal of Conflict Resolution* 59(5): 794–823.

Organski, A. F. K., and Jacek Kugler. 1980. *The War Ledger.* Chicago: University of Chicago Press.

Patterson, Thérése, and Kristine Eck. 2018. "Organized Violence, 1989-2017." *Journal of Peace Research* 55(4): 535–547.

Pearlman, Wendy. 2009. "Spoiling Inside and Out: Internal Political Contestation and the Middle East Peace Process." *International Security* 33(3): 79–109.

Phillips, Brian J. 2014. "Terrorist Group Cooperation and Longevity." *International Studies Quarterly* 58(2): 336–347.

Piazza, James A. 2008. "Incubators of Terror: Do Failed and Failing States Promote Transnational Terrorism?" *International Studies Quarterly* 52(3): 469–488.

Poe, Steven C. 1990. "Human Rights and US Foreign Aid: A Review of Quantitative Studies and Suggestions for Future Research." *Human Rights Quarterly* 12:499–512.

Popkin, Samuel. 1991. *The Reasoning Voter.* Chicago: University of Chicago Press.

Powell, Robert. 1996. "Uncertainty, Shifting Power, and Appeasement." *American Political Science Review* 90(4): 749–764.

Powell, Robert. 2004. "The Inefficient Use of Power: Costly Conflict with Complete Information." *American Political Science Review* 98(2): 231–241.

Powell, Robert. 2006. "War as a Commitment Problem." *International Organization* 60(1): 169–203.

Rabasa, Angel. *Ungoverned Territories: Understanding and Reducing Terrorism Risks.* Vol. 561. Santa Monica, CA: RAND Corporation, 2007.

Ramsay, Kristopher W. 2011. "Revisiting the Resource Curse: Natural Disasters, the Price of Oil, and Democracy. *International Organization* 65(3): 507–529.

Reiter, Dan. 2003. "Exploring the Bargaining model of War." *Perspectives on Politics* 1(1): 27–43.

Roggio, Bill. 2009. "Taliban Contest or Control Large Areas of Afghanistan." *Long War Journal.* http://www.longwarjournal.org/archives/2009/12/taliban_contest_or_c.php.

Ross, Michael. 2006. "A Closer Look at Oil, Diamonds, and Civil War." *Annual Review of Political Science* 9:265–300.

Ross, Michael. 2013. *The Oil Curse: How Petroleum Wealth Shapes the Development of Nations*. Princeton, NJ: Princeton University Press.

Russett, Bruce. 1985. "The Mysterious Case of Vanishing Hegemony; or, Is Mark Twain Really Dead?" *International Organization* 39(2): 207–231.

Salehyan, Idean. 2008. "The Externalities of Civil Strife: Refugees as a Source of International Conflict." *American Journal of Political Science* 52(4): 787–801.

Salehyan, Idean. 2009. *Rebels without Borders: Transnational Insurgencies in World Politics*. Ithaca, NY: Cornell University Press.

Salehyan, Idean, and Kristian Gleditsch. 2006. Refugees and the Spread of Civil War. *International Organization* 60(2): 335–366

Sambanis, Nicholas. 2004. "What Is a Civil War?" *Journal of Conflict Resolution* 48(6): 814–858.

Sandler, Todd. 1995. "On the Relationship between Democracy and Terrorism." *Terrorism and Political Violence* 7(4): 1–9.

Sarkees, Meredith, and Frank Wayman. 2010. *Resort to War, 1816–2007*. Washington, DC: CQ Press. See: http://www.correlatesofwar.org/data-sets/COW-war.

Saunders, Elizabeth N. 2015. "War and the Inner Circle: Democratic Elites and the Politics of Using Force." *Security Studies* 24(3): 466–501.

Schelling, Thomas. 1960. *The Strategy of Conflict*. Cambridge, MA: Harvard University Press.

Schelling, Thomas. 1966. *Arms and Influence*. New Haven, CT: Yale University Press.

Schmid, Alex P., and Albert J. Jongman. 1988. *Political Terrorism: A New Guide to Actors, Authors, Concepts, Databases, Theories, and Literature*. 2nd ed. Abingdon: Routledge.

Schultz, Kenneth A. 2001. *Democracy and Coercive Diplomacy*. Cambridge: Cambridge University Press.

Serle, Jack, and Jessica Purkiss. 2017. Bureau of Investigative Journalism. "Drone Wars: The Full Data." https://www.thebureauinvestigates.com/stories/2017-01-01/drone-wars-the-full-data.

Shapiro, Jacob N. 2013. *The Terrorists' Dilemma: Managing Violent Covert Organizations*. Princeton, NJ: Princeton University Press.

Shavell, Stephen. 1979. "Risk Sharing and Incentives in the Principal and Agent Relationship." *Bell Journal of Economics* 10(1): 55–73.

Shepsle, Kenneth. 1979. "Institutional Arrangements and Equilibrium in Multidimensional Voting Models." *American Journal of Political Science* 23(1): 27–49.

Sobel, Andrew C. 2012. *The Birth of Hegemony: Crisis, Financial Revolution, and Emerging Global Networks*. Chicago: University of Chicago Press.

Spence, Michael, and Richard Zeckhauser. 1971. "Insurance, Information, and Individual Action." *American Economic Review* 61(2): 380–381.

Small, Melvin, and J. David Singer. 1982. *Resort to Arms: International and Civil War, 1816–1980*. Beverly Hills, CA: Sage.

Stedman, Stephen J. 1997. 'Spoiler Problems in Peace Processes.' *International Security* 22(2): 5–53.

Steil, Benn. 2013. *The Battle of Bretton Woods: John Maynard Keynes, Harry Dexter White, and the Making of a New World Order*. Princeton, NJ: Princeton University Press.

Sundberg, Ralph, Kristine Eck, and Joakim Kreutz. 2012. "Introducing the UCDP Non-State Conflict Dataset." *Journal of Peace Research* 49(2): 351–362.

Thiel, Joshua and Joyce Hogan. 2011. "The Statistical Irrelevance of American SIGACT data: Iraq Surge Analysis Reveals Reality." *Small Wars Journal*. April 12, 2011. Available at: https://smallwarsjournal.com/blog/journal/docs-temp/732-thiel1.pdf.

Thomas, Sydney, and Richard A. Dawe. 2003. "Review of Ways to Transport Natural Gas Energy from Countries Which Do Not Need the Gas for Domestic Use." *Energy* 28: 1461–1477.

Toft, Monica D. 2010. *Securing the Peace: The Durable Settlements of Civil Wars*. Princeton, NJ: Princeton University Press.

U.S. Energy Information Administration. 2015. Data obtained May 2015 via infoctr@eia.doe.gov. https://www.eia.gov/beta/international/regions-topics.cfm?RegionTopicID=WOTC.

U.S. Energy Information Administration. 2017. Data obtained May 2019 via infoctr@eia.doe.gov. https://www.eia.gov/beta/international/regions-topics.cfm?RegionTopicID=WOTC.

U.S. State Department. 2003. "National Strategy for Combating Terrorism." February, pp. 15–22. https://2001-2009.state.gov/s/ct/rls/wh/71803.htm.

Wagner, R. Harrison. 2000. "Bargaining and War." *American Journal of Political Science* 44(3): 469–484.

Wagner, R. Harrison. 2007. *War and the State: The Theory of International Politics*. Ann Arbor, MI: University of Michigan Press.

Walter, Barbara F. 2002. *Committing to Peace: The Successful Settlement of Civil Wars*. Princeton, NJ: Princeton University Press.

Weber, Max. 1919. *Politics as a Vocation*. Munich: Duncker and Humblodt.

Weingast, Barry R., and Mark J. Moran. 1983. "Bureaucratic Discretion or Congressional Control? Regulatory Policymaking by the F. E. C." *Journal of Political Economy* 91(5): 765–800.

Weinstein, Jeremy. 2007. *Inside Rebellion: The Politics of Insurgent Violence*. Cambridge: Cambridge University Press.

White House. 1974a. Gerald R. Ford Presidential Library and Museum. "National Security Adviser, Memoranda of Conversations, 1973–1977." Memorandum of conversation between President Richard Nixon, Secretary of the Treasury William Simon, and Major General Brent Scowcroft, July 9, 1974. https://www.fordlibrarymuseum.gov/library/document/0314/1552732.pdf.

White House. 1974b. Gerald R. Ford Presidential Library and Museum. "National Security Adviser, Memoranda of Conversations, 1973–1977." Memorandum of conversation between President Richard Nixon, Secretary of the Treasury William Simon, Assistant to the President Kenneth Rush, and Deputy Assistant to the President for National Security Affairs Brent Scowcroft, July 30, 1974. https://www.fordlibrarymuseum.gov/library/document/0314/1552737.pdf.

White House. 1975. Gerald R. Ford Presidential Library and Museum. "National Security Adviser, Memoranda of Conversations, 1973–1977." Memorandum of conversation between President Gerald Ford, Secretary of State Henry Kissinger, and Shah of Iran Mohammad Reza Pahlavi, May 15, 1975. https://www.fordlibrarymuseum.gov/library/document/0314/1553077.pdf.

Whitford, Andrew B. 2002. "Decentralization and Political Control of the Bureaucracy." *Journal of Theoretical Politics* 14(2): 167–194.

Wietfeld, Axel M. 2011. "Understanding Middle East Gas Exporting Behavior," *The Energy Journal* 32(2): 203–228.

Winecoff, William K. 2013. "Financial Power and the Global Crisis." PhD diss., University of North Carolina–Chapel Hill.

Wong, Andrea. "The Untold Story behind Saudi Arabia's 41-Year U.S. Debt Secret." *Bloomberg News*, May 30, 2016. https://www.bloomberg.com/news/features/2016-05-30/the-untold-story-behind-saudi-arabia-s-41-year-u-s-debt-secret.

Wood, Dan B. 1988. "Principal, Bureaucrats, and Responsiveness in Clean Air Enforcement." *American Political Science Review* 82(1): 213–234.

Wood, Elisabeth. 2003. *Inside Collective Action and Civil War in El Salvador.* Cambridge: Cambridge University Press.

Wood, Reed M., Jacob D. Kathman, and Stephen E. Gent. 2012. "Armed Intervention and Civilian Victimization in Intrastate Conflicts." *Journal of Peace Research* 49(5): 647–660.

Woodward, Bob. 2008. *The War Within: A Secret White House History, 2006-2008.* New York: Simon and Schuster.

Woodward, Bob. 2010. *Obama's Wars.* New York: Simon and Schuster.

Zamelis, Chris. 2015. "Syria's Sunnis and the Regime's Resistance." *Combatting Terrorism Center Sentinel* 8(5): 5–9. https://www.ctc.usma.edu/v2/wp-content/uploads/2015/05/CTCSentinel-Vol8Issue52.pdf.

Zahlungsausgleich, B. 2010. "Triennial-Central Bank Survey-Report on Global Foreign exchange market activity in 2010." *The Bank for International Settlements.* Available at: www.bis.org/publ/rpfxf10t.pdf.

Zartman, I. William. 1995. *Elusive Peace: Negotiating an End to Civil Wars.* Washington, DC: Brookings.

# INDEX

Note: Figures are indicated by *f* following the page number
*For the benefit of digital users, indexed terms that span two pages (e.g., 52–53) may, on occasion, appear on only one of those pages.*

9/11, 1–6, 8–9, 31–32, 37, 43, 47, 50, 56, 66, 71, 110, 117, 122, 142, 150
   Afghanistan, 1, 5, 32, 43, 56, 142, 150
   global energy market, 3, 9, 150
   Iraq, 1–4, 9, 32–33, 43, 70, 108, 142, 150
   Response, 1, 32

Abu Sayyaf, 35
Afghanistan, 1, 5, 24, 28, 32–34, 38–41, 43–44, 56–57, 61, 67–68, 72, 78, 80–81, 84–85, 93–110, 112, 118, 142–143, 150
   Pro-Government and Insurgency Fatalities, 2006–2012, 99*f*
   Taliban control over, 2009, 94*f*
African Gold Dinar, 112
African National Congress, 6
Ahmadinejad, Mahmoud, 68
al Nusra, 111, 133
Al Qaeda, 1, 3, 5, 8–9, 26–30, 32–37, 42, 44, 47, 55, 79, 85–93, 96–111, 114, 124
Al Qaeda in the Arabian Peninsula (AQAP), 124, 127
Al Qaeda in Iraq, 87, 114

Al Sadr, Muqtada, 85–93, 103
Algeria, 37
Anbar Awakening, 88
Anbar province, 88, 90–92
Angola, 37, 78
Arab-Israeli conflict, 29
Arab Spring, 66, 93, 106, 112–113, 115, 124, 132, 143
Arabian American Oil Company (ARAMCO), 19
Army of Conquest, 133–137
Assad, Bashar al, 111–114, 129–138
Awakening Councils 88, 90–92
   growth of, 90*f*

Ba'athist Party, 86–87, 130
Bab el-Mandeb 36–37, 42, 126–128, 146
Baghdad, 33, 45, 72, 79, 86–92, 142
   civilian fatalities in, 2004–2007, 86*f*
bargaining theory, 50
Bernanke, Ben, 103
Biden, Joseph, 95–96, 101, 178
Bin Laden, Osama, 27–29, 31–33, 100–101, 112, 142

Boko Haram, 1
Bretton Woods system, 10, 12–16
British pound, 11–12
Bush, George W., 2, 8, 42–44, 70–73, 76–79, 81, 85–91, 142, 145, 151

Canada, 145
Cape of Good Hope, 36–37, 126
Carter, Jimmy, 57
Castro, Fidel, 59
China, 15, 26, 36, 38, 57, 64, 144–147, 149, 153
Clinton, Bill, 26
Clinton, Hillary, 149
Cold War, 8, 24–26, 29, 31, 47, 57, 130, 136
commitment problem, 18, 53, 84, 91, 110, 129
Communist Party of Nepal, 38
corruption, 7, 47, 62, 66, 71, 85, 95, 97
counterterrorism, 35, 45, 48, 75, 81, 96, 101, 107

De Gaulle, Charles, 15–16
debt, 141, 149
default, 25, 33, 105, 145, 149
Democratic Republic of the Congo, 122
depreciation, 17, 20–21, 152
Djibouti, 36–37, 126, 146
drones, 73, 96
  in Pakistan, 98$f$
  in Yemen, 125$f$

Egypt, 16–20, 37, 40, 42, 61–62, 65–66, 107–110, 112, 115, 126, 128, 140, 143, 145
Eikenberry, Karl, 95–96
Eisenhower, Dwight, 19
El-Sisi, General Abdel Fatteh, 110
empirical implications of theoretical models (EITM), 5

Erdogan, Recep Tayyip, 131, 133, 136
Ethiopia, 37
Euro, 26, 29–33, 64, 102–106, 110, 139, 142, 144–145, 148, 151
European Union, 26, 29, 64, 130–136, 138, 144–145, 148–150

Fahd, King of Saudi Arabia, 28
failed states, *see* weak states
Faisal, King of Saudi Arabia, 21, 23
financial crisis, 103–105, 108, 110, 138, 143–145
  Dow Jones and, 104$f$
Forces démocratiques de liberation du Rwanda, 38
Foreign aid
  Effectiveness, 47
  perverse incentive, 56, 67
Ford, Gerald, 22, 77–78
France
  cooperation in North Africa, 112
  opposition to U.S., 15–16
Free Syrian Army 111–112, 133

Game theory
  Model of American Strategy in the War on Terror, 49$f$, 82$f$
Ghawar oil field, 52–53, 121
Glaspie, April, 27
Global terrorism Database, 2–3, 35, 40, 44, 125
gold standard, 11–12, 17
  Bretton Woods system
    (*see* Bretton Woods system)
  Nixon shock, 16
Greece, 105
Greenspan, Alan, 22
Guatemala, 58–59
Gulf of Aden, 28, 126
Gulf War I, *see* Operation Desert Storm
Gulf War II, *see* Operation Iraqi Freedom

Hadi, Abrabbuh Mansur, 124, 126–127, 129
Hamas, 6
Haqqani Network, 101
hegemony, 4, 7, 10, 16, 19, 24, 26, 29, 31–39, 60–61, 79, 140, 142–153
Helmand province, 93–100
Hezbollah, 119, 121, 134
Houthi rebellion, 36, 42, 123–140, 146
Hussein, Saddam, 3, 9, 20, 25–33, 86–87, 135, 142
hydraulic fracturing (fracking), 145

India, 38, 41, 56, 118–119, 148
Indonesia, 34–35, 42
inflation, 12, 16, 18, 21, 23–24, 62, 67
insurgency, 1, 15, 41–42, 68, 79, 84, 86–87, 90, 93, 95, 97–98, 101–103, 114, 117–118, 120, 123–124, 130, 137
International Monetary Fund (IMF), 13, 62
International Security Assistance Force (ISAF), 93–102
Fatalities, 98f
Internationalized civil war spread of, 113f
interstate conflict, 4, 7, 115, 123, 139, 153
armed interstate conflicts, 115f
Iran, 18–20, 22–26, 30, 36, 57, 59–61, 66, 68, 79, 87, 91, 93, 111, 114, 121, 124, 126–140, 145–146, 148, 151
Iraq, 2–4, 9, 18–20, 25–27, 30–41, 43–45, 67–68, 70, 77–81, 84–93, 95, 102–103, 107–108, 110–115, 130–137, 142–143, 150–151
civilian fatalities in, 86f
Islamic State in Iraq and Syria (ISIS), 1, 9, 111, 124, 133–140, 145, 150
Territorial control, 135f
Israel, 6, 16–17, 21–22, 27, 29, 65–66, 108, 119, 121

Japan, 12, 26, 36, 144
Jemma al-Islamiya, 34, 42
Jordan, 114, 120–121

Karzai, Hamid, 85, 94–97, 101–102
Kashmir, 41, 118–119
Kenya, 28, 37
Khomeini, Ayatollah, 57
Kissinger, Henry, 22
Kuwait, 25–27, 131

Libya, 112, 115
light footprint, 73, 80, 96, 106, 112, 114, 137, 139, 143

Malaysia, 34–35
Maliki, Nuri al, 79–93
moral hazard, 39–40, 73–76, 81, 91, 102, 112, 120
hazard of terrorist group collapse, 46f
Moro Islamic Liberation Front (MILF), 35
Moro National Liberation Front (MNLF), 35
movement for the Emancipation of the Niger Delta (MEND), 64–65
Mubarak, Hosni, 37, 61, 65–66, 107–114, 126, 143
Murtha, John, 71–72, 80
Musharraf, Pervez, 41, 56

National Army for the Liberation of Uganda, 38
natural gas, 38, 130–133, 136
pipelines, 132f
New Silk Road, see One Belt, One Road Initiative
Nigeria 1, 37, 61–65
Nixon, Richard, 16–18, 21–22, 78
North Atlantic Treaty Organization (NATO), 101, 136

Obama, Barack, 1–2, 70, 95–98,
    100–108, 112–114, 124, 126–127,
    132–135, 140, 148, 150
oil, 3, 9, 16–32, 34, 36, 38, 41, 52, 60–64,
    66–69, 73, 79–80, 92–93, 106,
    108, 112, 116–117, 120–121, 130,
    133–138, 141–142, 145–146,
    148, 151
    Price of Persian Gulf Oil per Barrel
        in USD, 2002–2008, 68f
    Trade Routes and Chokepoints
        and Spread of al Qaeda, f34
One Belt, One Road Initiative
    (OBOR), 147–148
    Proposed, 147f
Operation Ajax, 19
Operation Desert Fox, 30
Operation Enduring Freedom,
    32–34, 118
Operation Enforcing the Law, 89–90
Operation Gothic Serpent, 31
Operation Iraqi Freedom, 2, 39, 45
Operation Neptune Spear, 100
Organization of the Petroleum
    Exporting Countries, 9, 17,
    20–31, 33, 61, 64, 77, 141, 149

Pahlavi, Mohammad Reza, 19–23
Pakistan, 28, 40–43, 56–58, 68, 94,
    97–99, 101–102, 118–119
Peshmerga, 80, 92, 135–137
Petraeus, David, 95, 103
petrodollar recycling, 21, 24–27, 33, 39,
    41, 54, 60, 67, 71, 74, 80, 82, 102,
    105, 111–114, 126, 140, 148
Philippines, 34–35
predatory war, 122, 133–134, 138, 143
preventive war, 130, 134, 136, 138, 153
Putin, Vladimir, 41, 114, 130–132,
    135–136, 140, 144, 146

Qatar, 111, 115, 130–138

rational choice, 48
Reagan, Ronald, 57
Red Sea, 36–37, 126–128, 146
Renminbi (RMB), 64, 144, 146–148
reserve currency, 3, 9, 144, 146, 148, 151
Rice, Condoleezza, 79–81
Roosevelt, Franklin, 15, 19
Russia, 26, 38, 41, 94, 111, 114, 129–140,
    144–146, 148–149, 151, 153
Rwanda, 38, 122–123

Sadat, Anwar, 65
Saleh, Ali Abdullah, 36, 42, 55, 124,
    126, 146
Salman, King, 127
sanctions, 30, 75, 147–148
Saudi Arabia, 17–32, 52–53, 58, 60–61,
    77, 102, 106, 111, 115, 121, 126–127,
    131, 138
seigniorage, 11
Simon, William, 17, 20–23
Sinai Peninsula 16, 42
Somalia, 31, 37, 81
Sons of Iraq, *see* Anbar Awakening
Soviet Union, 10, 14–15, 18, 20,
    24, 27
State Department, U.S., 5, 33, 38, 43,
    81, 172
Strait of Hormuz, 36, 126, 133, 146
Strait of Malacca, 34, 36
Suez Canal, 16, 19, 36–37, 42, 61, 66,
    107–108, 126
Syria, 16–17, 111, 112–115, 128–140,
    145, 150

Taliban, 1, 3, 5, 9, 28, 33, 41, 56, 68,
    93–102, 112, 114, 118, 142
Tanzania, 28, 37

terrorism, 1–9, 31–61, 66–67, 71, 75, 77, 82, 85, 93, 102, 116–123, 139, 150–153
   active groups 2001-2006, 45*f*
   attacks over time 1998–2011, 2*f*
   attacks in Middle East, Africa, and Asia 2002–2007, 40*f*
   attacks and Fatalities in the Iraq War Period 2003–2011, 44*f*
   definition of, 5–7
   fatalities compared to motor vehicle accidents, 3*f*
Trans-Pacific Partnership (TPP), 149
Truman, Harry, 14, 57
Trump, Donald J., 140–141, 146–150
Tunisia, 106–107
Turkey, 111, 115, 131–140

Uganda, 37–38
United Nations (U.N.), 30, 100, 172–173
United States economy, 11–15, 18, 22, 24, 26, 29, 61, 103
   Job Losses and Rising Unemployment in Financial Crisis, 104*f*

Uzbekistan, 32

Venezuela, 145–146
Vietnam war, 15–16, 22, 78, 99
Volcker, Paul, 24

war on terror, 1–5, 7–9, 35–36, 38–40, 49, 56, 70–72, 74, 76–78, 82, 84, 103, 112, 123, 140, 143, 145–146, 148, 150–153
   cost of, 71*f*
   fatalities 2003–2007, 72*f*
weak states, 5, 41, 44, 67
Westphalia, Peace of, 116
World Bank, 13, 148

Yemen, 20, 36, 40, 42, 55, 102, 111, 115, 123–129, 145, 146
   civil war in, 127*f*, 129*f*
   drone strikes and fatalities, 2012–2015, 125*f*
   terrorist attacks and fatalities, 2012–2015, 125*f*
Yom Kippur War, 65

Made in the USA
Columbia, SC
27 June 2023